Anthropology & Education

The major objective of this series is to make the knowledge and perspective of anthropology available to educators and their students. It is hoped and believed, however, that it will also prove valuable to those in other professions and in the several disciplines that compose the behavioral sciences.

In recent years some educators have discovered that anthropology has much to offer the areas of professional training and educational theory and practice. In its cross-cultural comparisons of human behavior and in its inductive, empirical method of analysis is found a conceptual freshness that is intellectually liberating.

There are four major areas of anthropological theory that have direct relevance for education. These are the regularities of behavior and belief that we call culture; the transmission of cuture and learning processes; the ways in which individuals group themselves for the accomplishment of communal purposes, from which comes organization theory; and the processes by which transformations occur in human behavior and groupings that can be explained by a theory of change. In addition, there are the subject-matter areas of child rearing; community and the relationships among institutions within it; the rites of passage; the cultural categories of social class, ethnic group, age, grading, and sex; and others. These several areas of theory and substance provide a rich source for this series. It is believed that the availability of such a storehouse of knowledge in the several volumes in the series will contribute immensely to the further improvement of our educational system.

Solon T. Kimball, General Editor

Anthropology & Education

Series

THE WAY TO MODERN MAN

Fred T. Adams

PERSPECTIVES FROM ANTHROPOLOGY

Rachel Reese Sady

BECOMING A TEACHER

Elizabeth M. Eddy

THE CULTURE OF CHILDHOOD

Mary Ellen Goodman

LEARNING TO BE ROTUMAN

Enculturation in the South Pacific

Alan Howard

Teachers College Press

Teachers College, Columbia University
New York, New York

DU
600
.H68

Manufactured in the United States of America

To Stephen Boggs and George Spindler
Two teachers who made a difference

Foreword

Increasingly, educators are beginning to recognize the need to break out of the narrow restrictions that their specific cultural perspective has imposed on them and to seek the broadened understandings that emerge from learning about the educative process in societies other than their own. Hopefully, this trend will gain further momentum, for only from the vantage point of cultural comparison can we ever expect to gain the new insights that are so vitally needed for understanding the consequences of our own educational enterprise and for consciously directing its transformation. This book makes a large contribution toward the attainment of these objectives.

Learning to Be Rotuman is significant because its author, Alan Howard, has succeeded in weaving the environmental, historical, cultural, and social strands into an account that illuminates the many congruencies between community and the educative process. Furthermore, it provides a contrast between the indigenous methods of inducting the young into full maturity and the alien, formal system of schooling sponsored first by missionaries and later by a colonial government. Missionary education, under the guise of bringing "pagan" natives to a worship of the true God and of civilizing their manners and morals was, in its initial phases, an arrogant and insensitive imperialism, however kindly and well-intentioned the purveyors of Western ways may have been.

Before the fingers of Western expansionism reached their island haven in the Pacific in the nineteenth century, the Rotumans followed practices of child rearing that were for them fully successful as transmitters of culture from one generation to the next. But the Rotumans are no longer isolated. They are now linked to the modern world politically and economically. Some of the young seek schooling beyond that provided on their island, and some of the adults live and work elsewhere. Formal schooling has acquired a new importance as the influence of Western society has intruded itself in their lives ever more deeply.

The basic relevance of this schooling to the culture from which the children come and to the world in which they must live is as fundamental for the Rotumans as it is for all of the other peoples of the world who find themselves in a comparable situation. This book contributes greatly to the conceptual formulations and strategies that the teaching process must incorporate in those situations in which teachers and students come from divergent cultural backgrounds. Only thus can those who bear the responsibility for teaching the young become more effective in their efforts.

The genesis of any book is deeply connected with the author's career and so it is with *Learning to Be Rotuman*. Dr. Howard's initial probing of Rotuman life began a decade ago as part of the requirements for his doctorate in anthropology at Stanford University, which he received in 1962. He has taught at colleges in California, New Zealand, and Hawaii, and at present is anthropologist at the Bernice P. Bishop Museum in Honolulu. In 1964 he took the first steps toward organizing what has become an intensive study of Hawaiian culture, community, and behavior.

The findings of this recent research and those reported about the Rotumans are of immediate significance for those who make policy for or work with people who reside in pluralistic cultural settings. The message is particularly relevant for educators, for Dr. Howard has established that biculturalism is both possible and desirable. Schools can contribute to the development of those skills that are utilized in the public world of work, but the traditional assault by teachers on the native behavior of the culturally divergent is both unnecessary and harmful.

Solon T. Kimball

May 1970

Introduction

Seeing the *Yanawai*, the inter-island copra boat that took me to Rotuma, fade out of sight on the evening of December 17, 1959, was one of the most anxious moments of my life. The next boat was not expected for several weeks, perhaps even months. Not only was I a stranger on an isolated island among people whose language I did not understand, but I was without the benefit of a role that would make sense to them. During the first few days I was treated well, but cautiously, while my hosts waited for me to reveal my "real" purpose in being there. The situation was made much more pleasant by the beauty of the place, and the more I explored the more impressed I became. The overall impression I had received of the island when approaching it from the sea—white sandy beaches offset by majestic coconut trees and deep green luxuriant vegetation—gave way to more specific impressions—a variety of trees, flowering plants, and an almost infinite variety of subtle hues. This was the tropics of my most revered romantic dreams, and the assortment of buildings, some with tin roofs and whitewashed limestone walls, hardly detracted from the imagery.

To explain what I was doing there, I relied on the typical anthropologist's offering—that I was there to learn about their history and customs, to write them down so that the Europeans could know something about Rotuma. This was understood by only a few of the more sophisticated individuals. The majority preferred the explanations offered in rumors: that I was a spy, or more pleasantly, that I was the grandson of a Rotuman man who left the island some thirty years before, ostensibly for America. His surname was the same as mine, for he was a descendant of Charles Howard, a renegade American seaman

who jumped ship in Rotuma early in the nineteenth century and remained to establish a sizeable progeny. It was tempting to answer in
the affirmative when asked directly whether I was indeed a descendant
of this romantic figure; it would have made over half the people on
the island my relatives! But ethical considerations overpowered the
Machiavellian scheme that flashed through my mind.

It is perhaps indicative of the respect the Rotumans have for education that the explanation that ultimately made sense to the majority
of them was that I had been sent there by my university to do a
"lesson." My role thus became one of a student, albeit a student of
unusually high rank. This was most fortunate, for it put me in the
position of one who was ignorant and needed to learn, and I found
myself with many teachers. They began by teaching me such obvious
things as the names of objects and places, the routine of specific customs, and the canons of interpersonal etiquette. At first my bumblings
and offenses against protocol were excused and not even brought to
my attention, but after I was around a while those who had become
close let me know when I had done something wrong. I really knew I
had been accepted, however, the first time someone got angry at me
for failing to behave appropriately. By that time they expected me to
know better, and were subjecting me to the same socialization pressures they use with one another. I might add that by this time I was
no longer merely attempting to emulate correct behavior in order to
learn about Rotuman culture. I had come to care for these people and
what they thought of me. I wanted their approval and they used this
motivation to socialize me.

In writing this book I have therefore not only relied upon my
observations about how Rotumans socialize and educate their children,
but also upon my own socialization experiences on the island. In fact,
I did not really concentrate my research efforts on the educational
process, although it is a topic in which I have always had a great deal
of interest. My dissertation was on land tenure. Nevertheless, my work
with George Spindler at Stanford University had done much to prepare
me for making observations in this area and although I did not
systematically gather data on education in the way I would have liked
if I had planned in advance to write a book on the subject, I did not
entirely neglect the topic.

In writing the book I have had to make some strategic decisions.
Perhaps the most difficult was how much ethnographic detail to include
in order to give the reader a good feeling for what life on the island
is like. My first temptation was to include a great deal more than is
currently included, but at the urging of some of my colleagues I have
eliminated much that is marginal to the central theme. What remains

is the minimum amount of information that I feel to be necessary in order to gain a basic understanding of Rotuman culture.

I have dedicated this book to two men who in my estimation are great teachers. At a time when I was intellectually floundering as an undergraduate student, Stephen Boggs provided the stimulation that turned me toward social science as a serious pursuit. It has been my good fortune to work with him recently as a colleague in Hawaii, where he has continued to provide stimulation and encouragement. He has read a draft of this book and provided valuable suggestions. George Spindler was my first anthropology teacher, and after taking his courses I never considered becoming anything but an anthropologist. Many of his ideas are no doubt reflected in this volume, although it would be difficult to distinguish them from my own.

Two other colleagues have contributed much to the ideas reflected in the book. Robert Levy and I have been engaged in a continuous dialogue for several years over theoretical issues related to psychological anthropology and the ethnography of Polynesian societies. His lengthy field work in Tahiti has given him a remarkable insight into Polynesian character, and my understanding of the Rotuman material has markedly appreciated as a result of our discussions. If the reader discovers that many of my generalizations are couched in the language of social learning theory, it will be the result of my association with Ronald Gallimore, a psychologist who is my current partner on a research project among Hawaiians of Polynesian ancestry. I only hope he has learned as much anthropology from me as I have learned psychology from him.

Innumerable persons have gone out of their way to make this study possible. Felix Keesing, perhaps the man who knew more about Polynesian ethnology than anyone else, first drew my attention to the area and personally assisted me in preparing for field work. His death while I was still in the field was experienced as both a personal and professional loss. To Alex Spoehr I also owe a great debt, for it was through his personal efforts as the United States representative to the South Pacific Commission that I was permitted to go to Rotuma at a time when the Government of Fiji was apprehensive over the turmoil that had been created by an unpopular land reform. The understanding attitude of His Excellency Sir Kenneth Maddocks, the Governor of the Colony of Fiji, is much appreciated. I hope that this book proves to be of some value to his successors, thereby justifying his confidence in my ability to carry out meaningful research without incident. Christopher Legge, the Commissioner, Eastern, under whose jurisdiction Rotuma falls, was not only understanding, he went out of his way to provide me with useful data. A great deal of scholarly and practical assistance was also provided in Fiji by Dr. H. S. Evans, a former District Officer on Rotuma; Dr. Lindsey Verrier; and the Reverend Allan Tippett. All are excellent scholars in their own right. Ian Diamond, the Archivist in Suva, made it possible through his extraordinary efficiency for me to find my way through the great wealth of historical documentation on all aspects of Rotuman society that is housed there.

The Rotumans who contributed both tangibly and otherwise to this study are so numerous that I hesitate to try to mention them all. I ask forgiveness from those whose names I fail to mention. In words that I learned on the island, "Please blame the pen but love the writer." Alex Rae, Josef Rigamoto, Fred Ieli, Wilson Inia, Mamao Managreve, Father Kitolelei, Sister Madeleine, Aisea Aitu, Hanfiro Kitione, and Paul Manueli all did much to further the research and make my stay enjoyable. In Suva, Faga Hoeflich took me into her house and treated me like a son; in Rotuma, Sakimi, Seferosa, and Akeneta Farpapau put up with me for a whole year. It must have been a terrible strain having to educate a post-teen age adolescent foreigner to act decently so as not to bring shame upon their household. Amai Sakimi and Rejieli Pasepa worked as my assistants and did a superb job of gathering data. Some of the life history material presented in Chapter VII was obtained by them in Rotuman and translated into English. Finally, to Father Beattie I owe a very special debt. He offered his mission house as a place for me to work, and not only provided much needed intellectual stimulation but tea twice a day and marvelous cookies sent by his mother from his home in New Zealand. And how does one thank a wife who provides an atmosphere that makes writing fun, and a secretary, Marcia Heighton, whose patience is unbounded.

Contents

Photographs follow page 114

I

Education in a Changing World

Like so many others in the world today, the people of the South Seas are caught in the tides of change. Although they have been spared the overwhelming effects of rapid industrialization and urbanization, even those on the more remote islands, such as Rotuma, are very much aware that they live in a dual world. One is the world of their Polynesian ancestors, whose way of life was worked out over centuries in a relatively bountiful, but limited, island environment. It is true that this way of life has been modified by more than a century and a half of contact with the white man, but the change has been slow and selective, and the original character of this life is still very much in evidence. The other world is that of the modern city, from which emanate strong pressures for cultural change, and whose promise for a more prosperous, interesting, and exciting life the Rotumans can no longer ignore.

In this book we shall be concerned with both of these worlds, and the ways in which Rotumans learn to cope with them. Our focus is on education, not merely in the narrow sense of schooling, but in the broadest sense, in which growing individuals are influenced by their total environment. In Rotuma we find the individual being shaped by two distinctly different teaching strategies. One, employed by his parents, relatives, and friends—indeed by everyone who is dear to him—is rooted in the traditional way of life and relies upon personalized, informal influence. The proper ways of doing things are learned by observing more what others do than what they say, and the most important reward for successful learning is community acceptance. The punishment for failure is ridicule, shame, and ostracism. In contrast to this approach are the techniques of the school, which are rooted just as firmly in the traditions of Western European culture. Here teaching is formal and essentially impersonal. Information is explicitly transmitted, and to be successful students must learn to focus on what teachers say rather than on what they do. The rewards for success are periodic displays of symbolic recognition and the hope of expanded opportunities. The punishment for failure is a constricted personal horizon.

Part of our task will be to gain an understanding and appreciation of the cultural contexts that have fostered these contrasting approaches to education. We shall be concerned with the ways in which Rotuman teachers have adapted formal teaching strategies in order to make allowance for the kinds of children they are instructing, and we shall evaluate the efficiency with which school is preparing these people for a place in the modern world.

Before I ask the reader to embark with me on an imaginary emigration to Rotuma, I should like to clarify the meanings of two important concepts, "education" and "culture." Both of these terms have been given a wide range of meaning by laymen and behavioral scientists alike, and it will help us to communicate if we can arrive at an understanding now, before we begin the analysis. I have already mentioned that we shall be concerned with education in its broadest sense, the sense in which individuals are shaped by their total environment. More specifically, as an anthropologist I have come to think of education as synonymous with the transmission of culture, i.e., the process by which an individual learns to behave in an appropriate and effective way within particular environments. It encompasses covert patterns that are transmitted without awareness, as well as overt content that is handed down intentionally from generation to generation. It incorporates the influences exerted not only by teachers and parents, but also by relatives, friends, neighbors, and even strangers. In short, it includes all those processes that mold the individual into a social being.

The concept "culture" requires more elaboration. When using the term I refer to a shared body of concepts, ideas, and feelings that are transmitted through the process of symbolic communication. In saying that culture is "shared," I do not mean that all persons who share a common culture are necessarily members of the same group. In this respect the concept of culture differs from the concept of society. If a person plays a part in the functioning of a society, he can be considered a member of that society; if he does not play a part, he cannot be considered a member. Societies are distinct social units with distinct memberships; it is possible to define their membership boundaries in a way that is not always possible for cultures. At the highest level one can speak of pan-human culture, since all known human beings share certain understandings (e.g., extreme anger, fear, and sexual arousal). At a somewhat lesser level of inclusion all English-speaking peoples share common understandings not shared by non-English-speaking peoples. By the same token all Catholics, whether or not they speak English, share common understandings not shared by non-Catholics.

Cultures thus often cut across societies, and many societies contain a number of sub-cultures. Within American society, for example, it would be quite appropriate to speak of a Japanese-American sub-culture, a professional sub-culture, a working-class sub-culture, a teen-age sub-culture, and even a female sub-culture. If we carry this usage to the extreme we can speak of each husband and wife as constituting a sub-culture, for surely each set of spouses shares certain understandings that are not shared by others. I have elaborated this point because it is all too easy to think of people in other societies as confined to one culture, particularly if that society is such a small Pacific island as Rotuma. But in fact most Rotumans do learn to behave appropriately in various cultural contexts. Indeed, the whole purpose of formal education on the island is to make them competent within modern urbanized world culture. The problem, as I shall point out later on, is one of becoming bi-cultural, of being able to be *both* Rotuman and modern rather than having to choose between the two.

Let us now suppose that an individual from urbanized America were going to Rotuma with the intention of staying there and becoming a fully accepted, productive member of that society. His goal is to learn the style of life so thoroughly that he is able to assimilate completely, to become a Rotuman in every possible way. To give the game some stakes let us say that his economic and his social well-being depends on how well he learns. If he fails he will be condemned to poverty; if he fails completely he might even starve. With such a journey in mind we can consider our initial concern, which is the transmission of culture content. *What* does he have to learn in order to be successful?

The most sensible way for him to begin is to learn the Rotuman language. Minimally this involves mastering the rules of grammar and learning the denotative meanings of words, i.e., building a working vocabulary. He must learn how to identify and classify objects that are familiar to Rotumans. Since Rotuman categorization does not always coincide with English categorization, simple translation is not sufficient; he has to learn a whole new set of rules for categorizing certain kinds of things, including, for example, his relatives. He also must learn to identify many kinds of items with which he was unfamiliar, such as varieties of taro, bananas, and yams.

At this same "formal" level of learning he is expected to master

Rotuman customs. These include, for example, knowing which door one uses to enter a house, what types of gifts are appropriate on what occasions, and proper behavior at ceremonies. It also includes the principles of etiquette—knowing how to behave toward whom and under what circumstances. Customary ways of performing such tasks as planting crops, cooking, weaving mats, and fishing must also be learned if the individual is to play an acceptable social and economic role in the community.

Knowing these things—the fundamentals of language and custom —is absolutely basic; assimilation is impossible unless they are thoroughly mastered. These are the overt aspects of culture and are consciously taught to children by adults. If our visitor were to get himself a good Rotuman teacher and studied diligently he could probably learn most of this information without great difficulty. Even if he were to learn all this, however, his assimilation would be far from complete unless he also mastered the subtleties of Rotuman behavior.

Let us reconsider language. We all realize that there is a vast difference between learning to produce grammatically correct sentences in a foreign language and developing sufficient mastery to pass as a native speaker. To do the latter one has to eliminate one's "accent," or those phonetic qualities of speech that are beyond the normal range of sound patterns for native speakers. But even this is not enough. To be indistinguishable from a native speaker one also has to develop an awareness of the connotative, or expressive, content of words and phrases. One has to learn the proper use of idioms, colloquial expressions, and so on. That is, if he is to avoid offending people, or more basically, if he is to communicate effectively, an individual must be aware of the emotional loadings of the things he says. A concept that is neutral to the members of one cultural group may be highly loaded to the members of another, even though they speak the same language. For example, it has been pointed out by several writers that the term "compromise" has a generally favorable connotation to Englishmen, for whom it implies an honorable and sportsmanlike agreement, whereas to Americans it has a generally unfavorable connotation, implying that one has had to yield from a position of principle. At an even more complex level of subtlety is paralinguistic behavior, e.g., voice intonations, gestures, subtle body movements, that convey important information. Although all this is ordinarily covert, or sub-cognitive, a Rotuman would feel that something was not quite right about a person who had failed to master this aspect of communication, even though he might not be able to specify exactly what was wrong.

Now let us suppose that after an intensive course in learning the language, both denotatively and expressively, our aspirant has mastered the art of verbal communication to the point at which he can pass for a native speaker without trouble. He has learned the meaning of gestures, facial expressions, and other body movements and can employ them appropriately. What other subtle aspects of communication must be learned? For one, he needs to learn some things about space and time. How far should one be from someone when talking to him? At what angle does one stand? Where does one focus one's eyes? How long is it appropriate to speak when given an opportunity and at what point should one disengage from an interpersonal encounter? In every culture there are comfortable modalities of spacing and timing of interpersonal engagements.[1] In the most general sense, to fit into a culture inconspicuously one must learn to anticipate the rhythm of life—the normal arrangement and movements of people and things. Not knowing these things is apt to lead to awkwardness and embarrassment.

Thus far we have distinguished aspects of culture that every child in Rotuma learns and that mark him as a Rotuman. But there is yet another kind of information that a person has to learn in order to be successful. Even if he controls all the information we have discussed thus far he may still fall short of social competence, to the extent that competence involves the successful manipulation of interpersonal relations and resources. To become a truly competent participant in Rotuman culture requires that he learn the *strategies* that are most likely to work to advantage in situations of problematic outcome. That is to say, although there is a wide range of behavior that may be acceptable in given instances, not all of it is likely to be effective for achieving one's ends. Strategy involves learning at a rather complex level and is not mastered equally well by all persons in a culture. It involves both overt and covert knowledge, a capacity to anticipate the responses of others, and an ability to see the relationship between fragments of information. But although there are gross differences in the success with which individuals master the complexities of strategy, the basic principles are culturally shared, just as all professional quarterbacks are familiar with the strategic importance of punting on fourth down when deep in one's own territory. To use the example of language again, one may be able to communicate flawlessly, yet be unpersuasive or unconvincing when trying to persuade or convince. Strategy involves saying the right kind of thing in the right kind of way to the right kind of people. The successful mastery of strategy differentiates the people in a culture whose behavior is *effective* from those whose behavior is merely adequate.

If our aspirant were to master all this information he might be able to assimilate, but he still would not be a Rotuman. It would not be just a matter of race or ancestry either. He would differ from Rotumans because he would have learned the information in a different way from the way they had learned it. His Rotuman "self" would be grafted on to a previous personality, or set of characteristic responses. He would be much more conscious of how he was acting than a Rotuman is; in effect he would be choosing to act as a Rotuman, whereas a person raised in that culture would have been conditioned to act that way. Chances are he would be most unlike the people he was imitating in the ways he felt about things. The symbols, sights, and sounds that the Rotumans had learned to love and hate would not have the same impact on him. The Rotumans' anxieties would be different in many respects and so would their pleasures. Swear words in Rotuman would not arouse the same emotions in him, for he would not have learned them in the same anxiety-producing circumstances in which Rotuman children learn them. To him they would be words denoting certain things in his own language, but the impact, if it came through at all, would be experienced only after translation and then only if the equivalent words in his language were powerful. He would also probably differ from Rotumans in his response to new experiences. Perhaps after living among them for a long enough time, if he were a sensitive and empathetic person, he might come to anticipate their responses, but unless he were extremely unusual it is unlikely that he would ever be able to respond likewise in a completely unself-conscious way.

I have several reasons for asking the reader to consider this imaginary emigration to Rotuma. In part it is to define the scope of education from the perspective of cultural transmission. As should now be evident this goes well beyond formal schooling, even in its most inclusive forms. Nevertheless, I should like the reader to keep the relationship between formal schooling and cultural competence constantly in mind as he reads on, for one of the goals of this book is to assess the role of schools in multi-cultural situations. I have also chosen this pedagogical strategy because it reverses the Rotuman situation. If Rotuman children are going to learn to cope successfully with the modern world they must learn culture content just as complicated and subtle as that an immigrant to Rotuma has to learn if he is to participate successfully in their culture. It is my hope that by imagining the educational processes that an immigrant would have to endure in order to master Rotuman ways the reader will be better able to empathize with what Rotumans experience in trying to learn "our" ways. For them the stakes are in fact high. Because of a recent dramatic increase in population, the island has surpassed its capacity to support all Rotumans in the traditional way. This surplus population must go off to urban centers, where they are forced to rely on wages for support. Success in acquiring the necessary social and economic skills means a good job, steady employment, and a decent standard of living. Failure means poverty.

So much for the *what* of cultural transmission. Our second major concern is *how*. If the processes were the same in every society we could account for cultural differences on the basis of content alone, but such is not the case. As I have pointed out, merely learning the content of Rotuman culture does not make an immigrant a Rotuman. His feelings about things and response patterns to new stimuli differentiate him, having been shaped by the ways in which they were learned in his original culture. This is not to deny that such basic principles of learning as reinforcement and imitation are pan-human, but the way in which these principles operate is shaped by culture. For example, the kinds of behavior that become cues to others—in fact the very need to be sensitive to social cues—are patterned by repetitive forms of communication, i.e., culture. Cultural values also help to shape reinforcement schedules, which in turn have differential effects on the learning process and on character formation. We shall therefore examine education in Rotuma not only from the standpoint of transmission of cultural information, but also from the standpoint of its effects on the character formation of individual Rotumans.

The approach we shall take is to examine the modal life pathway traversed by Rotumans, from birth through childhood, the school years, youth, adulthood, and old age. In tracing this course we find the maturing individual becoming enmeshed in a constantly broadening physical and social universe, beginning in a house in Rotuma containing close family members, expanding to include the neighborhood and eventually the whole island of Rotuma, including a large network of kinsmen; for some the process culminates in their induction into the world-wide urban milieu of bureaucracy and ephemeral multi-ethnic relationships. While following this pathway we shall explore the complications introduced by the fact that Rotuman children are expected to learn competency in at least two differing cultural contexts, one the Polynesian culture of their ancestors, in which appropriate behavior requires a knowledge of kinship rules, traditional etiquette, and a characteristically Rotuman rhythm of life, and the other, the urban market economy of Fiji, in which appropriate behavior requires an understanding of contractual relationships, English rules of etiquette, and a characteristically Western rhythm of life.

We shall discover that the Rotuman world view and system of values contrast markedly along several dimensions with the one prevailing in the urbanized West. In Rotuma the cultural emphasis is upon the maintenance of interpersonal harmony and cooperation; conflict is to be avoided and individual competition is therefore tightly restrained. Whereas Western individualism has fostered a view of man that places a heavy emphasis on such aspects of human functioning as personal ideology (i.e., individual belief systems) and motives, the Rotumans are more behavioristic. They are concerned with the pragmatic consequences of behavior rather than the inner dynamics that generate it. We constantly ask *why* people do things and evaluate their actions largely in terms of their intentions; the Rotumans observe how a person's behavior affects his relationship with others and judge it accordingly. Our primary commitments are supposed to be to principles and ideals; the Rotumans are supposed to be to other human beings. We value individual achievement above everything else; the Rotumans place a similar emphasis on obtaining the approval of their fellows.

Throughout this book we shall continually contrast Rotuman culture with that of middle-class Western, and particularly American, culture. My reasons for doing this are twofold. One is that most of the people who read this book will probably be participants in this middle-class culture, and hopefully they will better be able to appreciate the character of Rotuman culture by contrasting it with their own. A second reason is to highlight the dilemmas confronting the Rotumans as they become enmeshed in the Western urban market milieu: Is it possible to be both a good Rotuman and a successful Westerner? In order to be economically successful and gain respect in the modern world how much of their Rotumanness must they relinquish? I shall attempt to answer these questions in Chapter VII.

The dilemmas created by multi-cultural environments are not confined to Rotumans, nor even to non-Western, industrializing societies; they also exist in the United States, although I do not believe we have properly recognized their nature. It is to the problem of educating culturally different children in the United States that I address the concluding chapter. My hope is that by presenting the case of the Rotumans I can convince a few American educators that all children need not be cast into the same cultural mold in order to become competent, productive citizens in a technologically complex industrial society.

NOTE

[1] For an excellent introduction to the cultural significance of spatial arrangements and timing see Edward T. Hall, *The Hidden Dimension* (Garden City: Doubleday & Company, 1966).

The Island and its People

Any attempt to understand education without a grasp of the historical factors that have influenced it is like trying to understand calculus without having been exposed to basic mathematics. Culture is the product of history, and cultural transmission is itself an historical process. Even before the presence of white men, the cultures of the South Seas were evolving and influencing each other. It is true that we do not have documentation of the changes that were taking place, but the results are reflected in the racial, linguistic, and archaeological records. What appears to have emerged is a culture whose dynamics were well suited to island environments, a culture emphasizing cooperation and capable of adapting to changing conditions.

The coming of missionaries and traders lent impetus to change and altered its direction. The missionaries brought with them new problems, new resources, and new ideas. They also attacked some elements in the traditional culture; with only a few exceptions, however, the peoples of the South Seas adapted to the pressures without changing the fundamental character of their life style. But history has also brought Rotuma into the orbit of the modern world and the island can no longer be looked at in isolation. Economically, religiously, and politically Rotuma is now part of the modern world and is changing with it.

In this chapter we shall set the stage for examining educational processes by sketching the historical background that has shaped Rotuman culture. We begin by describing the location and geographical environment of the island, and some of what is known about its prehistory. We then discuss the changes that were induced by the first century of contact with Europeans, culminating in the establishment of colonial rule toward the end of the nineteenth century. Finally, the major trends of the twentieth century are described, ending in a description of the current (as of 1960) socio-economic structure of the society.

THE SETTING

Geography

The island of Rotuma is located at 12° South Latitude and 177° East Longitude, some three hundred miles north of the Fiji group in the South Pacific. It is a similar distance to the south of the Ellice Islands; Futuna, its "neighbor" to the east, lies about 240 miles away. The nearest islands to the west are the New Hebrides, approximately 500 miles distant. Rotuma is therefore somewhat isolated, a factor that helps to account for some of the unique cultural features of its people. Isolation has also insulated Rotuman culture to some extent from the overpowering influence of the Western world, and during the time when research was being carried out, the island community gave every indication of having maintained its cultural integrity despite over a century and a half of exposure to Western culture.

Geologically Rotuma is of volcanic origin, with its highest crater rising about 840 feet above sea level. A glance at the map on page 13 shows the island to be divided into two main parts, joined by an isthmus. Tradition holds that the two parts were once separate, and the geological evidence supports this contention; indications are that the isthmus was formed by sand being washed upon an intervening reef. Taken as a whole, the island is about eight miles long, and, at its widest, approximately three miles across. It comprises a land area of 17½ square miles. Surrounding the island is a fringing reef; within a short distance from the mainland are several off-shore islets, none of which is now inhabited.

Rotuma possesses an extremely rich soil, in which nearly all tropical plants flourish. From the sea the island casts a dark green hue, appearing almost black, so luxuriant is its vegetation. The entire island is covered with coconut trees, including the slopes of the volcanic craters, and virtually all the interior lands are suitable for cultivation. There is no natural supply of fresh water, with the exception of a small springlet, which supplies only the smallest district, Itumuta, when rain has been plentiful. The rainfall is sufficient most of the time, however, so that there is rarely a shortage of fresh water; provision is made for its storage in iron or concrete tanks. In addition, scattered over the island are a number of wells, whose water, though somewhat saline, can be used for washing and bathing if rainwater runs short. Droughts never affect the drinking supply, for the people always have access to the sweet nectar of young coconuts.

The climate is tropical, but rarely uncomfortable. Hardly ever does the temperature rise above 90°F nor fall below 70°F. From April through November the tradewinds blow steadily from the southeast. During this part of the year temperature and wind variations are minimal. From December through March the winds shift to the north and northwest. During this period the weather is less predictable; the wind may die down to a whisper, leaving the island sweltering, or it may occasionally rise to hurricane force.

Rotuma's geographical location is particularly interesting because of its nearness to the conventional intersection of the cultural areas known as Micronesia (containing the Caroline, Marshall, Mariana, and Gilbert Islands), Melanesia (containing the New Hebrides, Solomon, Santa Cruz, and Fiji Islands), and Polynesia (containing New Zealand and the Hawaiian, Samoan, Tongan, Cook, and Society Islands groups). The physical characteristics, language, and culture of the Rotumans show influences from each of these regions, as one might expect.

The People

Physically the Rotumans manifest a considerable amount of variation, but first impressions lead one to classify them as essentially Polynesian. Most are quite light-skinned, with black wavy hair and Polynesian facial features. They are a well-formed people, but generally smaller in stature than the Tongans or Samoans. Obesity is common, but not prevalent, among the middle-aged group. Upon closer examination one notices a number of individuals with features characteristic of the Melanesian peoples to the west—darker skin, wooly hair, and narrower aquiline nasal forms. Still others manifest the more Mongoloid features of the Micronesians to the northwest, and it is not uncommon for visitors to Rotuma to ask if some of the people are of Oriental extraction. From a Western point of view, a high proportion of Rotumans are attractive in both physical bearing and facial features.

The Language

The Rotuman language also reflects the island's geographical location, and as a result of extensive influence from several distinct sources has developed its own unique character. According to C. M. Churchward, a Methodist missionary who spent many years on Rotuma and

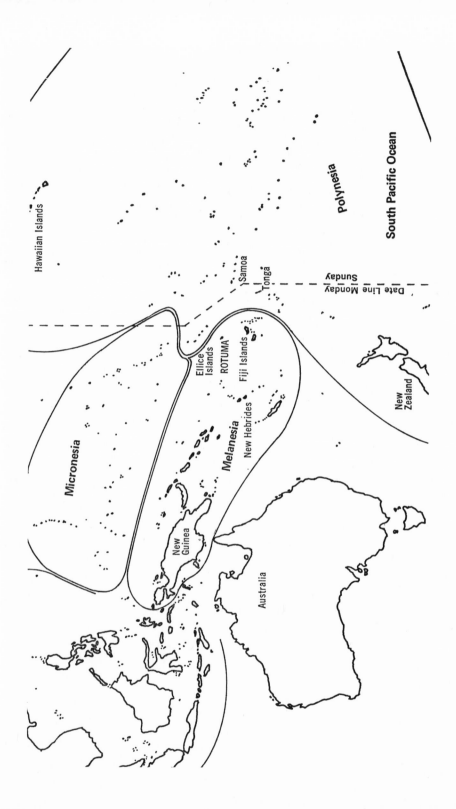

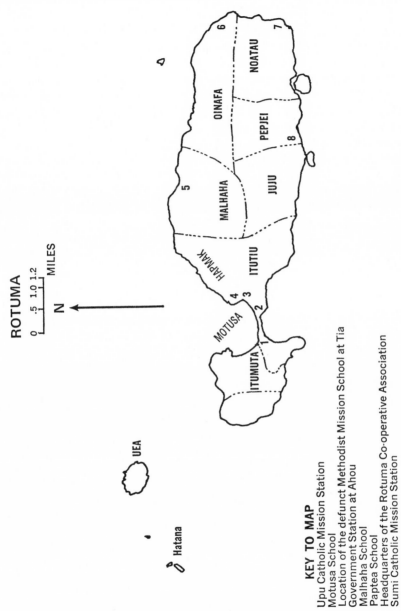

ROTUMA

0   .5   1.0 1.2
MILES

N

Hatana

UEA

HAPMAK

MOTUSA

ITUMUTA

ITUTIU

MALHAHA

OINAFA

JUJU

PEPJEI

NOATAU

5

6

7

8

4
3
2
1

KEY TO MAP

1. Upu Catholic Mission Station
2. Motusa School
3. Location of the defunct Methodist Mission School at Tia
4. Government Station at Ahou
5. Malhaha School
6. Paptea School
7. Headquarters of the Rotuma Co-operative Association
8. Sumi Catholic Mission Station

made an extensive study of the language, Rotuman is in no sense a dialect of any other known language, but can best be explained as the result of a fusion of several earlier languages. In contrast to the Polynesian languages, which, like Spanish and Italian, have relatively few vowels, the Rotuman language is more like French or German in its elaboration of vowel sounds. Also un-Polynesian is the use of consonants at the end of words, which gives the listener the impression that the language is less relaxed and musical than such languages as Hawaiian, Samoan, or Fijian. Ironically, although the language is spoken by less than six thousand persons, three separate orthographies have been developed since the island's discovery, and all three are still in use. The first two were developed independently by French priests and English ministers who missionized the island during the latter part of the nineteenth century. Each orthography reflects the phonetics of the writer's mother tongue. The third spelling, introduced by Churchward, uses phonetic symbols and, although more complicated, it is more accurate than either of the others and will be used in this work to designate Rotuman words (see Appendix A).

Prehistory

Until the archaeological sites on Rotuma have been excavated and their materials analyzed, speculations about the island's pre-historic affiliations must remain highly tentative, but indications are that it was initially settled prior to Polynesia proper by a people who spoke a proto-Polynesian language. We have no way of knowing the physical characteristics of these people, but it seems probable that they were darker-skinned than the current population, and generally more similar to present Fijians. This early group probably remained somewhat isolated, with an occasional lost canoe arriving from another island. Then, as the Pacific island populations grew and explorations (planned or accidental) increased, the number of canoes arriving from other lands must have increased accordingly, in some cases with profound effect. The most significant cultural "invasions" evidently came from Samoa and Tonga, in what has sometimes been called the westward Polynesian "backwash."[1] The founding legend of Rotuma states that the island was originally "produced" and settled by a Samoan chief named Raho. Another legend tells of a Tongan invasion, led by the chief Ma'afu, that took place less than one hundred years before the European discovery of the island. According to this tradition the Tongans conquered the island and proceeded to allot the various parts of Rotuma to their own men. The Rotumans, so the legend goes, found their conquerors overly demanding and oppressive and rebelled, eventually defeating the Tongans. Nevertheless, even today the highest chiefly title on the island is "Marafu," a Rotuman adaptation of the Tongan invader's name.[2]

The effects of the Samoan and Tongan intrusions have been sufficient to give Rotuman culture a decidedly Polynesian character, but the mixture of other influences has given it a flavor that is neither Polynesian, Micronesian, nor Melanesian, but simply Rotuman.

THE EUROPEANS AND COLONIZATION

Rotuma was "discovered" in 1791 by Captain Edward Edwards in H.M.S. *Pandora* while he was searching for the mutineers of the *Bounty*. The vessel, according to the accounts of Captain Edwards and the ship's surgeon, Dr. George Hamilton, was received with great suspicion. The Rotumans approached the ship with caution and were prepared for war, but through constant coaxing and offers of presents the crew managed to lure the reluctant natives on board, and successfully negotiated for supplies. Before the eighteenth century had ended, the island was visited by a second European vessel, the missionary ship *Duff*, but the Rotumans were not eager to trade, and after a minor incident provoked by an attempt by one of the islanders to make off with a non-negotiable item, all trading ceased.

The first half of the nineteenth century was a time of increasing contact with agents of European culture, and any reluctance to engage in trading gave way to an eagerness for the acquisition of European goods. Whalers found the luxuriant island as excellent station for replenishing their stores, and it became a favorite stopping place. In addition to the whalers there were labor recruiters, who were responsible for transporting scores of young men to plantations in all parts of the Pacific. Other young men eagerly signed on board visiting ships as crew members, and sailed to the far corners of the globe. In addition to these influences, contact with European culture (or at least a highly specialized segment of it) was rendered continuous by the large number of deserters who found their way to Rotuma's hospitable shores. Several of the latter took Rotuman wives and left a substantial progeny—a factor that has contributed to diversification of physical types among the people.

Soon after the middle of the nineteenth century missionaries from the Wesleyan (Methodist) and Roman Catholic Churches established themselves on Rotuma. Unfortunately, the French priests and English ministers were somewhat less than tolerant toward one another's labors, and a religious factionalism resulted. Each mission marked off its own territorial domain and jealously guarded its converts from the "evil" influences of the other side. An increasing number of disputes arose between adherents of the opposing faiths, often over the question of the right to build churches on communally held land. Antagonisms between the Wesleyans and Catholics continued to mount until 1878, when they culminated in a war between the two groups, in which the Catholics were defeated by the numerically superior Wesleyans.

The unrest that followed this religious war led the paramount chiefs of Rotuma's several districts to petition England for annexation, and in 1881 the island was officially ceded to Great Britain. The Crown decided that Rotuma should be administered as a part of the Colony of Fiji—the nearest Crown Colony—rather than as a separate unit. A Resident Commissioner was appointed to govern it along with an advisory body comprising the seven paramount chiefs. Fortunately for the Rotumans, government under English law had the desired effect of reducing religious conflict, and eventually harmony between the two religious factions was restored.

In the years following cession the administration did what it could to foster the growth of trade and to bring the "benefits" of civilization, including the luxury of Western material culture, to this remote Pacific island. Prior to the advent of Europeans, the Rotuman economy was based upon dry land agriculture, fishing, animal husbandry (pigs and chickens), and a system of ceremonial exchange. For subsistence they depended upon the characteristic Polynesian root crops—taro and yams—supplemented by fruits and seafood. Pigs and fowl, though sometimes used as food staples, were usually reserved for ceremonial occasions. These commodities were exchanged most abundantly during weddings, funerals, and other life-crisis ceremonies, but they were also used as a means of apologizing for wrongs and as a technique for expressing gratitude (see Chapter V).

There was little opportunity for extensive trade relations with other islands, and although some contacts were almost certainly maintained, the economy of the island was essentially a closed system. The arrival of European vessels "opened up" the system and paved the way for Rotuma's current participation in the world economy. The early visitors needed supplies, and exchanged such items as metal tools and cloth for them. The Rotumans soon came to value European goods to a considerable extent, and trade with visiting ships flourished.

Sometime between 1860 and 1870 the first commercial traders established themselves in Rotuma, and in all probability the island's first commercial product was coconut oil. It was not long before the copra trade sprang up, however, and by 1875 copra had replaced coconut oil as Rotuma's chief export.[3]

Kava, a root from which a beverage with a mild narcotic effect can be brewed, was also exported in small quantity. In 1881—the year of cession—Rotuma exported 446.5 tons of copra, 2 tons of coconuts, 104 gallons of coconut oil, and 3 tons of kava, with a total estimated export value of £2,800 (approximately $11,200). Imports for the same year were valued at £2,076 (approximately $8,300), and included tools, clothing, food, and sundry other articles of civilization.

The nineteenth century was thus a time of rapid socio-cultural change on Rotuma. During that period the society underwent an extentive transformation from its pre-contact state, though not without a good deal of social upheaval. By the beginning of the twentieth century, however, this transformation was virtually complete, and the Rotumans had adjusted to the alien culture. They had been "Christian" for nearly half a century, had engaged in commercial trading for a comparable period of time, and had submitted to English law for nearly twenty years. They wore European clothes, used European tools, and supplemented their native diet with tinned meats, tea, biscuits, and innumerable other items of European food. They also paid taxes to the government, applied for marriages and divorces through government offices, sought medical aid from the Resident Commissioner, and sent their children to mission schools.

This does not mean that Rotumans simply adopted Western culture uncritically and made no efforts to retain their own customs. It would be more correct to characterize the nineteenth century as a period of selective cultural borrowing, in which the Rotumans adopted into their society a considerable number of foreign elements, and managed to attain a new integration.

THE TWENTIETH CENTURY

During the twentieth century Rotuma has continued to change, but it has changed more as a part of the modern world than as a distinct entity. Although the Rotuman community has retained its unique cultural identity to a considerable degree, economically and socially it has become thoroughly integrated with the rest of the Colony of Fiji. Today Rotuma is in the position of a hinterland community to Fiji's urban centers, particularly the city of Suva, which is the center of government, commerce, and communication for the colony. Information, goods, money, and people continually flow into Suva from all over Fiji and it serves as a center for the dispersal of the commodities that are necessary to maintain modern social life.

The Economy

Economically Rotuma has remained dependent on copra as a commercial product. As the market for coconut oil and kava dropped away, copra became, in fact, the island's only source of income. Various attempts have been made through the years to introduce such secondary crops as cocoa, coffee, rubber, and tobacco, but so far none has met with success. Were Rotuma closer to Fiji's markets, it could profitably export such perishable commodities as bananas, oranges, and other surplus foods, but the problem of lengthy storage and the high cost of transportation render such a trade impractical.

Rotuma is nevertheless a prosperous island. Except during periods when the copra market fell badly, as it did during the Great Depression of the 1930's, the Rotumans have always had access to an abundance of goods. The average income per family now ranges somewhere between $250 and $500 annually, and since subsistence expenses are low, most people have ample money to spend on clothes, household articles, food luxuries, improvements to their houses, or whatever else may take their fancy.

Rotuma's subsistence economy itself has not been changed drastically by the advent of commercialism, except for the addition of money as a medium for exchange. But access to European products over a span of nearly two centuries has completely altered the standard of living, and has resulted in Rotuma's overall economy becoming inextricably tied to that of Fiji. Many European products are now considered absolute necessities rather than luxuries, and if Rotuma were cut off from them for an extended period of time, it would suffer as much as would communities in rural Europe or the United States under comparable conditions. To obtain such commodities requires money, and to get money Rotumans must cut copra, which is exported to Fiji. The result is an economic dependence on the urban commercial market.

This economic dependence on commercial exports has many ramifications for life in Rotuma. For example, fluctuations in the price of copra (a consequence of world market conditions) touch upon many areas of Rotuman life by affecting the amount of money available. Expensive Rotuman-style weddings may be deferred or even eliminated in times when copra prices are low, and since the cost of manufactured goods remains more or less stable, a fall in the price of copra must be compensated for by an increase in production in order to maintain the same standard of living; or men may decide to delay cutting their copra in the hope that prices will rise. In these ways the price of copra, though it is determined by factors completely external to Rotuma, affects the daily routine of the people.

The advent of the government-sponsored co-operative movement following World War II has had a great impact on the Rotuman economy and has projected it into a new phase. Prior to 1947 the business of the island was carried out exclusively by two or three established firms and a few independent traders. The people themselves were merely customers. Now, with the co-operative movement firmly entrenched on the island and handling the bulk of the business, each member has become an integral part of a business organization, and is gaining a working knowledge of business affairs. This broadening of economic responsibility, which is one of the primary goals of the co-operative movement, has in no way weakened economic affiliation between Rotuma and Fiji. Rather it has placed the interaction on a more extensive and democratic basis through wider participation in economic affairs.

Rotuma's ties with Fiji have been further reinforced by the growth of Rotuman colonies in Fiji. Like so many Pacific islands, Rotuma underwent a period of depopulation following contact with Europeans. Having neither resistance to newly-introduced diseases nor the knowledge to treat them, such relatively mild diseases as measles took a heavy toll. But a combination of modern medicine and the processes of natural selection has led the population to rebound with great vitality, and now the Rotumans are increasing at a rate approaching the upper limits of human capability. As a result the island faces a population problem. Rotumans are being put under great pressure by land shortages to emigrate to Fiji in order to find wage employment. In 1921 only 5.5% of the Rotuman population lived in Fiji (123 of 2,235); by 1956 the percentage had swelled to 32.3% (1,429 of 4,422). The majority live either in the capital city of Suva or in the gold-mining community of Vatukoula.

With the growth of these colonies has come a more intense interaction between Rotuma and Fiji. Travel back and forth has greatly increased, as has the flow of information and ideas. Almost every adult Rotuman has been to Fiji one or more times, and the young people who were born and raised in Fiji are eager to visit their home island. Goods and money are constantly being exchanged between kinsmen and friends in the two places. It is quite common for relatives in Fiji who are earning a good wage to send money to Rotuma for special occasions, or simply to help their families. Husbands or sons may even do this on a regular basis, sometimes sending a weekly sum by telegraph. Such goods as furniture, clothes, and personal effects are also sent to Rotuma by successful urban residents, and proud is the son or daughter who, upon returning, can provide his parents with the funds for a new iron roof on their home.

Goods and money are also sent from people in Rotuma to those in Fiji. Every ship returning from the island carries baskets of oranges and other fruit for delivery to relatives and friends; mats and gifts, and a complement of pigs and fowl are also in evidence, destined for a wedding or other festive event. Then, too, many a Rotuman who has failed to succeed in Fiji has resorted to sending for passage money home, obliging his relatives to go into the bush and cut the necessary copra.

The Settlement Pattern

A survey of the island reveals that house-sites were previously scattered through the interior as well as along the coast, but before the turn of the twentieth century the entire population had settled near the shore. Soon after cession the colonial administration completed a road for horses around the circumference of the western section of the island, and along the northern shore of the eastern section. In 1927 the road was improved to accommodate motor vehicles. With the increased significance of commercial trading, these roads have become the economic lifeline of the island, and at the present time houses are scattered along them, making it difficult to distinguish villages as distinct entities.

The main commercial center is at Motusa, on the isthmus joining the eastern and western parts of the island. Two prominent South Pacific trading companies have their central Rotuman branches there, although each maintains small stores at various points around the island.[4] Three Indian tailors also operate shops in Motusa, and a Rotuman family runs its own retail business and operates a motion picture theater. Motusa owes its prominence to the fact that the northern anchorage at Motusa Bay is favored by visiting sea captains because it provides maximum protection during most of the year. Rotuma has no natural harbors and visiting ships must anchor off the reef, discharging and loading their cargo by launch. More recently Noatau, on the opposite end of the island, has become a commercial center, it being the location of the Rotuman Co-operative Association (R.C.A.) headquarters. Ships bearing co-op goods use the anchorage off Oinafa, which, although it is not regarded as satisfactory from a nautical point of view, has the advantage of permitting around-the-clock loading and unloading. This is impossible at the Motusa anchorage because the reef creates an impassible barrier during low tide.

Transportation is provided by government trucks and buses, trucks owned by the firms and R.C.A., and private taxis operated by two of the Indian tailors. The only electricity on the island is produced by generators at the Government station, the two Catholic mission stations, and the firms, all for private consumption; there are no telephones for intra-island use.

Religion

One result of missionization was that the people on one side of the island converted to Methodism and those on the other side, quite possibly in reaction since they were political rivals, converted to Catholicism; this pattern has peristed into modern times. Catholics are concentrated in the districts of Juju and Pepjei (which together are known as Faguta) and the adjacent sections of Itutiu and Noatau, although a few Catholic families are scattered around the rest of the island.[5] Likewise a few Methodist families live in the Catholic area. Despite this territorial arrangement, the areas served by the two missions overlap to a considerable degree. Thus the Catholic mission not only maintains a station at Sumi, in the heart of Faguta, but one on the Motusa isthmus as well. The latter, the Upu station, serves a territory that is predominantly Methodist. Both Sumi and Upu have large concrete churches built in Gothic style, complete with gargoyles, stained glass windows, and organs. They were designed according to patterns common in European towns, and constructed over a long period of time under the guidance of resident French priests around the turn of the century. To the newcomer these structures seem somewhat incongruous in a tropical setting among the coconut trees, but before I left they appeared as much a normal part of the landscape as the sandy beaches and thatched roofs.

The Catholic churches are under the supervision of Marist priests; in 1960 Upu was under the direction of Father Beattie, a New Zealander, and Sumi was in the hands of Father Maguire, an Irishman. Father Kitolelei, the first Rotuman to become a priest, assisted Father Maguire at Sumi, which is the larger of the two parishes. Both Catholic mission stations maintain schools and support a staff of teaching nuns and lay brothers, most of whom are Rotuman, although a few of the nuns at Sumi are from European or North American countries.

The organization of the Methodist mission is more complex. The island is divided into two circuits, each containing six "churches." [6] A resident minister is in charge of each circuit, and one or more catechists are attached to each church. There are also lay preachers, church stewards, leaders (Sunday school teachers), and deaconesses. All the people occupying these positions are Rotuman, including the ministers. The churches maintain a full schedule of activities, including prayer meetings, youth group evenings, choir practice, and so on. Although the Methodists ran schools for some time following the establishment of their mission, they relinquished this function to the colonial government in the 1920's (see Chapter IV).

Government

The central figure in the government of Rotuma is the District Officer,[7] who is appointed by the Governor of Fiji. He presides over the Council of Rotuma, is in charge of the administration of the island, and has the power of second class magistrate. In 1945 the first Rotuman was appointed District Officer, and with the exception of a few short intervals, Rotumans have been appointed to the post ever since. Thus the island's immediate administration is entirely in the hands of the local people, although they are ultimately responsible to the Colonial Administration in Suva.

The Council of Rotuma comprises, in addition to the District Officer, the chiefs of the seven districts, one elected representative from each district, and the senior medical officer on the island. The purpose of the Council is "to consider all such questions relating to the good government and well-being of the natives in the island as may be directed by the Governor or may seem to them to require their attention."[8] The Council is empowered to make regulations relating to:[9]

(a) the keeping clean of Rotuma and the promotion of public health;
(b) the social and economic betterment of natives;
(c) the performance of communal work by natives and other communal activities of natives;
(d) the control of livestock on Rotuma;
(e) the care of native children and aged persons; and
(f) the conservation of food supplies on Rotuma.

It also has authority to impose fines for breaches of its regulations.

The Council meets quarterly and decides issues by majority vote, with the District Officer having the deciding vote in case of a tie, in addition to his original vote. Meetings are conducted in the Rotuman language [10] and according to the rules of parliamentary procedure. Prior to the meal a kava ceremony is held, in which members are served in rank order, beginning with the District Officer. After meetings a feast is prepared and a kava ceremony held, with each district hosting the event in rotation.

The District Officer is responsible for maintaining the following facilities: a hospital and dispensary, the schools, a post and telegraph department, the police force, and a Court of Justice. All departments, with the exception of the schools, have their headquarters at the Government station at Ahou, which is located on a picturesque bluff overlooking Motusa Bay. It is a separate little community, consisting of the administration buildings, homes for government officials, a hospital and dispensary, a jail, and a wireless station.

The hospital and dispensary are located in a neat wooden building surrounded by a veranda. An Assistant Medical Officer (A.M.O.) is in charge; his staff includes some six or seven nurses, an ambulance driver trained as a dresser, and a hospital maintenance crew. The A.M.O. during 1959 was a Rotuman who had been trained at the Suva Medical School, an institution serving the entire Pacific region. He was replaced in 1960 by a Fijian with comparable training. Both were conscientious and able men who performed their duties well.

The Rotumans make ample use of the medical facilities provided them, and their confidence in modern medicine is great. This is not to say that they have entirely abandoned their belief in native practices, however. The latter mainly consist of highly specialized massages and herbal medicines, administered by anyone who is learned about such things, possibly with the help of ritual formula. Most people seek both native and modern medical treatment, just to be on the safe side.

A program of child welfare is administered by the nurses, who visit the districts at regular intervals. In order to increase the incentive of mothers to take proper care of their children, an annual baby show is held in which prizes are given to the parents of the healthiest and most blemish-free infants and children. The program has met with considerable success and the rate of infant mortality, which was once very high, has declined to an insignificant level in recent years. This decline in infant mortality is but one aspect of an overall drop in the death rate. Prior to 1930, when the first systematic public health program was initiated, the annual death rate approached 50 per 1000. Between 1930 and the early 1950's, the rate dropped to about 25 per thousand, and by 1960, as a result of the introduction of penicillin and other wonder drugs, the rate had dropped still further, to about 5 per thousand. Since the birth rate has remained relatively constant throughout the entire period (at approximately 45 per thousand), the population is increasing at an accelerating rate. Thus the health problem has given way to the problem of over-population, and a need for family planning is becoming apparent.

The post and telegraph department is responsible for handling mail and operating the wireless station on the island. Mail is delivered and picked up by each vessel, and it is processed at the post office at Ahou. In 1960 some 106 bags of mail were delivered to the island and 21 bags were taken to Fiji. This imbalance in the flow—fully five times as much coming in as going out—can be accounted for mainly by the inflow of magazines, newspapers, and pamphlets. They constitute a major source of news about the outside world for people living in

Rotuma. Most of them are received by the few well-educated persons, who disseminate the news to their less literate friends, who in turn spread it around the island. Quite understandably, such information is often exaggerated or misinterpreted to suit special interests. For instance, a French priest wrote into his diary for the year 1940:

Defeat of France and the signature of the armistice of the 24th of June. A tremendous surprise to the Europeans. One of them spoke badly of France and soon the Wesleyans began rejoicing and announcing everywhere the defeat of France, not understanding anything of this very complicated situation.[11]

Much of the mail, however, is personal correspondence with friends and relatives in Fiji, exchanging the mundane news of everyday life.

A wireless installation was inaugurated in 1933 and maintains daily contact with Suva. It includes both a telegraph and radio-telephone service, permitting intimate and extensive communication between the two points. These services make rapid transmission of information possible and are used to convey messages of arrivals and departures, births and deaths, and requests for money or goods. Government personnel, missionaries, and business managers also use them to communicate information and requests, and to receive orders and advice. In addition, the telegraph is used to transmit meteorological data to Suva.

The Fiji Police Department maintains a minimum staff on the island; in 1960 there were only a corporal and a constable, both Rotumans. Neither was overworked, for serious crime is quite rare. A jail is nevertheless maintained at the government station with a warden in charge, and there is usually a prisoner or two to help mow the lawns or paint the buildings on the station grounds. When a violation of a Rotuma regulation or the penal code is reported, the police investigate, and if they conclude that an offense has indeed occurred, they issue a summons to the suspected party. He is then required to appear before the District Officer's Court to plead his case. If the offense is minor, not requiring an indictment, the case is heard solely by the District Officer and his judgment is final. In serious cases requiring indictment, evidence is taken by the District Officer and recorded in English. The transcript is then sent to the Chief Justice in Suva, along with any recommendations the District Officer wishes to make, for a verdict.

In addition to criminal cases, the District Officer's Court also hears land cases, divorce suits, and any civil action that is brought to its attention.

Finally, it is the responsibility of the District Officer to keep records, to make reports to the administration in Fiji, and to communicate directives from them to the people on the island. As a result of Rotuma's isolation the District Officer is endowed with extraordinary decision-making powers, but fortunately the men who have occupied the post have almost all been of the highest integrity. They have made mistakes and at times created ill-will, but their errors have been rooted in ignorance and at times inadequacy, virtually never in a willful abuse of power.

SUMMARY

This, then, is the geographical, historical, and political context within which Rotuman children are educated. It is a world as yet uncomplicated by the massive bombardment of new information and products that the urbanized middle-class American has to cope with daily. It is a world of familiar faces and a sense of community. But although the island itself is isolated and confined, its people are currently being absorbed more and more rapidly into the modern world. They are being exposed to mass media at an accelerating rate and are travelling more freely. Like other emergent peoples their aspirations are rising accordingly and they have hopes of attaining a standard of living of which their grandparents, or even parents, would not have dreamed. They are a people still swirling in only an eddy of the frantic tide of modern change, but they are aware that they will be swept out to sea someday, and are looking around for something Rotuman to bring with them.

NOTES

[1] This presumes the settlement of Polynesia to have been predominantly a west to east movement; the "backwash" refers to post-settlement east to west movements.

[2] For an account of Rotuman legendary history and mythology, see C.M. Churchward, *Tales of a Lonely Isle* (Sydney: Oceania Monographs, No. 4, 1940).

[3] Copra is the dried meat of the coconut, from which a commercially valuable oil is extracted.

[4] I have recently received word that the success of the Rotuma Co-operative Association has been so great that the two firms have been forced out of business on the island.

[5] The only district that does not contain any Catholic families is Oinafa, whose chief during the time of the religious war of 1878 vowed not to

permit Catholics to reside there. His oath is still taken seriously by the present leaders of the district.

[6] This does not refer to church buildings, but rather to congregations. In actual fact there are fourteen church buildings and two houses that are used for that purpose.

[7] Rotuma is single district within the administrative structure of the Colony of Fiji.

[8] Colony of Fiji Ordinance No. 4 of 1958, p. 3.

[9] *Ibid.*

[10] As long as the District Officer was a European, an interpreter was used. Even now, however, an account of the minutes is translated into English for transmission to the central Administration in Suva.

[11] *Historique de la Station St. Michel Upu Rotuma.* Unpublished manuscript. Translated from the French by Irwin Howard.

— *III* ——————————————

The Early Years:
The World of
Household and Kinsmen

Well before a child enters school he is expected to know a good deal that is fundamental to living in his society. He must learn how to walk and talk, how to do what is necessary to take care of himself, and, most importantly for Rotumans, how to get along with other people. Not only is he brought into the world amidst ceremony that places him immediately into a network of social obligations, but he is himself part of his parents' social network, and his behavior implicates them. Although parental love engenders considerable indulgence, the weight of obligation requires restraint, and therein lies the problem of socialization for Rotuman parents.

BIRTH

From the time it is known that a woman is pregnant, social processes are set in motion that are designed to facilitate the child's adaptation to the society that awaits him. Expectant mothers are a focus of attention and are carefully looked after by husbands and relatives. They are apt to be pampered and urged to get plenty of food and rest, so that the baby will be strong. Every effort is made to satisfy pregnant women's cravings, for it is believed that their babies will be adversely affected if they are not. During first pregnancies women like to be with their mothers and usually return to their parental home for the first few months after conception and again shortly before confinement. Today most first births are delivered at the hospital by the Assistant Medical Officer and nurses; subsequent births take place in the home with a trained mid-wife in attendance.

For some time now the Rotumans have been aware of modern practices regarding prenatal and postnatal care, and most of their aboriginal practices in this area have been abandoned. It might be of some interest nevertheless to relate a description given in 1899 by H. E. Leefe, then Resident Commissioner:

For some weeks before confinement the mother is dosed with native medicines. As soon as the child is born & the umbilical cord cut & bound up, a woman gives the child a native medicine . . . to make it vomit & empty its stomach which they believe to be full of unclean matter. The child is then either rubbed all over with a wet cloth, or else washed in a wooden bowl, cold water being used. The infant is then given to some woman who is suckling a child, no matter what age her child may be or whether she smokes, drinks kava etc. It is then dosed with coconut oil or milk of the nut, this done it is covered up so that not a breath of air can get near it, as is also the mother. On the 4th day the child is given to its mother to suckle. . . . When the first dose of herbal medicine is given, if the child vomits the natives say that it is a sign that the child is healthy. If the child is not healthy, they call in different wise (?) women each of whom has a medicine of her own, & these are tried one after another if the first does not cure it. . . . They consider the mother's milk unfit for the child to drink until after a period of four days, in the meantime they feed the mother well on young coconuts until her milk becomes richer, as they say at first she has only bad water in her breasts. If the child does not thrive on its mother's milk, they get in some instances a native wise woman to secure all the mother's milk into a tin which they boil, & when it boils they place two hot stones in it, if the milk clings in white flakes to the stones it is considered good, but if it is thin and watery & has an unpleasant odour they consider it to be bad. If bad they dose the mother with coconut oil & give her nothing to eat; about a quart would be an ordinary dose—After the first bath the child is not washed again for a considerable period of time —sometimes for a month or more.[1]

Today the guiding principles of postnatal care are determined by the Fiji Department of Health, with a corresponding reduction in infant mortality. Bottle feeding, the use of powder and other baby cosmetics, and most of the paraphernalia familiar to an American mother for the care of her baby are known and used by Rotuman mothers.

When a child is born, or possibly before it is born, someone may come to the parents and request that the child be named after him. Alternatively, the parents may ask a particular person to be the child's namesake (sigoa). This establishes a special relationship between the person giving the name and the child, one that simulates the grandparent-grandchild relationship. The name-giver is expected to indulge his namesake and grant him considerable personal license. In all subsequent life-crisis ceremonies a person's *sigoa* has a special role to play.

It is customary to consider the first child as belonging to the father, the second to the mother, the third to the father, and so forth. If the child belongs to the father, it is up to his family to select a namesake; if the child belongs to the mother, her side of the family enjoys the privilege. This arrangement simplifies divorce or separation procedures, among other things, for the father can simply take "his" children and the mother "her" children.

Only after the birth of a first child is it appropriate to have an elaborate ceremony. This is called *'of'aki*, and initially involves the family of the father bringing a ceremonial food offering (*koua*) to the place of birth. Customarily, the child is held, or carried about, by the father's relatives until the food has been delivered. They may carry the infant for a few hours, a day, or several days, depending upon how much they wish to emphasize the significance of the event. A more elaborate ceremony, the one for which the custom is named, is held within a week or so following birth, usually on the fifth day. This involves a ceremonial exchange of food and mats by the families of the parents and their mutual participation in a feast.

THE HOUSEHOLD

The household into which a child is born is likely to be a large one. A census taken during 1960 by myself and some Rotuman assistants revealed an average of 6.9 persons per unit for 417 households containing Rotumans or part-Rotumans. For the purposes of definition, a household was considered to consist of individuals occupying the same or adjacent sleeping houses, and sharing a common hearth (i.e., cooking and eating together). The Rotuman term for such a social unit is *kau noho'ag*.

The core of the majority of these households consists of a nuclear family. Attached to this basic unit may be any bilateral relative, from parents to unspecified relatives. Those persons who are not members of a nuclear family—including widowed and divorced persons, orphaned children, offspring of unwed mothers, and unmarried adults— tend to have a high rate of residential mobility, moving from household to household. An elderly widow, for example, might spend time in the homes of each of her several children.

Ideally, a newly-married couple lives at the bride's home, but numerous factors may mitigate against this choice. Actually the ideal rule presumes special circumstances—that both the girl's parents are alive and that she has been living with them, that the marriage has been properly arranged, and that her family possesses sufficient resources (especially land) to accommodate a new family. The initial choice of residence is rarely a final one, and most newly-married couples make several moves before establishing themselves. They may eventually end up on land belonging to either the husband's family or the wife's—the final choice being one of expediency. A few persons have established themselves on land that they obtained through purchase or gift.

Physically, a household minimally consists of a sleeping house and a cooking house. Some also include a separate eating house, wash house, storage shed, or even a second sleeping house. In addition, each household is required by law to maintain adequate toilet facilities. Domestic compounds may be arranged in whatever fashion the household head decides; there is no set plan.

Sleeping houses are always the most elaborate structures, and are used to entertain guests. They are built upon raised platforms, which serves to keep them dry in rainy weather. In pre-European times the height of one's platform (fūag rī) was an indication of rank. Thus ordinary people built their houses upon platforms two or three feet high, whereas chiefs built theirs on much higher platforms. A number of remains of such platforms can still be found in the bush, measuring between ten and fifteen feet in height. Traditionally houses were built entirely of thatch, but shortly after contact with Europeans lime was introduced as a building material, and houses with limestone walls and thatched roofs became popular. As the prosperity of the island increased, lumber and corrugated iron were imported and used in varying combinations. Today, houses vary in construction, some having thatched walls and thatched roof, some limestone walls with thatched or iron roof, some wooden walls with thatched or iron roof, and others with iron walls and thatched roof.

Each house has at least two doorways, the distinction between them being of social consequence. The front door, which generally faces the sea, is used for receiving formal visitors, or men of rank. All ceremonial interaction concerning the household, including the removal of a corpse, takes place through this passage. The back door, which generally faces away from the sea, is used only by persons of the household, close friends, and relatives. To enter a house by the rear door is a form of social license, and hence an indication of intimacy with the members of the household. If the house is built perpendicular to, instead of parallel to, the sea, the front door may face a village green (marä'e), and the back door away from it.

The interior of each house is covered with mats, and today almost every family owns a table and a few chairs, and at least one bed. Most people, however, sleep on a neat pile of mats, carefully stacked at either end of the house. Incongruous as it seems to the visitor, heavy Victorian furniture is favored. The high four-poster beds seem strangely out of place in this Polynesian setting, but the posts provide an ideal frame over which to place mosquito netting. Some homes are rather lavishly furnished, containing all the essentials of a European dwelling, including wardrobe cabinets, dresser drawers, and a settee. A survey of household interiors indicated that about 30% contained sufficient furniture to be considered essentially European in standard, a reasonable indication of the prosperity of the island when one takes into account the expense of shipping furniture from Fiji.

More than most other Polynesian peoples, Rotumans are concerned with personal privacy, even within the household, and drapes may be hung to section off the sleeping areas. If a family is large, both ends of the house may be draped off, only the middle being exposed to visitors.

In comparison to sleeping houses, cooking houses are usually quite crude. Most consist of little more than an open frame of logs and a thatched roof, with iron or thatched siding from the ground to a height of perhaps two feet. The openness serves the purpose of letting the smoke out from the oven. If rain or wind becomes a problem, mats are hung for protection on the weather side. Cooking houses have no flooring, since the traditional style of preparing food in an earthen oven (*koua*) is still nearly universal, although virtually every family also owns a primus or kerosene stove.

Some families have a separate eating house, generally built along the same lines as the cooking house, whereas others reserve a section of the latter for eating. The majority of people eat their meals off banana leaves placed on mats that cover the floor, but a few families own tables and benches or chairs.

Other household compounds also contain a washing house, which at its crudest simply consists of 3½ walls of iron about five feet high, and no roof. More elaborate types include concrete structures with an iron roof. Only a small percentage of households have a separate washing unit; the majority of people bathe in the open, waiting until dark if they want to make a thorough job of it.

The toilets are of two types: pit latrines in the bush with thatch or iron structures built around them, or pier types, built on platforms extending over the beach beyond the high tide mark.

Aside from the elaborateness of facilities, households differ in the care that is given the physical structures and the immediate grounds. Some are kept neat and immaculate, with iron, wood, or limestone surfaces carefully painted or whitewashed, the grounds kept free of rubbish and neatly trimmed, and perhaps containing a small flower garden. One can predict that the inside of houses in such compounds have also been swept clean. Other people are not so meticulous, and a few seem to pay little attention to the physical appearances of their homestead, or the cleanliness within. These differences reflect the personal habits of the occupants rather than social status, and although little direct social pressure is exerted on those whose homesteads are not well kept, the meticulous housekeeper is often praised and the slovenly one subjected to periodic criticism. Men are also concerned with the state of their compounds since this, along with the state of their food plantations, is the clearest indication of a man's ability as a worker and a family provider.

Each household is a self-sufficient economic unit, capable of maintaining itself without outside aid. This is made possible by the abundance with which the island is blessed. A husband and wife alone can generally supply the subsistence needs of a fairly large family; many households contain more than two economically productive persons, however, and are able to maintain themselves with a minimum of effort. The head of a household is usually the eldest male member, but if he is senile or infirmed, he may turn over the main responsibilities to a son, his daughter's husband, or any other male of sufficient maturity. In some cases older women are regarded as household heads, but this ordinarily occurs only when no sufficiently mature males are present.

INFANCY

Indulgence of Children

As a general rule infants and young children are a focal point within each household and are indulged by everyone. During infancy this indulgence takes the form of constant caressing and soothing, in addition to feeding upon demand. Infants are nearly always in someone's arms; if the mother is busy then an obliging aunt, grandmother, or sister is generally around to take over. Even men and young boys seem to take great pleasure in holding an infant in their laps and fondling it. Demonstrations of affection by physical means continue long after the child has begun to walk, and children come to seek physical contact with those whose affection they desire. Indulgence also takes the form of gift giving. A good parent is one who grants his children's every reasonable request; if he can anticipate their desires, so much the better. Toys and other presents are given to youngsters whenever there are a few spare shillings, and it is not unusual for parents to sacrifice much wanted household effects in order to buy their child a toy. In most households this pattern of indulgence extends to eating behavior—children are fed first and are given the best food; the elders content themselves with leftovers.

This indulgent attitude on the part of parents is clearly reflected in the reminiscences of a Rotuman woman about her childhood:

When I was young my parents treated me very well. They always tried to give me everything I wanted. I remember one time at Christmas when I went with my father to buy a Christmas present for me. I saw a nice toy in the store. It was a pretty doll with a pretty dress, and I wanted my father to buy it, but at that time the price of copra was very bad, and it was a hard time for everyone who had to earn their money from cutting copra, like my father. It wasn't bad for the people who were earning their money from jobs—it was easy for them—but for the people who had to cut copra it was a hard time. My father wanted to buy me an umbrella, but I liked the doll better. The two were the same price, and finally my father bought both of them, because he did not like to make me worry about the toy, and the umbrella was a useful thing. He knew I liked the toy better, and that's why he bought both of them for me.

The association of affection with material giving is continually reinforced, and is reflected in the connotation of the word *hanisi* (the nearest Rotuman equivalent to the English word "love"). *Hanisi* implies willingness to give tangibly, rather than an emotional state. This emphasis has some interesting implications. For example, since loving is more strongly associated with behavior than with emotion, the statement, "I'm punishing you because I love you; it's for your own good. . .", which is perfectly understandable to an American parent (although one wonders whether it is understandable to the American child), would be incomprehensible to a Rotuman parent. When one is punishing, one is not loving. Kindness and generosity are the measure of love, not the degree to which feelings are aroused. Perhaps one of the most important implications of *hanisi* is that it is an unselfconscious love. There is no need to ask oneself whether he loves someone (such as his parents or spouse) or to ask others whether they love him. This is determined by the way people behave. A further implication is that Rotuman parents *must* indulge their children if they are to avoid being accused by their neighbors of being unloving parents. Thus childhood indulgence is backed up by generalized social pressure.

The affection displayed for children does not signify a possessive love. As in many other Polynesian societies adoption is a common practice and serves to distribute children from those who have too many to those who have too few.[2] Often an older couple whose children have already grown, or a childless couple, approach expectant or recent parents with an adoption request. If they are close relatives, it is enough simply to ask, but more distant kin or non-relatives usually solemnize a request by bringing a ceremonial food offering. When asked how they felt about giving away their children, parents invariably answered something like this, "As long as the people love my child (i.e., are kind and generous to him) why should I mind?" Particularly if the natural parents are poor or already have a large family to support, they welcome an adoption. "They will be able to give our child so much more than we can," is a typical comment by parents under these circumstances.

Adopted children are regarded as grandchildren (*ma'piag*) and are indulged even more than most children. As one Rotuman informant summarized, "An adopting parent must be especially loving so that the little one will not always be thinking of his real mother and father and want to return to them."

Formerly it was the custom for children to be sent to a grandparent's home at about one year old for weaning. The child would remain away from home until he was completely weaned, with substitute indulgences from the grandparents for compensation. In some instances the grandparents adopted the child permanently and raised him. Today the pattern is for mothers to begin to feed a baby solid food, usually mashed tapioca, at from 3 to 6 months, gradually weaning the child (from breast or bottle) by the end of the first year. In some cases the old custom is still followed, the child being sent to a grandparent for an extended period of time to complete the weaning process.

Discipline

This overall description of childhood indulgence is not to imply that children are not disciplined, however. Soon after a child has learned to understand language he is encouraged to behave in culturally appropriate ways and is discouraged from acting badly. Socialization focuses upon teaching children how to behave in the company of different people. They are taught with whom they must be restrained and with whom they may take license. Particular emphasis is placed upon restraint in public, or in the company of high ranking persons. Rotuman etiquette forbids "showing off," and acting "proud" (*fakman'ia*) is one of the greatest social offenses. Ridicule is the dominant disciplinary technique, and it can be sharply derisive at times. The following descripton from my field notes epitomizes the socialization strategy:

We had come back from a picnic on Hatana, one of the offshore islands, around sunset and about thirty or so people gathered at Sakimi's place to cap off the day. Some of the young men had guitars and ukuleles and began to play, and before long individuals got up and began to dance in a spontaneous fashion. The entire mood was one of light-hearted gaiety. At one point Sakimi's four year old namesake began imitating the dancers and was making a pretty good job of it. He appeared to be quite unself-conscious and was making a serious effort to simulate the movements correctly. A couple of people called attention to his actions, praising and encouraging him. He responded to the praise by intensifying and exaggerating his movements; it seemed clear to me that he was no longer concerned with accurate imitation but with drawing attention to himself—with "showing off." As soon as this shift was sensed by the observers they ceased praising him and began to ridicule him instead. Instead of comments like, "Look at little Sakimi; he is a very clever dancer," they shifted to making remarks like, "Look how silly he is, acting like a showoff and making a fool of himself in front of everyone." The more little Sakimi intensified his antics the sharper the ridicule became, until he stopped entirely and went off by himself to sulk.

Mothers are the main disciplinarians and scold children or slap them when they are mischievous or disobedient. Only if a child does not respond to a mother's efforts, or if a particularly bad deed has been perpetrated, does the father take action. When parents are irritated by a child's behavior they may spontaneously scold him, or slap him on the legs. A more calculated form of punishment, used "to teach the child a lesson," is to make him kneel in one spot for a while.

Much can be learned about the values of a people by discovering what children are and are not punished for. My initial impression was that Rotuman parents were unusually harsh with young children who wandered away from their homes without permission. I thought that this reflected great concern for their welfare, rooted in a fear that they might hurt themselves or get into trouble. But other observations rendered such an explanation implausible. As long as children remained on the home compound they often engaged in the most dangerous pursuits without being stopped. It is common to see a three- or four-year-old tot swinging a razor-sharp machete in imitation of his elders. No one shouts in horror or even urges him to put the implement down, as long as he is handling the tool reasonably well. By the time they are five or six, youngsters have become proficient at climbing coconut trees thirty or forty feet high without inciting anxiety in their parents. In general, then, Rotumans seem to be optimists regarding childhood accidents, and do not share our attitude of caution. They simply do not seem to have a sense of impending danger. Why then do they punish their children for wandering? The answer became clear to me as I came to understand the culture better: if neighbors see a young child wandering about by himself they are likely to accuse the parents or guardians of neglect, of not caring enough about the child to watch after him. Such an accusation would be a bitter pill for any Rotuman parent to swallow. Hence it is apparently a parent's concern for his own reputation that leads him to punish strongly this apparently minor infraction.

On the other hand, whereas American middle-class parents tend to punish children for damaging household property, the Rotumans are very permissive in this area. Children are allowed to handle almost any item belonging to the household, and even the destruction of valuables rarely arouses anger or brings punishment. Destruction of neighbors' property is a somewhat different matter, though, since it may affect the relationship between the families. A similar situation prevails in response to children's fights. If the fighting takes place between siblings, or members of the same household, parents may ignore it or mildly scold the battlers, imploring them to love one another. When the fight takes place between children from different households, however, there is much greater concern because relations between families are involved, and parental punishment for fighting tends to be more severe.

Toilet training is rather casual and untraumatic. An infant in arms is generally held off to the side to urinate or defecate, although an increasing number of women are using diapers on their children. Chamber pots have also become common for infants who have learned to sit but do not yet walk well. By the time a child is about two years old he is encouraged to look after his own toilet functions; he may urinate in any convenient sandy spot, but is taught to go down to the beach to defecate below the high water mark. Failure to control himself is met with ridicule, or possibly a sharp slap on the leg if it occurs at an embarrassing moment for the parent. When a child is about five years old he is taught to use the proper latrines. In general there is little embarrassment regarding the natural functions of the body and although personal cleanliness is highly valued, there is little concern for the compulsive ritual that characterizes many middle-class American homes.

Language Development

I never noticed a Rotuman parent speaking to an infant in baby talk. From the very beginning adults address themselves extensively to the objects of their affection, but always using adult language and talking about sensible things. They may tell of their hopes for him, describe what is going on, or tell a story. As the child grows into the toddler age and begins to babble, parents do not make a big fuss about his first words. They continue to speak to the child patiently and to correct his errors, but although they speak simply and plainly to him, they do not resort to incomplete or incorrect grammatical forms. When they feel that he is ready they begin to teach him the names of things, not as a focussed event, but within the course of daily routine. The parents I observed seemed to have a natural sense of a developing child's curiosity, and they taught him things after his attention had determined the focus. It was as if they did not want to intrude on their children any more than was necessary for socialization, but were prepared to provide information at the child's discretion. I remember reflecting that in contrast to American parents, who seem to feel that knowledge is something like medicine—it's good for the child and must be crammed down his throat even if he does not like it— Rotuman parents acted as if learning were inevitable because the child *wants* to learn. Although I made no systematic observations, it appeared to me that Rotuman children learn to speak clearly and distinctly at an earlier age than do American children.

INTERPERSONAL RELATIONSHIPS

Among the most important things a child must learn as his speech develops is who the people are in his life. As different people come to visit his household, and as he is taken by his parents to other places in the community, he becomes familiar with many new faces, and he must learn what to call them and how to act toward them. A good many of the people he comes into contact with are kinsmen, and he is explicitly told what is expected of him: "Why don't you go outside and play with Fatiaki, he is your *sasigi;* or "You must show respect to Samuela, he is your *ö'fā*", are the kinds of things parents might say. He soon becomes familiar with a complete set of kinship terms and an associated set of expected behavior patterns.

For an anthropologist the way in which people from other cultures classify their relatives is of considerable interest, in large part because it provides an important clue to the principles by which interpersonal relations are structured. We, for example, distinguish lineal relations, such as father, mother, son, and daughter from consanguines such as aunt, uncle, and cousin. This reflects the importance we attach to the nuclear family as a social unit. The Rotumans, on the other hand, do not discriminate between relatives within the parents' and children's generations, except to designate sex. If we were to describe their system in our terms, we would say that they lump all the aunts with mother and all the uncles with father. Within one's own generation, however, distinctions are made on the basis of whether the person spoken about is of the same or opposite sex from the person speaking. This reflects a Rotuman concern for regulating relations between potential sex partners. For those who are interested, a description of Rotuman kinship terms is included in Appendix B.

Restraint and License

Learning how to act toward other individuals is an extremely complicated process involving extensive feedback and continual re-orientation, and it is beyond the scope of this book to present the details of this process as it applies in Rotuma. But the general principles that Rotumans employ in structuring their interpersonal behavior are quite easily described in terms of the degree of restraint an individual is required to exercise when interacting with another. At one extreme complete restraint may be required, virtually restricting the actor's initiative to zero; at the other extreme nearly unrestricted license is permitted. The rules governing restraint and license may be considered to apply in three areas of concern: activity, property, and integrity. Before presenting the rules of relationship, let me examine what restraint and license entail for Rotumans in each of these areas.

Activity. Exercising *extreme restraint* with regard to another person's activity involves never asking him to do anything, whereas *moderate restraint* involves contracting services on a wage basis. The most suitable form of wage is cash, but other commodities of a cash value may be offered. Such traditional commodities of exchange as pigs, mats, and kava are not regarded as suitable payment for a wage contract.

Kinsmen are rarely so restrained with one another as this, though. The very fact of kinship is sufficient to warrant at least *conditional license* over activity, which is signified by the word *faksoro*. In going *faksoro* to another, a person pleads for help in performing an important task that is beyond his own capacity. One recruits labor in this manner to build a house, to cut large quantities of copra, or to prepare a feast. The request should be made humbly, as a plea, and when so requested, a person should not refuse unless he has good reason to do so. The one who asks for labor creates an obligation to reciprocate when others come *faksoro* to him, and he is required to feed the helpers while they are working for him.

Moderate license involves requests for services or participation in an activity unaccompanied by a plea, and not directly implying reciprocation of the same kind. For example, a man may ask a close friend or relative in quite a casual manner to come fishing or to assist in the preparation of a feast. *Extreme license* over activity involves giving orders to another, as a parent might order a child to run an errand, but even at the extreme it is not considered appropriate to be emphatic; it is always regarded as proper to ask first, and to rely upon demand only if the person being asked is recalcitrant.

Property. When property is involved, *extreme restraint* involves complete avoidance of the property's use, whereas *moderate restraint* most usually implies purchase by cash or a cash equivalent. Commercial transactions are therefore dominated by *moderate restraint.*

Conditional license over property is an elaborated area in Rotuman relationships, and has at least three distinguishable gradients: (1) Closest to the restraint side of the continuum are requests for credit in commercial transactions. This involves, of course, a promise to pay, but it is regarded as a personal favor and does not include interest payments. (2) The intermediate form of conditional license over property is an institutionalized pattern signified by the word *fara*. To *fara* property is the counterpart of asking for *faksoro* labor, and the request is similarly made, humbly and in a pleading fashion. Need is implied in the request, and if it is done in the appropriate manner refusal is unwarranted unless there is a good reason. By its very nature, *fara* applies to useful goods rather than luxuries, and the nature of the commodity determines whether it is to be returned. Such durable goods as tools are expected to be returned following their use. Expendable commodities like food and money (or copra) do not require a direct return payment, but involve the obligation to reciprocate when the supplier is in need. The term *fara* is also used to describe requests for skilled labor (e.g., from a carpenter or mechanic) without compensation, which is equivalent to a request for money since the craftsman would ordinarily be paid for his services. The most frequent use of *fara* requests is to obtain ceremonial exchange goods (particularly mats and pigs) for presentation at weddings, funerals, and other ceremonies. (3) Closest to the license side of the continuum are informal requests (and hence not *fara*) for useful items. The need for the item is either understood or casually announced. A characteristic request of this order would be: "I would like to borrow your canoe for a few hours. Is it all right?"

Moderate license over property differs from informal requests only inasmuch as need is not a necessary criterion of use, and it therefore applies to more intimate commodities such as clothing, musical instruments, sporting gear, etc. *Extreme license* involves the use of another person's property as though it were one's own, without even making a request. In less extreme cases the intention to use an item may simply be announced to the owner as a fact.

Integrity. The third area of concern is with other people's integrity, or personal dignity. In Rotuma, *extreme restraint* implies an avoidance of interaction; one is specifically expected to exercise restraint in expressing personal opinions. If asked for an opinion by a person with whom one is supposed to be inhibited, it is considered better to be vague than specific. Under no circumstances should views previously expressed by the person be contradicted. If he has already expressed an opinion, or if his opinions are known, a noncommittal affirmation, humbly expressed, is in order. When in the presence of a person who commands such respect, walking in front of him should be avoided; if this is necessary, however, it should be done in a stooped position. It is also not proper to stand when the person is sitting, nor should one look directly at him. In general, when interaction is required with such a person, it is safer to abide by ritual or ceremonial protocol, but safest to avoid interaction altogether.

Moderate restraint involves the use of formal etiquette. One need not be reluctant to initiate interaction with people to whom one owes moderate respect, as long as the rules of formal etiquette are observed. Some of the most significant of these rules are as follows:

1. One should not talk too much, and when talking, should be serious; one should not joke.
2. If eating at the same time as the person, one should not commence before he does and when he has finished, one should stop eating.
3. When sitting on a mat, the proper position should be assumed. For males this means crossing one's legs in front of him, with knees down; for females this means sitting with legs folded to her side, pointing behind her.
4. Any request, including asking for an opinion, should be preceded by the word *figalelei* (please); when given something, one should reply with *faiak se'ea* (thank you).
5. One should avoid expressing one's own opinion unless called upon to do so; when asked, one can appropriately offer one's point of view, although this should be done humbly and should not contradict the opinion of the other person if it is known.
6. The person should be addressed by his appropriate title, or by the general term *gagaj* (signifying any person of high status).

In contrast *conditional license* over another person's integrity involves the possibilities for relaxed conversation, with permission to joke about things not directly implicating the person, but with restrictions upon joking *at* (i.e., about the person to him) the person.

Opinions may be freely expressed so long as they are not insulting to the other person, or imply that his own opinions are foolish. One should not pry into the person's intimate affairs, such as sexual and financial matters.

Moderate license over integrity involves complete permissiveness with regard to expressing opinions, and the possibility of joking at the person, or even approaching him physically, provided his consent has been given (either explicitly or tacitly). Sexual intercourse, when consented to, falls into this category. *Extreme license* over integrity includes swearing at the person, denouncing his competence or character, or attacking him physically. There are two degrees of *extreme license,* the less extreme done in a joking manner (but without consent implied), whereas the more extreme form is in a serious vein.

Interaction between Kinsmen

With these behavioral patterns in mind, let us examine the rules of interpersonal relations that apply between sets of kinsmen.

ö'fä *and* ö'hön-le'e *(parent-child; aunt, uncle-niece, nephew).* Parents possess extreme license over their children's activity, property, and integrity, but are expected to exercise these rights with kindness and consideration for their children's happiness. This involves, in part, the granting by parents of considerable license over activity and property, but children are expected to exercise some restraint continually with regard to their parents' integrity. In other words, they may be quite free with most of their parents' property and relatively unrestrained in asking their parents to do this or that for them, but they should never be disrespectful.

The same pattern applies between collateral relatives (those not in the same line of descent) in adjacent generations, except that a bit more restraint is expected from everyone, particularly if they do not live in the same household.

ma'piag-ma'piag *(grandparent-grandchild).* The rules governing the grandparent-grandchild relationship parallel those that apply between parent and child, although the expectation that grandparents will be indulgent is greater. Grandparents therefore tend to grant extreme license to their grandchildren and may even be tolerant of attacks upon their integrity.

sạsigi *(siblings or cousins of the same sex).* Siblings of the same sex are generally expected to take considerable license with one another in all areas. When it comes to serious tasks, however, elder siblings have the right to direct their younger siblings' activities. They can also demand respect with regard to property and integrity, whereas younger siblings are obliged to grant license in these areas.

The same holds for cousins, but in general the less they see of each other, the more restraint is exercised.

sågväväne-såghạni *(siblings and cousins of opposite sex).* Brothers and sisters are expected to exercise mutual restraint with one another. In traditional times, restraint was required to the point of avoidance, but today it is regarded as permissible for siblings of opposite sex to relax restraints considerably, at least when they are not in public. Adolescents avoid going to the same dances or parties as their opposite-sex siblings, though, as each would be obliged to be inhibited in the presence of the other. In the household, mutual license over property is permitted to some degree, but each is supposed to exercise restraint with regard to such personal items as articles of clothing. Also, since boys are their sisters' guardians, they have a special interest in restricting their sex behavior, and are expected to exercise control over their sisters' activities. They can also demand respect, and are permitted to punish a sister for threatening the family's honor by loose behavior.

Cousins of opposite sex are likewise supposed to be restrained with one another, but since boys are more concerned with their sisters' virtue than with their cousins', they can be more relaxed with the latter, and may even come to be able to joke with them about sexual matters.

väväne-hạina *(husband-wife).* Spouses have a right to demand respect from each other, but the general rule is for both to grant considerable license, at least within the home. In public they should show mutual restraint. A good husband is expected always to take his wife's welfare into account, and to consult her before making decisions that may affect her happiness. A good wife is expected to do likewise. Their granting of license to each other is therefore with the understanding that each will take the desires of the other into account.

mäe *(brother-in-law–brother-in-law; sister-in-law–sister-in-law).* A person is obliged to show respect to his siblings-in-law of the same sex, but may ask for assistance if in need. When such a request is made by one's *mäe,* a person must oblige if at all possible. The rule is thus one of mutual conditional license with regard to activity and property, whereas moderate restraint is in order with regard to one another's integrity.[3]

hạmfua *(brother-in-law–sister-in-law).* The rules of relationship between brother-in-law and sister-in-law are the same as those between *mäe,* mutual conditional license over property and activity, and mutual respect for one another's integrity. If it has an effect, the difference in sex between *hạmfua* increases the strength of the requirement for restraint.

Parents-in-Law–Children-in-Law. The rules of relationship between parents-in-law and children-in-law follow the same pattern as those between siblings-in-law, with the added vector of generational differences. This increases the requirement for showing respect by the child-in-law and decreases it somewhat for the parent-in-law.

First Encounters

When meeting a relative socially for the first time, the rule is to begin by exercising restraint. If the person encountered is of higher rank than oneself, it should be left to him to make the first moves toward removing the restraints and prescribing the limits of license to be permitted. If the other person is of lower status, it is one's own right to remove initial restraints and to prescribe the limits. If both are of equal status, either may initiate such steps.

Children also come into contact with non-relatives, and although the rules for relating to them are not as explicit as they are with kinsmen, definite guidelines do exist. Adults are to be respected, the more so if they are persons of high rank, such as chiefs, ministers, or government officials. This requires, above all, being unobtrusive when in their presence, and silence is the safest strategy unless the child is specifically addressed or asked to do something. With children one's own age, one is permitted considerable freedom to play and to joke, as long as there are no signs of overt conflict; when children's conflicts escalate to public view any adult present may admonish them, without regard for which child is responsible.

SUMMARY

In Rotuma, children are indulged and shown a great deal of affection and attention. Socialization is directed toward teaching the child whom he must respect and with whom he may take license, and to distinguish between those situations in which he may express himself freely and those in which he may not. In other words, right and wrong are not conceived as absolute, but are situationally defined. Thus aggression is not bad for its own sake, but only when it has disturbing effects on interpersonal relations. The idea of it being "sinful" is foreign to the Rotuman mentality, despite the influence of Christianity. In general the Rotuman child grows up in an interpersonal milieu that is easily mastered. He is likewise made to feel that the physical world is not particularly threatening, and in response most Rotuman children learn to master, without anxiety, physical tasks American parents would be most reluctant to allow their children to attempt, even at more advanced ages.

By the time a child is ready for school his character is already very much Rotuman. He is hardly an empty cup to be filled with the collective wisdom of the ages, but is a deeply inscribed individual in every respect. His motor skills, response patterns, and mode of thinking have been well formed and are tenacious, particularly since he returns from school every day to a home and community in which they continue to be reinforced. Above all he has developed a mode of interpersonal behavior in which he is restrained with strangers, particularly adults, unrestrained with his peers, and extremely sensitive to the opinions and evaluations of those around him. It is this "equipment" that he carries with him into school and with which teachers must work in order to educate him to the ways of the modern world.

NOTES

[1] Dispatch from Resident Commissioner H. E. Leefe to Colonial Secretary, January 14th, 1899. *Outward Letters, Rotuma District Office,* in the Central Archives, Suva.

[2] See Alan Howard, "Adoption in Rotuma," in Vern Carroll (ed.), *Adoption in Eastern Oceania,* in press.

[3] It is of some interest that the word *mäe,* when used as an adjective, means "to be ashamed, bashful, or shy, to feel uncomfortable in the presence of others, to suffer from stage-fright." C. M. Churchward, *Rotuman Grammar and Dictionary* (Sydney: Australasian Medical Publishing Company, 1940), p. 254.

— IV

School:
Preparation for a World Unseen

From a sociological point of view the school is an alien institution in Rotuma. The training it offers has little to do with life on the island, and the norms that govern its operation are foreign to Rotuman culture. From the beginning it was imposed by outsiders who strove to use it for their own ends, and historical changes have almost always been in response to outside influences rather than from within the culture. As we shall see, the effect of the school system is to introduce discontinuity into the socialization process. In many respects it is the fork in the road; some master the school's challenges and go on to a Western life style, whereas for others it is a source of extreme frustration from which they beat a hasty retreat to the more comfortable Rotuman style of life.

HISTORY OF THE SCHOOLS

The history of formal education in Rotuma dates from 1839, when Reverend John Williams of the London Missionary Society stopped there and left two Samoan teachers. The Samoans were not very successful either as missionaries or as teachers, largely because they failed to master the difficult Rotuman language, despite the fact that much of its vocabulary is shared with Samoan. Tongan teachers of the Wesleyan mission followed in 1841 and fared somewhat better, although progress was painfully slow. In 1847 a native Wesleyan teacher from Fiji paid a visit to Rotuma and reported that the Tongans had made some eighty converts. It was not until ten years after that the first Biblical translation was available in the Rotuman language.

The first classes using these written materials were held by a Fijian native teacher with the Christian name Zerubbabel. Their character is described by Churchward from written documents:

Every lesson was opened with prayer: their teacher saw to that: and when the pupils had made sufficient progress, the Gospels were distributed and from them they read. Before long the more thoughtful ones began to realize that this book had a message for them, and asked Zerubbabel to explain it. Like a true Christian, he seized the opportunity, and soon the reading lesson became a Bible class. By and by some of the pupils made their decision for Christ. Naturally the classes grew and interest spread, till even some of the chiefs came under its spell, and finally they decided to withdraw their opposition to the Christian religion.[1]

Churchward states that motivation to participate in these classes was stimulated by returning laborers who had been greatly impressed by the white man's "progressiveness" as compared with the backwardness of their own people:

So, on returning to Rotuma, they recounted their experiences, and endeavoured to show their fellow-countrymen, and particularly the young men, how important it was that they should wake up and seek the education, which was obviously the secret of the white man's progress and prosperity. "And the first step in education," they added, "is to learn to read and write one's own language."[2]

In 1864 James Calvert visited Rotuma and reported that 1,200 persons were professedly Christian and that 230 persons were meeting in class. At the time there were eleven chapels in "tolerable repair," four preaching places, and twenty-two local preachers.[3] Later that same year the Reverend William Fletcher and his wife established residence on Rotuma. Some time before, in 1847, a French priest came to Rotuma and remained for six years before he was withdrawn, but the arrival of Fletcher marked the beginning of sustained residency by European missionaries. The Catholics returned to establish a permanent mission in 1868. Fletcher and his wife supervised the teachers, who held classes in the various villages. The curriculum is reflected in a letter by Fletcher dated January 1866:

All the schools met, and gave us pieces of scripture, after their own native style, and any scraps of geography, or history they had managed to gain. All were well dressed. Evidently much pains had been taken by the teacher. . . . Before people dispersed, I collected all the children together. I asked questions on Scripture subjects, added a few simple questions in arithmetic. The whole then chanted together the multiplication table. This was followed by a hymn, and with a short address and prayer, we concluded.[4]

By 1870 Christianity had triumphed and the majority of the young people were receiving instructions. The Catholic mission also established schools and for the remainder of the century education on Rotuma was entirely in the hands of missionaries. The pattern that was established by the Methodist schools was for the children to meet with their teacher in a schoolhouse three days a week from six in the morning until nine. School attendance was compulsory and parents who failed to send their children were liable to a fine. Teachers were supplied by the mission, but every Methodist household was required to give something quarterly toward the teachers' support.[5] According to a report by Reverend Allen in 1895, "all the boys and girls on the island can read, write, and have some knowledge of arithmetic and geography."[6] This was perhaps an exaggeration, for the 1911 census of Rotuma recorded only 1,331 persons out of a total of 2,293, or 58%, as literate. Nevertheless, if allowances are made for very young children and those too elderly to have received instruction, it is apparent that the literacy rate was quite high.

During the first quarter of the twentieth century the Methodists established a school at Tia, near the main village of Motusa; it provided a higher standard of education than was available in the ordinary village schools. The school was run by European Mission Sisters together with a native assistant, and provided instruction up to the third standard (equivalent of third grade), although some students received education beyond this level. Promising students were sent to mission schools in Fiji where they could get advanced academic or vocational training.

The Government of Fiji took over responsibility for educating native peoples in the late 1920's. They established standards and provided supervision and grants-in-aid. Although the Catholics continued to administer their own schools after this reorganization, the Methodist mission relinquished its educational role in favor of government-run institutions. In 1936 school was made compulsory for children between the ages of six and fourteen, and since then all Rotumans have received a minimum of eight years education. Failure to send children to school was made punishable by a fine, or in default of the fine, by short-term imprisonment.

In general, the government officials who administered Rotuma did a great deal to encourage education, but there were exceptions. One was W. Carew, who wrote in his annual report for 1930:

Higher Education is not needed by the Rotumans. The manufacture of a number of so-called highly educated Natives means, in a small island like Rotuma, only a deposit of discontented units—useless for the ordinary Native duties and, with no scope for the higher ideas, they fall back as "know-alls" and bush lawyers amongst their people, with a disturbing effect.

This is evidenced even now in the case of those returning from Fiji after some years at Davuilevu and other schools. What the Rotuman requires is to be taught "conduct" in relation to his native duties.

It is even doubtful if the majority are any better for a smattering of the three R's. His business in life lies close at hand, and he really has only one business i.e., the production of his native crops and his duties entailed therein. I do not suppose that he ever hears in his school hours one word calculated to draw his attention to any such conception of his future duty.[7]

ORGANIZATION OF THE SCHOOL SYSTEM

In 1960 there were seven schools in Rotuma. Three of these, two primary and one secondary, were Catholic. The other four, of which three were primary and one secondary, were under government control. All the schools, with the exception of the Catholic secondary school, were co-educational.

The government-run primary schools are divided into three administrative districts: (1) the Motusa School District, which includes Itumuta and all of Itutiu except Hapmak; (2) the Malhaha School District, which includes Hapmak, Malhaha, and Lopta (Oinafa); and (3) the Paptea School District, which includes all of Oinafa except Lopta, and Noatau. The Methodist children from Pepjei and Juju may go either to the Paptea or Motusa schools. Since the vast majority of people in these latter districts are Catholic, there are only a few children from these districts attending the government schools.

In addition to these three districts, which administer the primary schools, there is a Central School district, which administers the secondary school. The Central School includes grades 7 through 10 (Form IV); it is located in Malhaha, on the same grounds as the primary school, and for all practical purposes is integrated with it. It should be noted that the school districts do not coincide with any normal political division in Rotuma. They each include at least one whole political district (*itu'u*) and adjacent parts of others. The names given to two of the school districts, Motusa and Paptea, refer to villages in which the schools are located.

The District Officer, as chief administrative executive on the island, manages the government schools. Each school district has a committee, theoretically appointed by the Governor of Fiji, but in fact mainly consisting, for the primary school districts, of the chiefs (*gagaj 'es itu'u*) and sub-chiefs (*fa 'es ho'aga*) residing in the area. The Central District committee consists of the *gagaj 'es itu'u* of the five predominantly Methodist political districts—Itutiu, Malhaha, Oinafa, Noatau, and Itumuta—with the District Officer acting as chairman. The chairmen of the primary school district committees have generally been the highest ranking chiefs in the area. The duties of the committees, as prescribed by the Education Ordinance of 1929, are:

1. To visit the school under its supervision and report to the manager (District Officer);
2. to inspect and verify all records and registers required to be kept by the teachers of the school;
3. to inspect and report on the sanitary and structural condition of the school;
4. to use every endeavor to induce parents to send their children to school;
5. to give advice on any educational matter which may be submitted to it by the Board of Education concerning its district;
6. to consider applications for admission of people; and
7. to keep statistical and financial records for the district.

For most of these purposes the committees are inactive. The majority of chiefs lack sufficient education to understand academic affairs, and their role has been to consider labor and financial matters pertaining to the maintenance of school buildings and grounds. The Motusa committee had not met for four or five years prior to my arrival. Apparently a problem regarding the management of funds had arisen, and the headmaster of the school carried on by himself. Whereas the committees were intended to be policy-making bodies, in fact they have been little more than instruments for acquiring labor and cash for projects suggested by the headmasters. Technically headmasters are only supposed to report to the committee and are not even entitled to vote, but as a result of the discrepancy in educational levels between them and the members of the committee, they invariably emerge as dominant policy-makers.

The three Catholic schools are supervised by the Catholic Education Secretary, operating from the Bishop's office in Suva. One, a primary school including grade 1 through grade 7, is located at the Sumi Mission in Juju. The other primary school, and the secondary school, are located at the Upu Mission in Itutiu. The Upu primary school includes only grades 1 through 3, after which the children in that parish must attend school at Sumi.

Provided they meet the standards set by the Fiji Board of Education, two-thirds of the teachers' salaries are paid by the Government and one-third by the Rotuman Development Fund, a self-imposed tax on copra exports. Unqualified teachers are paid entirely from local sources, but the large majority of teachers in both the government and Catholic schools are qualified. Families are charged twenty shillings (about $2.50) per term for each child, although moderate reductions are made for families with three or more children attending school.

The school year runs from mid-February to mid-December, and hours are from 8 a.m. to 3 p.m., Monday through Friday. School buses are operated by the government and take children from their villages to school and back again.

The basic curriculum in all schools is set by the Board of Education and is modeled after the Australian and New Zealand modifications of the standard English curriculum. The history and geography of the British Empire are stressed, with special attention given to the south sea area that includes Rotuma. English is taught as a second language from the first grade, and by the third or fourth grades most of the instruction is in that language, with Rotuman resorted to mainly to explain concepts. The available literature is virtually all in English; with the exception of the Bible and some government pamphlets, very little has been translated into Rotuman. In addition to academic subjects, children receive instruction in religion, and in the government-run primary schools a few hours a week are spent on learning traditional Rotuman customs and lore.

Island-wide final examinations are given periodically to the students in the first six grades of the government schools. Each teacher takes a subject, prepares an exam for it, and scores the results. Grading for the more advanced grades is the responsibility of the individual teacher. The majority of students pass each year, but there is little reluctance to hold poor students back, and a substantial minority repeat at least one class in their academic careers. If a student progresses normally, he will complete the eighth grade by age fourteen, after which he may leave or go on to a secondary school. If he has not completed the eighth grade by that time, he may continue for an additional two years, up to age sixteen. Secondary school in Rotuma (Forms III and IV, the equivalent to our grades 9 and 10) is largely oriented toward passing the Fiji Junior Examination, a standard exam given throughout Fiji. Passing this exam is a prerequisite for continuing one's education in the more advanced schools in Fiji. After completing Form V (grade 11) a student may take the Fiji Senior Examination, and if he is successful can obtain a School Leaving Certificate that qualifies him for a variety of positions in government and private enterprise, or he may go on to one of the professional schools in Fiji, which offer training in such things as teaching, agricultural science, and medicine. All of these schools are oriented toward creating a cadre of quasi-professionals for the government service who can fill the needs of the Colony. Still another possibility is to sit for the University Entrance Examination. If he passes this exam, a student qualifies for entrance to most Australian and New Zealand universities.

Education beyond Form IV is expensive and not very many continue past that point. A student must travel to Fiji and either live with relatives or board at school. Besides tuition and books, the cost of clothes and incidentals is increased over what is required in Rotuma. Advanced education thus may cost several hundred pounds per year, creating an insurmountable barrier for many families. Nevertheless, most Rotuman parents are willing to sacrifice a great deal for their children's education and if they can possibly afford it they usually make an effort. Scholarships are also available from government sources, and The Rotuma Council of Chiefs has created a Rotuma Scholarship, which is awarded annually.

ADJUSTMENT TO THE SCHOOL ENVIRONMENT

Going to school represents a rather sharp discontinuity for most Rotuman children. After having experienced a period of nearly unqualified indulgence, they enter a situation in which they have to compete for approval with dozens of others. They are extremely sensitive to cues indicating approval or disapproval, but they have not learned the skills required to *earn* a teacher's approval. Their strong need for acceptance facilitates learning when they are reinforced, but it is difficult for teachers to avoid frustrating some children's overbearing demands for attention, or to eliminate the arousal of jealousy. Strong anxiety is frequently exhibited when children are called upon to perform in the early grades, especially if they are unable to perform well. I frequently observed children break into tears if asked to recite when they were unprepared.

The most important job that teachers have in the elementary grades, therefore, is to socialize children to the school milieu, and to do so without destroying the children's willingness to make an effort. In their favor is the initial sensitivity of the children to approval; what teachers must watch out for is the tendency of Rotuman children to withdraw when confronted with difficulties. This tendency seems to be part of a general response pattern that might best be described as a low tolerance for frustration. It is apparently rooted in the unconditional indulgence experienced at home. Since children are rarely required by their parents to endure frustration, they are badly equipped to put up with it when it comes. As a general rule, children do well when confronted with problems over which they can easily achieve mastery by an initial effort, but when difficulties are experienced, or when first attempts fail, their overwhelming tendency is to give up. Furthermore, the tendency to give up involves very little punishment outside school. Just as in early childhood, parents do not make their love and approval contingent upon achievement. They encourage education and are proud when their children are successful, but if a child fails in school he is more likely to be treated with sympathy than to be admonished. Parents feel sorry for a child who has failed or is not doing well. They respond as though he has been deprived of something valuable (perhaps the teacher's approval) and they seem to want to make it up to him.

Although this tendency to withdraw in the face of frustration is a hindrance to scholastic achievement, teaching levels are generally adjusted so that a fair proportion of the better students are able to achieve mastery over the large majority of tasks they are required to perform. As a result, the better students have their sense of mastery reinforced in the scholastic area, and are encouraged to maintain high aspirations, whereas the less able students tend to drop aspirations of scholastic and occupational success. Consequently, according to teachers' reports, there is a clear tendency in almost every class for students to divide quite sharply between high achievers and low achievers, rather than to form a gradual continuum reflecting differential ability.

Another area in which inability to endure frustration well is manifest is athletic competition. Rotuman children are very keen competitors, and they take their sports seriously. As long as a game is close, both sides struggle very hard to win, but as soon as one side gains a substantial advantage, their opponents tend to give up, but instead of withdrawing, as they do when adults are the object to their frustration, they respond with anger and aggression as well as tears. This is understandable in terms of the rules of social relations; with adults they are supposed to be restrained, whereas they can express themselves more readily with their peers.

It is interesting to note the way in which social relations are affected by the placing of children on opposing teams. Sister Madeleine, a young Rotuman nun, said that when she first began teaching she put all the boys on one team and all the girls on the other for playing games at school. She abandoned this idea when she noticed that the boys and girls became antagonistic toward each other, whereas before they had gotten along quite well. They ridiculed each other, joked in an ungracious manner, and even came to physical blows. These antagonisms affected the relations off as well as on the school grounds, and even brothers and sisters became abusive to each other. As a remedy, Sister Madeleine arbitrarily divided the class into two teams composed of an equal proportion of boys and girls. According to her account, the alignment of friendships and antagonisms immediately changed; teammates became buddies regardless of sex, and began to abuse members of the opposing team. The only satisfactory solution was to change team alignments often, in order to keep patterns of friendship and antagonism from becoming "institutionalized." This is perhaps a rather common problem among children throughout the world; it is certainly not peculiar to Rotumans.

TEACHING METHODS

Interviews with Rotuman teachers made it clear that they were aware of contemporary issues being discussed in Western urban society concerning teaching goals and methods. At one point during a monthly meeting of the teachers at the Malhaha School a discussion of the merits of "progressive" versus "traditional" philosophies developed, generated by a brief talk that I gave on educational practices in America. The headmaster stated that teachers in Rotuma were currently confronted with the problem of deciding which techniques best suited their situation. He said that they had collectively agreed to use the new techniques (those oriented toward overall adjustment goals) as much as possible, but that whenever they got anxious they tended to fall back on the old techniques (those oriented toward immediate mastery of lesson content). He pointed out that since the Fiji system was based upon standardized competitive examinations there were strong pressures toward drilling students on the subject matter covered in the exams.

Class size ranges from a minimum of five or six students to a maximum of near forty, with an average of about thirty. Most teachers organize their classes into work groups of five to ten individuals for at least part of the time as a means of facilitating interaction and perhaps, although they did not explicitly say so, as a means of de-emphasizing individual competition. In the majority of cases the groupings were based on ability, with students of comparable performance levels placed together. Several teachers remarked that this allowed them to pay more attention to the slow children while the faster ones could learn readily by themselves and from each other. Each group had a leader appointed by the teacher. Some teachers appointed the brightest child in each group; others rotated leadership in order to give each child a chance. Those who selected the first strategy emphasized the teaching role of the leader, whereas those who rotated the position emphasized the significance of leadership experience for each individual's education. Teachers also differed in the extent to which they emphasized competition between the groups. Some used competition as an incentive, making games out of many of the lessons, whereas others chose not to utilize the competitive framework at all.

The following are descriptions of group work methods used by various Rotuman teachers:

(S.F.R., first grade). In Class One, the teaching of subjects like Vernacular Speech Training, Vernacular Reading, Vernacular Spelling, etc. and Number Work were based mostly on Group Work. The Class is divided into four groups. The best child becomes the Group leader. New work is taken with the whole class, then they work in groups. One group remains at the blackboard while other groups move to places where various Reading activities or Number Work activities have been set out. The teacher must go around checking their work and helping the weaker ones. They change groups after a few minutes.

(E.S.E., first grade). Group Work or working together in groups is the main method used in this class for most subjects. There are 4 groups with 8 in each group. The children are divided into their groups according to their knowledge e.g., by putting the bright ones together and the dull ones together. This allows the bright ones to go ahead rather than having to lose a lot of time waiting for the dull ones to catch-up. In other cases grouping of the class is mixed instead (bright ones with the dull ones). This is done only when most of the class is found too far behind the bright ones. By doing this there may be a chance for the dull ones to pick-up far quicker than by having to wait for the teacher's help.

The brightest one in the group is always selected leader for she is expected to help the others when in difficulty while the teacher is busy attending another group. All activities given for group work are introduced to the class as a whole first.

In this class the groups do not compete against each other for each group has a different activity to do, changing when told. Groups are changed now and again.

(A.F.K., seventh grade). My class is divided up into five different groups of mixed sexes according to their abilities or knowledge. There are seven to a group. The leaders in each group are selected for a fortnight which gives everyone a chance in the training to be good organizers for the future, as some of them are likely to leave this class at the age of fourteen and it will give him or her every possibility of organizing his or her fellowmates in their various fields. These groups work with each other in every subject taught.

Regarding the value of group work methods in alleviating the adjustment problems of elementary school children, one teacher made the following comments:

(Sister M., third grade). The best way to get the children to work is to give them group projects. This is especially true of the slower children. If left to work individually, the slower children get frustrated and stop making an effort. At times I become impatient with individual children and this becomes a further cause of frustration and slows down their progress. But if they are divided into work groups, with the brighter children acting as leaders, they do not get frustrated so easily. For example, I have the whole group read together instead of each child performing individually. This way the slower children can follow along with the group. I find that individual reading skills improve by using this technique. With arithmetic I have each group give answers to the problems. They have to work it out together and reach a single decision. After doing this for several days I hold a competition between the groups, adding up the sums of correct answers for each group. During the competition each child works out the answers individually and the correct answers are added up to get the group score. I find great improvement in individual skills by using this technique.

The curriculum is broken up into weekly units for most subjects, with new lessons introduced at the beginning of the week and exercises given afterwards. As a general rule new materials are introduced to the class as a whole before assignments are given to the children in groups. Visual aids are not readily available, but teachers are conscious of their value and use them whenever possible. In teaching written English, words are printed on cards or on the blackboard, with appropriate objects, pictures, or sketches to illustrate them. Dramatization is also used to communicate English meanings.

Since virtually all the educational materials used in Rotuman schools are in English, mastery of that subject is essential, and the teachers in the early grades devote a great deal of attention to it. Following are some descriptions of methods used by elementary school teachers in handling English as a second language:

(F.M.O., second grade). In teaching English Reading new words are used in many sentences. Words like *run, jump, hop,* etc. are dramatized to communicate their meanings. With nouns, like *box, door, mat,* etc. real objects are shown. The word is printed on the blackboard several times for children to see and say. Then, they go to their seats and copy it four times, saying it at the same time. After writing it down, they go to group corners to do activities set out for them, like word matching, sentence matching, flash cards, etc. Group leaders are in charge.

One group will stay with me at the blackboard. After each in the group has read two lines from the passage, I'll leave them to the group leader, but go and check the other two groups, after which they change to the next activity. When all the groups have had a turn in reading the passage, the apparatus are put away and the children come down to the floor. I will read the passage over to them or sometimes get the best reader to do so.

If the Reading matter is suitable for dramatization, then the children can dramatize it. If not, then I ask them questions about it. Sometimes I get a few children to tell it in a story form in Rotuman. The rest can add on to it or say it's not true.

(S.F.R., first grade). In teaching Oral English no words are printed on cards or on the blackboard. The words are taught in sentences by dramatization, use of real objects, pictures, drawings, and blackboard sketches. The children hear the new word in sentences. They pronounce the new word and use it in sentences, acting out while saying what he or she is doing.

The teacher asks questions and the children try to answer. Later on one child comes in front to be the teacher and asks the other children questions. They must not answer in unison. They put up their hands and the teacher calls on one child to answer. They may answer together after individual children have already given answers.

There are two problems that make teaching English particularly difficult. One is the lack of adequate visual materials, so that many of the concepts the children must learn have no meaningful sensual referents. The other is that there are few opportunities to practice speaking English outside the classroom. As I have pointed out previously, "showing off" is severely censured, and speaking English is considered by most Rotumans to be a form of showing off. Not only are attempts to speak the language frowned upon, but mistakes, when caught, become the focus for an intense form of banter that borders on ridicule and is the source of considerable embarrassment. The problems of teaching English in Rotuma are aptly summarized by one of the better educated teachers:

(A.A., ninth grade). In teaching English, my greatest difficulty—in fact the greatest difficulty in any non-English speaking country—is to encourage children to think in English as they speak it. This is a real problem as the need to speak English in Rotuma is almost negligible. Children can do very well without English in the home and, consequently, they have to make a conscious effort to think in English while they are speaking it. To counteract this, I ask children to write the following for me to mark:

        1 composition
        1 letter
        1 geography composition
        1 comprehension test

These four constitute what I call a *must* in English in the week's work. Incidental and other work consists of talks in the morning given by the pupils, reading of poetry and prose, debates and grammar work and exercises.

As far as formal grammar is concerned the Department of Education lays down no definite ruling as to how the subject should be taught except that the teaching of the subject should be planned in such a way that it does not become a meaningless and unnecessary task. The idea behind this is that no formal grammar should be taught until the *need* arises. In Rotuma, however, I believe that the pupils will need to have a firm grasp of the rudimentary mechanics of English because they do not live in an environment of full or rich and correctly spoken English. "Learn to speak by speaking" is quite all right if one speaks and hears correct English frequently enough, but as this is impossible in Rotuma, Rotuman pupils should not depend entirely on this method to enhance their knowledge of English. In this connection, I can say that perhaps I teach a bit more grammar than is required by the department but I feel that I am justified in doing so because my experience both as a pupil and teacher in Rotuma led me to believe that the "learn to speak by speaking" method is inadequate in Rotuma and that a good background in English grammar is necessary to implement the teaching of English.

In my correction of pupils' work in English, I simply use a system whereby a symbol is put in the margin where a mistake occurs on the same line. The wrong word or words are crossed out. The pupil is expected to correct and rewrite the corrected version of phrase or sentence and show it again to me. This procedure applies to all written work in English, whether it be English Composition or a geography essay.

The shortcomings of language background, in conjunction with the extreme isolation of the island and the limited material environment it provides, create problems of conceptualization that are familiar to people concerned with so-called "culturally deprived environments" within our own society. Following are some of the ways in which Rotuman teachers attempt to cope with these difficulties:

(A.A., ninth grade). Because of the extreme shortage of reading matter such as newspapers, magazines, etc. and the fact the radio set has not found its way to the average Rotuman home, many subjects such as social studies have to be taught using the direct method of really *teaching* or *telling* children what has to be taught. At times one or two children may have heard about the subject but otherwise the teacher has to do his or her best to convey a mental picture either by descriptions or diagrams or both. The teacher is very fortunate if what she or he is teaching has its picture available. I am thinking particularly of geography when one has to teach, say, the various types of forests. Pictures of each type would obviously be the best that we in Rotuma can hope for, for without these, description and diagrams and characteristics will, at best, only convey to the children a distorted picture of say, what a monsoon forest really is.

(E.I., seventh grade). In lessons such as history, geography, natural science, and hygiene, I usually arrange my work in at least three steps. These are:
Step I. I ask a few questions at the beginning of the lesson to prepare the children's minds for the new subject. It is impossible for them to learn anything completely new. They learn by linking a new idea to an old one.
Step II. After refreshing the children's minds with some familiar ideas on which they can connect the new ones, the new ideas are presented to them. I find that if I tell them everything they are likely to have forgotten everything I said by the following week, and that is of very little value in developing the powers of the children. The telling method is good for the lower classes, but in my class the finding out method is best. Of course I have to tell them some things which are too hard for them to find out, or if my questions fail to lead them to the facts. In this "Presentation Step," *questions* help them to reason out some facts. Demonstration is important, and *teaching aids* help to make my teaching more effective. I have only a few pictures cut from some magazines; brown paper maps which I made myself because our school can't afford to buy maps for each class; no globe either. Drawings and sketches on the blackboard are very helpful indeed.
Step III. Lastly the children do something with the ideas presented to them. "No impression without expression." The children answer oral revision questions. They may draw something from the lesson or retell the story; they may draw maps or diagrams, etc.

(A.F.K., seventh grade). In all my presentations, particularly of a new topic, I always apply the teaching techniques which I gained from a couple of years training with slight alterations, i.e., I always introduce my lessons along these few points:
1. Teach from simple to difficult. This is the only way which I have learned from my experience that will arouse the interest of the pupils and maintain it right through the lessons. From being taught the simple at first, I notice that they are anxious to learn and as the lesson progresses, and links up to difficulty, they frequently apply their initiative and imagination.
2. Teach from the known to the unknown.
3. Teach from the concrete to the abstract. In the course of my lesson, I try my very best to ask questions on the facts mentioned so that the pupils will remember them. I also find that by framing my questions properly and asking them at the right time the students are enabled to discover the facts for themselves. I avoid doing all the talking and always keep in mind not to lecture them so long as to cause boredom.

REWARDS AND PUNISHMENT

If teachers in the primary grades are to prepare students for optimal learning within the school context, they must find ways to establish themselves as "significant others" for the children. That is, they must develop in the children a concern for the teachers' approval and disapproval, for only if children care about teachers' responses can the latter provide effective social reinforcements for learning. With middle-class American children this is not usually much of a problem, for parents of such children generally dispense rewards and punishments in achievement-related activities in much the same way that teachers do, providing a considerable measure of continuity from home learning to school learning. Children learn to care about adult approval and to work to obtain it.

For Rotuman teachers, however, the problem is more complex. It must be kept in mind that most Rotuman parents dispense love unconditionally to their children, and punish them only for violations of well-defined rules. Children do not have to achieve or perform in order to obtain love at home, and therefore school involves a discontinuity. Teachers have the advantage of the children's initial sensitivities, but they must be careful not to "turn children off" by frustrating them too much. On the other hand, they must teach the children to inhibit intense approach or dependency responses that would disrupt the classroom. In the early grades, therefore, if they are to be successful in preparing children for effective learning, Rotuman teachers must be nearly as sensitive and responsive as their pupils. The following are responses to a question regarding rewards and punishments by primary school teachers in Rotuma:

(Sister E., first grade). If the children do very well at a lesson I may give them religious pictures or Christmas cards. I also praise them for good performances. Sometimes the other children clap when one of them does something well; sometimes the child who does best gets to go to the front seat. The children like the front seat and try hard to "win" it.

If they do poorly at something I show them how to do it. If they misbehave I scold them and tell them the right way to act, but if they continue to act bad I might use the stick, or make them kneel, or make them stand on their desk in front of the others, which makes them ashamed. Sometimes I punish them if they refuse to do the work. If they fight I give them the stick right away.

The small ones don't get angry when you hit them because they want you to love them. They come right back to you. If they cry when I hit them I threaten to hit them again and they stop. It's not good for the children to be frightened of the teacher, so I try not to hit them much. If they are afraid of the teacher, it's not good because they won't tell her things.

Sister E. gave her response in an oral interview, and her sensitivity to children was dramatized by tearfulness when she spoke of punishing them. Her colleague, Sister M., showed similar sensitivities:

(Sister M., second and third grades). I praise good work by one of the students in front of the others; sometimes I pet them when they have done good work. If I've punished a child earlier in the day I make a special effort to reward him if he does something good later on. If the whole class does well on an assignment, I sometimes give the class some extra recess time —something they like very much. Sometimes, if a few of the children do well at an assignment, I give them religious pictures as a prize.

To punish children if they've been bad, I usually begin by scolding them first and warning them; the second time I also scold them, but the third time I give them the strap. It's not good to hit the little ones right away because they might not know the right way, but after I have told them the right way and have warned them, I use the strap. I used the strap, for example, when the children disobeyed me several times and ran to the bus before it had stopped. I had to do it or someone might have been killed. For school work I punish them for being lazy or not working well by shaming them in front of the class, usually just by speaking loudly to them. For general work the European system of report cards to the parents, and grading of individual assignments is used.

If the children fight, I hold an inquiry to find out what happened and who started it. If nothing serious has happened, like if they were only pulling each other, I let it go with a scolding. I give weekly lessons on proper behavior and use the children's misbehavior as examples. If one of the children gets malicious, like striking another child with a stick, I use the strap.

If a child acts "cheeky" to me, I bring them in front of the class and scold and shame them. They don't like that. It's a good means of keeping control.

Sister M. said that being a teacher is very important because it affects the lives of the children so much. "A good mother can do a better job, but the mothers in Rotuma don't know many things. The important thing is not only to teach English and arithmetic, but to teach them to be kind and friendly and to get along with each other." In talking about punishments after the interview, Sister M. said that you can't punish them too much, because you want to teach them to be kind, and how can you do that if you are not kind to them yourself? "They remember what you taught them, and sometimes they come back to you after a year or more and remind you of something you taught them a long time ago and something you've forgotten about. . . . I love teaching very much." She said that children are wonderful and that she can understand why the Bible teaches that it is easy for a child's heart to find the way to heaven. "You can learn a lot from children."

The teachers in the Government schools likewise emphasized praise and recognition for good performance and scolding, shaming, and physical punishment for poor work or misbehavior. The use of corporal punishment is supposed to be under strict control, but in fact it is used freely. According to Board of Education regulations in the Colony of Fiji, corporal punishment can only be given with the permission of the headmaster, but the headmasters in Rotuma have given general authorization permitting teachers to use it at their own discretion. In Catholic schools the Bishop has restricted the use of corporal punishment to "native" school teachers, but the latter, like Sister E. and Sister M., are permitted to use it as they see fit. Most Rotuman teachers feel that corporal punishment is necessary for the effective disciplining of Rotuman children. One teacher expressed her attitude this way:

(A.F.K., seventh grade). European children are different from the Rotumans. With European children you may be able to spare the rod without spoiling the child, but not with Rotuman children. Rotuman children cannot learn without the aid of the rod. Once we stop using the rod, our children will turn out to become lazy and will never learn. Although I punish my pupils at times, I always see that I don't give corporal punishment so as to inflict injuries. All minor misbehaviors I punish with my pointer and they never show me any sign of misbehavior or laziness. Serious offences such as stealing, fighting, etc., I always forward to the Headmaster for consideration. Sometimes I growl at them instead of using corporal punishment. When I am about to give corporal punishment, I always think for a while whether it is fair for me to give it or not.

This same teacher emphasized the necessity of giving rewards for good work, and listed three techniques that she frequently employed:

(A.F.K., 7th grade). 1. *praise:* For children a word of praise is very highly valued. They like being praised by others, and by praising them inside the classroom they give their finest effort. They always try to please the teachers and to win their favors.

2. *Display:* Pupils like to show to the public that they create things, so any good thing that is done by them I try to display inside the classroom so that everyone will attempt their best to have one on the wall. A "roll of honour" on the wall showing their marks on each test also gives them great competition daily at a very high standard.

3. *Changing Seats:* I have special seats in my class known to them as "Excellent Seats" which only the excellent pupils occupy. Everyone tries their best to occupy one of these seats.

Other rewards employed by teachers in the intermediate grades include the dispensing of such privileges as allowing students to work independently and giving the better performers positions of responsibility as monitors and prefects. In general there is a gradual transition in emphasis from the lower grades to the higher ones on using such non-social rewards as marks. Thus one seventh grade teacher stated that "the biggest reward they have is the ability to solve problems from their sums, and the good marks they get from their everyday lessons," and a ninth grade teacher responded to the question of rewards by writing:

(A.A., ninth grade). With me, these are very rare. Perhaps the only form of rewards that I frequently use is that written at the end of an exercise which I mark in their books. The following are used: "Good," "Very Good Work—keep it up." This last one was of course rarely given.

Other semi-reward, half threat phrases & clauses that I use are: "This is not your best," and "writing poor—look out!"

Perhaps the greatest reward my pupils can hope for is to have one's work read to the class. I believe there have been only two such readings so far this year.

Teachers vary in the degree to which they rely upon positive incentives and threats of punishment to control students, but from my observations of ongoing classrooms all appeared to maintain firm discipline within the classroom. The rules were clearly laid down and vigorously enforced, but the children appeared to be naturally well disposed toward appropriate classroom behavior. None of the teachers interviewed felt that their children presented disciplinary problems. A seventh grade teacher summed up the situation in her classroom this way:

(E.I., seventh grade). In order to ensure orderly behavior in my class, and to give them self-control and the ability to live in happy relations here in the school-room as well as in their villages when they grow up, I must maintain good discipline. I do not have troubles in keeping my children disciplined. As a fact I have not come across two in my class fighting one another; partly because they are at an age or a state in which a social disapproval from the class is felt very greatly by the offender and partly because the weekly visit of the local minister has done a lot in helping the children to love one another. It is the aim of his visit to develop in the children characters as far as possible like that of Jesus. But in case there is one who makes life miserable for others in my class, I won't suppress that sort of self-assertive instinct, but try to find some outlet for it, e.g., putting him in charge of a game or a certain job. I have few rules in my class and I insist that they are obeyed from the beginning. If they fail to obey the rules they are punished. I found out that corporal punishment although on the lowest plane is the highest form of punishment to which the children may respond. If they do their work badly they are scolded and then must do the work properly.

Failing to do it means a very unpleasant punishment for the offender, e.g., leveling the playground.

SCHOOL AND SOCIETY: A SUMMARY

As an institution, school is something of an anomaly in Rotuman society. In contrast to the informal educational practices of the household, which are directed toward behavior modifications that are situationally relevant, the learning that takes place in school constitutes preparation for a world the children have never seen—a world as remote to them as it was to their ancestors. In the artificial setting of the schoolroom they learn, in a language they rarely speak outside of school, about places, things, and events for which their own experience provides almost no referent. The startling thing is that they do learn; in fact many of them learn well enough to go on to higher education in Fiji, New Zealand, and elsewhere and succeed in competition with Europeans.

That this is so is a tribute to the Rotuman teachers, most of whom are aware of the stakes of formal education for their people and are extremely dedicated. Although their main purpose is to transmit the kind of "denotative" information required to pass standard examinations—examinations that will permit their students to get a higher education and eventually good positions—they are also aware of the expressive code that prevails among the students, and they are knowledgeable as to strategies that are effective in getting them to perform. They have, in effect, adapted the school to their community by taking note of the way in which their children respond to cooperation and competition, to various forms of punishment and reward, and to different teaching rhythms. They have often taken steps that are not condoned by their Western colleagues because they recognize the inapplicability of techniques standardized within Western society for persons raised in Rotuma. In sum, what the teachers have done is to alter their teaching techniques to accomodate the expressive code and influence strategies characteristic of Rotuman culture.

During the school years children are not required to do more than a minimal amount of serious work in their homes or community, particularly if they show promise as students. Parents encourage their offspring to study as long as they anticipate success, but if the children are obviously uninterested and not faring well, they may be encouraged to learn subsistence tasks instead—to become farmers or fishermen or weavers, and to care for a family in Rotuman fashion. After having completed the last grade on Rotuma, those students who have passed the Fiji Junior Examination go on to attend advanced schools in Fiji. The others terminate their schooling at about age 16, or upon having completed the most advanced grades in Rotuma. They then assume the status of young men and young women, which most Rotumans regard as the prime of life.

NOTES

[1] C. M. Churchward, "One Hundred Years of Christian Work in Rotuma," *Missionary Review*, Sydney, August 5, 1939.

[2] *Ibid.*

[3] Thomas Williams and James Calvert, *Fiji and the Fijians; and Missionary Labours among the Cannibals,* 3rd ed. (London: Hodder and Stoughton, 1870), p. 585.

[4] *The Wesleyan Missionary Notices,* No. 37, October 1866.

[5] William Allen, "Rotuma," Report of Australian Association for Advancement of Science (sixth meeting, January 1895), pp. 556–579.

[6] *Ibid.*

[7] *Annual Report of the Resident Commissioner for the year 1930,* Outward Letters, Rotuma District Office, in the Central Archives, Suva.

V

Youth to Old Age: Rotuman Style

Dropping out of school does not end the educational process. There are still many things to learn, and skills acquired throughout childhood need to be practiced and polished. As one makes transitions from youth to adulthood, from being single to married, from non-parent to parent, he must learn new roles and accept new responsibilities. As individuals mature they are drawn more and more into the economic and political life of the community, and their prestige and standing depend on the degree to which they master the more subtle aspects of culture, including successful strategies for coping with problems. This is the kind of learning that comes from living with people and being part of a community. One absorbs the information informally, usually without anything being made explicit. The process contrasts dramatically with the formal explicitness of school, where learning is so artificially separated from life.

YOUTH

Unlike the dislocations that accompany entrance to school, the transition from schoolchild to youth is easy and requires no startling readjustment. Youth is a period during which individuals learn to perform adult tasks—the men to plant and fish, to build houses and make canoes, to prepare food for native feasts; the women to weave mats, to care for a house, to fish, and to prepare everyday meals. These are tasks they have observed from early childhood, and by the time an adolescent is expected to perform them competently he has already seen them performed thousands of times. An adult or older youth might correct an error or teach a specific technique from time to time, but for the most part learning adult tasks is contingent upon imitating familiar actions.

The Young Men

The most important interpersonal relations during this period are among the members of one's own age group, and boys in particular do not spend much time with their families. As soon as a lad leaves school he begins to associate with the older boys. At first he is expected to be a passive observer, and is somewhat marginal to group activities. He listens to the older boys talk about their experiences and helps them when they work. During this socialization period there is not much pressure on him to participate in events; the degree to which he gets involved is mostly up to him. He may form a close alliance with another boy his age, or perhaps several other boys, thereby establishing a separate sub-group within the larger group of youths in the neighborhood. By the time a boy is seventeen or eighteen, he and his age mates have usually become core members of the local gang. They have learned expected behavior gradually, by listening to the older boys, by helping them do things, and by imitating their actions.

During this stage males ordinarily sleep away from their parental homes, although each customarily continues to eat with his own family. There is nothing formal about this arrangement, as is the case in some other societies. The sleeping house used by boys may be nothing more than a structure in temporary disuse, or they may habitually go to the home of a receptive bachelor or widower. In only a few villages did the boys build their own structure, and none projected an image of permanence. Likewise, there is no formal organization to the groups that form, and no hazing or initiation ritual prerequisite to participation. Membership in the groups is unspecified, and it would be difficult to determine their composition. Relationships within the groups are basically egalitarian, although older boys frequently ask younger ones to do things for them and the latter are expected to comply; between kinsmen, the rules of kinship priority act as a guideline.

Despite the optimal degree of freedom alotted them, young men are not entirely free from societal responsibility. They form the nucleus of communal labor in every village, but even this obligation is not regarded as an imposition since most events requiring their labor involve feasting and fun as well as work. The opportunity to work together with one's friends is looked upon with relish rather than dismay. For example, while discussing the preparations in progress resulting from a hurricane warning, my informant, a young man of twenty years old, exclaimed, "we [the young men] are really hoping there will be a storm. Then we'll all get together and go from house to house, tying things down, fixing roofs and doing whatever needs to be done. It's lots of fun." Their attitude was not shared by their elders, who stood to lose much in the way of copra (and hence money), crops, and property if the storm were severe.

The young men also do some farming and fishing, but since they do not have to provide for families in most cases, there is little pressure on them to produce regular supplies. Usually they maintain a plantation that they farm together, on ground requisitioned from one of the larger land-holders in their locality. Each boy develops a plot of his own and disposes of the produce as he sees fit. Some food is contributed to the households in which they live, some is cooked and eaten on special occasions, and some is donated toward community feasts. In the latter case the boys present food as a group, rather than as individuals.

A second set of activities that occupies unmarried men is sports. These primarily include soccer, rugby, cricket, and the indigenous sports of wrestling (*hula*) and dart throwing (*tika*). As with other activities, imitation plays a major role in learning sports, but instruction is now also given in school. Most Rotumans are well coordinated and learn to perform quickly and with a good deal of skill. For competitive events they train in earnest, usually giving up smoking and having team practice several times a week. During a "season," a soccer, rugby, or cricket team is likely to practice for two or three hours every afternoon, sometimes under the supervision of a teacher who has learned the finer points of the sport from European coaches in Fiji or New Zealand. There is rarely any discussion of strategy or formal teaching of techniques, however, and most practice sessions simply consist of playing an intra-squad game. As a result, athletes tend to reach peak performance quickly, but do not improve beyond their gross abilities. This may begin to change, though, as an increased number of school teachers return to act as coaches after having participated in organized collegiate sports.

Games of European origin are played between sports clubs, ephemeral organizations that come into being when a particular sport generates sufficient interest. A season is usually initiated by a group of young men who casually take up a sport. When I was on Rotuma in 1960, a number of groups were formed for the purpose of playing table tennis and soccer. It all began when a ping-pong table was set up at the Government Station. At first only a few Government workers and their friends played in their spare time, but before long, interest increased to the point at which a regular group formed for the purpose of holding informal competitions. The idea caught on and tables were built elsewhere on the island—one at the Rotuma Cooperative Association headquarters in Noatau, one at the Catholic Mission Station at Sumi, and one in the main village of Motusa. These places became the headquarters for sports clubs, which quickly included most of the young men on the island (including many who were married). At irregular intervals challenges were sent out and an inter-club competition was held. Interest in table tennis waxed strong for a while, and within a remarkably short time many boys who had never even seen the game played became excellent competitors. Matches were held in complete earnest and the equipment used met European competitive specifications. During competitions international rules were in effect, and infractions were punished accordingly.

About six months after the table tennis craze began, interest gave way to soccer. Each club purchased uniforms and equipment, and held regular practice sessions. Eventually cricket may replace soccer. Ultimately interest in any one sport can be expected to wax and then to wane to a point at which the clubs no longer function. Girls' clubs, organized for the purpose of playing basketball and field hockey, emerge and dissolve in approximately the same way.

Contributing to the disintegration of sports clubs are the feasts that accompany competitions. It is customary for a host club to provide refreshments; initially this may include only a beverage and some cakes, but eventually one of the groups invites others to share a meal as well. This may occur during a multi-club competition that consumes the better part of the day, requiring a meal in between. The visiting clubs feel obliged to reciprocate, indeed, not simply to reciprocate, but to prepare something more elaborate. Each club escalates in turn until the demands become excessive, and members start dropping out. This process is not unknown to hostesses in our own society.

At the height of interest, club organization may become quite complex. The Ahou club, to which I belonged, was perhaps the most elaborate. Officers were elected, including a chairman, secretary, and treasurer, and meetings followed parliamentary procedure. A committee was assigned by the chairman to frame a constitution, and this was done. When money was needed to purchase equipment, three methods of raising it were initiated: (1) a subscription fee was levied upon each member, (2) European-style dances were held and the proceeds from admission and the sale of refreshments put into the club treasury, and (3) members were fined for missing practice sessions and meetings, or for being late. Eventually these meetings took on a business-like flavor, with the major portion of the time being spent in discussing finances. This contributed to making participation less enjoyable for most of the members, and to a general diminishing of interest.

Two traditional sports are still played, dart throwing (*tika*) and wrestling (*hula*), but they are organized differently. Both are initiated on the basis of spontaneous interest, but instead of clubs being formed, formal matches are held between the two sides of the island. The "sunrise" side includes Oinafa, Noatau, Pepjei, and Juju; the "sunset" side comprises Itumuta, Itutiu, and Malhaha.

Tika matches are generated in the following way: A few youngsters in one of the villages begin throwing darts and play among themselves. Darts are made of straight reeds about three feet long, with hardwood tips; the object is to throw them as far as possible along a sandy stretch of road. Distances are calculated from the point at which the darts are thrown to their final resting place, a good proportion of the throw being a slide along the ground. As interest mounts, more and more young men participate, and villages may challenge one another to informal matches. Whole districts get involved, and eventually the men from one side of the island agree among themselves to issue a challenge to the other side. They make their desire known to the chiefs of their districts, and if the chiefs agree, negotiations are carried out through formal channels until a time and place have been arranged for the meet.

A good deal of ceremony surrounds these sectional competitions, and they are often attended by the vast majority of the island's population. The host side (the one that accepts the challenge) must feed everyone, and each family is expected to contribute food. All chiefs who are able attend, and they are afforded the traditional courtesies owed them. They in turn make speeches of thanks, appreciation, and apology.

The game begins with members of the visiting team throwing first, followed by the host team. A point is scored each time a throw by the host team exceeds the longest throw by the visiting athletes. A number of the visitors' longer throws are left on the course while the remainder are picked up. If none of the host team's throws are farther than the longest of the visitors', the latter gain a point for each of their efforts exceeding the longest throw of their opponents. After all the players have thrown from one end of the course, they go to the other end and throw in the opposite direction, the order in which the teams throw being reversed. They go back and forth until one team reaches a score of twelve, ending the game. The first team to win two games wins the match. A challenge is ordinarily reciprocated by the other side, after which interest in the sport wanes.

Wrestling is introduced in an almost identical way, by the casual play of young men in one of the villages. Eventually, as the seriousness of play increases, intra-village, intra-district, and intra-sectional meetings are informally held, and the best man is determined. Then, as in the case of *tika*, the young men request their chiefs to challenge the opposing side of the island formally. A meeting consists of a number of individual matches, resulting from spontaneous challenges, but the only one that really counts is between the best men from each side. It is this match that determines which side has won. The mode of wrestling, incidentally, is similar to sumo wrestling in Japan; the first man thrown to the ground loses.

In general, sports competitions are played with considerable seriousness, and a will to win is clearly apparent. Like their younger siblings, the young men do not usually take well to the frustrations of losing. It is quite common for fights to break out near the end of a game, initiated by short tempers on the part of the losers. The more important the game, the more likely such flareups are to occur.

The Young Women

Adolescent girls are under much greater restriction than boys, and they do not form peer groups of quite the same intensity. They are not permitted to sleep away from home and are expected to contribute more regularly than males of the same age to household activities. Nevertheless, girls do form close friendships with others their own age and, provided their parents are not too strict, spend some time in mixed groups, but the most significant education they receive during late adolescence is at home from their mothers and aunts. They assist in cooking, washing clothes, cleaning the house, making mats, and fishing on the reef. Adolescent girls are also given much of the responsibility for taking care of infants and young children. This they do enthusiastically, with as much indulgence as parents and grandparents.

Except for differing tasks, the activities of unmarried women parallel those of unmarried men. Thus, just as the young men form a nucleus of male communal labor in a district, the young women form a nucleus of female communal labor. On any occasion when a village or district hosts visitors, the young men prepare and cook most of the food, and the young women do most of the serving and cleaning up. The spirit of comradeship that pervades boys' work gangs also characterizes those of girls. Another parallel is that girls are enthusiastic about sports and are equally keen competitors, and equally temperamental losers.

As far as parents are concerned, the goal of an adolescent girl's education is to groom her to become a desirable spouse. Although this requires that she learn to perform all the chores associated with the role of housewife, it also requires, more importantly perhaps, learning a manner of decorum and self-presentation that appeals to Rotuman men. The traits associated with such decorum are modesty, with a touch of shyness; considerateness for others, including parents; and respectfulness. A subtle sense of humor and unobtrusive coquettishness are also assets, but they must not be salient. Olfactory sensations are particularly stressed and adolescents learn to use a wide variety of perfumed toiletries. The importance of learning to be a "desirable" wife cannot be underestimated, for it is the only honored role open to a woman if she remains on the island. Success means attracting a man who will be a considerate husband, a warm and loving father, and, most important of all, a good provider. The ways in which a girl learns the essential aspects of self-presentation and the strategy of getting a desirable husband are varied and complex; some are overtly taught by parents, but much is learned by unconscious imitation of culturally approved models. Then again, it would not be surprising if some of this female behavior were instinctive to our species!

COURTSHIP

The nature of courtship and pre-marital sex in such societies as Rotuma is often misunderstood by Westerners, who interpret such matters ethnocentrically. Indeed, perhaps no other feature of non-Western culture has been as thoroughly misunderstood as the sexual customs of Polynesians. In order to gain a proper perspective, we must start from the vantage point of Rotuman culture.

The Rotumans maintain a double standard with regard to pre-marital sex. Boys are expected to pursue sexual gratification, and, within limits, are encouraged to do so, whereas girls are discouraged and in most cases are closely guarded. Restrictions upon unmarried girls date back to pre-missionary days, when some brides were required to undergo virginity tests at marriage. The traditional control of pre-marital sex was social as opposed to moral, however, and the teachings of the missionaries have not seriously modified this emphasis. The rationale behind restraint in traditional times was that virgins were more desirable as wives, since their husbands would not have to face the embarrassment of meeting other men who had taken sexual liberty with their spouses. Such restraint, by increasing a girl's desirability, enhanced her chances of making a suitable match, to the benefit of her entire kinship group, in some cases yielding social, economic, and political benefits.

The basis of the current Rotuman attitude toward pre-marital sex is similar to the traditional one. It is rooted in the conception that sexual intercourse involves a male taking license with a female. Whether or not she consents is not the issue. Sexual license is considered justified only when a boy accepts the corresponding responsibilities, which means, in effect, that he support her economically. To state this arrangement in terms of social economics, sexual license over women is a valued "commodity," and for a boy to take it without paying the appropriate price (assuming economic support) is equivalent to stealing. In traditional times a girl's sexuality was "owned" by her local kinship group; it was they who benefited by a favorable marital transaction. Correspondingly, it was the members of a girl's local kinship group who had greatest interest in controlling her behavior, and by taking sexual liberty with an unmarried girl, a boy was committing an offense against the entire group. In the current social system, however, localized kinship groups no longer operate as effective social units, and no other clearly circumscribed group stands to gain in a comparable way by a "good" marriage. But pre-marital chastity is still valued for girls, and for a boy to take sexual liberties with a girl and not pay the price is regarded as more than just an offense against her; it is an offense against all those who are concerned with her integrity. This is likely to include her immediate family and a number of close relatives. It is they who implore a girl to remain virtuous so as not to bring shame upon the family, and who attempt to restrict her behavior so that she does not have the opportunity to do so. Nevertheless, girls have many opportunities for fun and recreation during this period, and familial restrictions are not severe enough to keep them from getting involved in romantic episodes.

An understanding of Rotuman courtship behavior requires more knowledge than this, for as with many cultural practices, it is influenced by shared personality traits. Since common experiences during the socialization period lead toward a sharing of personality traits, we can look for clues to characteristic courtship patterns in the child-rearing methods already described. Three child-rearing practices in particular appear to play an important role: the high degree of bodily contact and physical demonstrations of affection, the association of affection with material indulgence, and discipline by ridicule.

As an apparent consequence of early physical contact, adolescents are motivated to express affection toward their peers physically. One frequently sees adolescent boys as well as girls walking hand in hand. It looks a bit strange to a Westerner to see husky young men walking hand in hand, but the implication of homosexuality that might be inferred in New York or London does not apply in Rotuma. There was, in fact, no evidence of exclusive homosexuality among males at all.[1]

The point simply seems to be that when Rotumans get to like each other they express their fondness physically, regardless of sex. As far as courtship is concerned, this means that romances quickly become physical and hence "sexualized."

The association of emotional commitment with material indulgence carries over into adolescence with two important ramifications. The first is that "giving" becomes instrumental for the gratification of emotional needs. Thus young men, in order to express affection to a girlfriend, periodically give presents bought with money earned from cutting copra. Girls are in a somewhat different position, however. They too feel a need to express love by giving, but being economically dependent, the only "commodity" they have to give is their sexual favors. They are therefore motivated to grant sexual license to a boy-friend, having no other property with which to express love in a culturally suitable manner. Thus, for the relationship to be "balanced," each person must both give and receive. A girl who permits sexual license without reciprocation is considered a *larrikin,* the implication being that she enjoys sex for its own sake instead of using it as a gift of love. Girls with such reputations are regarded as fair game for anyone. The second ramification is that girls who are materially deprived may seek to alleviate their condition by forming alliances with boyfriends. This by no means should be interpreted as prostitution, for the element of kindness is fundamental. A boy who coldly offered money or gifts in exchange for sexual intercourse would be refused in virtually every case.

Discipline by ridicule has an even more direct effect on courtship patterns. As a result of its salience, children become extremely sensitive to the opinions of others. This leads Rotumans scrupulously to avoid situations that might expose them to ridicule, and since court-ship behavior is a prime target for teasing and banter, there is a strong tendency to avoid its public display. Affectionate behavior is particularly inhibited in public, since it is regarded as a form of showing off. As one young man put it, "If a boy and a girl are affectionate in front of others it would be just as though they were saying they are the only people in the world in love." In effect, they would be inviting ridicule by tacitly suggesting that they cared so much for each other that they would be impervious to the taunts of their follows. There are few Rotumans who are so insensitive. Even married couples take care not to express affection in front of others.

For these reasons courtship tends to be surreptitious, and careful efforts are made by lovers to conceal their alliances. As a corollary to this situation, unrelated boys and girls take care not to be seen talking to one another in private. If they are, it may be inferred that they are lovers, or are in the process of becoming lovers. Social pressures would then be brought to bear urging that the presumed affair either be legitimized or terminated. The pattern at European-style dances is indicative:

> The dances usually take place in a meeting house or a house that is temporarily unoccupied. Usually only unmarried men and women attend, but sometimes married couples participate. The music is provided by guitars and ukes, with a persistent Polynesian rhythm accompanying every song, although many tunes can be recognized as American "pop" hits.
>
> The girls sit around on chairs and at the beginning of each dance, boys trickle over and ask a girl to dance by tapping her on the knee, usually looking away rather than at her. During the dance couples do not talk to each other. Their faces are fixed and rigid, with somewhat empty stares. After each dance the boys escort their partners back to a chair, usually without a word, or perhaps with a polite phrase of thanks. Between dances the boys go outside where they joke with their friends and discuss various girls, etc. If someone has beer or a bottle of liquor it is kept outside and the boys pass it around. The reason given for drinking is frankly to relieve nervousness and to gain sufficient courage to ask the girls to dance. Boys rarely dance with the same girl more than two or three times in an evening, for fear it will be thought that he likes her and will be teased for it.[2]

These social pressures do not result in a suppression of courtship behavior; in fact, they often have the reverse effect. A boy and girl may be seen talking together in innocent conversation, but when gossip and joking start they may decide to go ahead and have an affair since people are talking about them anyway. Rather than suppress courtship, social pressures lead to an elaboration of the process, bringing into play all the ingenuity that boys and girls can muster. A game of intrigue is continually in operation, with notes being passed through trusted friends and clandestine meetings being arranged on the spur of the moment. Boys usually make the first approach, although they may be reluctant until they have had some indication that their advances will be accepted. Often time is short, involving only a few seconds in which the boy can make his intentions known. In this precious time he must profess his love and attempt to arrange a meeting, but if the girl is willing, if she has been waiting for his approach, a great deal can be decided very rapidly. Meetings usually take place in the bush, where the chances of being caught are minimal, but girls may also arrange to sneak out of the house at night for a rendezvous in a nearby cooking house or other building. More rarely, since it involves maximum risk of discovery, a boy will sneak into a girl's house with the expectation of leaving before her parents or guardians awake.

All this is not to indicate that girls are ready partners to such affairs. Even if a girl likes a boy who approaches her, she is likely to be very much concerned about her family's wishes and sincerely will try to avoid casual involvements. A great deal of seduction may be required before a girl can be persuaded to grant sexual favors. The favored seductive strategy is for the boy to proclaim his love as intense, and to promise to marry the girl as soon as the time is right. She responds with the tactical assertion that he is not really sincere—that he only wants to have intercourse with her and will then leave, making a fool of her. He responds by giving presents to demonstrate his sincerity, and unless something interferes, the "negotiations" continue until the girl has extracted sufficiently intense promises to justify, in her own mind at least, her submission, or until the boy gives up. In addition to the near-universal techniques of flattery and expression of intense desire (e.g., "Your eyes are more beautiful than the stars; I cannot live without you," etc.), one other approach is especially likely to be successful—playing upon the emotion of compassion. Whereas boasting and showing off are frowned upon and provoke ridicule, acting helpless and forlorn arouses sympathy and generosity. To aid those in want is a dominant Rotuman value, and the word *hanisi* (love) connotes not only material giving, but pity as well. A boy is therefore much more likely to be successful in his seduction if he can convince the girl that he is a poor, unloved, mistreated fellow.

Interpersonal relations between lovers are of special interest and would be confusing to someone unfamiliar with the dynamics involved. Sweethearts rarely joke with each other; they exercise considerable restraint and are careful not to attack one another's sense of personal integrity. If a boy were to joke with his girlfriend it would be seen as an indication that he was taking the relationship lightly, and that he was not sincere with his promises. One might say that a girl, by getting involved in a romantic affair, makes herself vulnerable to devastating ridicule, and her boyfriend must reassure her by demonstrating that he regards her seriously. Only a *larrikin* girl permits her lovers to joke with her without taking offense. If a girl and boy joke freely with one another, therefore, it is an indication that there is no romantic interest between them. Correspondingly, if one person has a romantic interest in another he is likely to react to joking with embarrassment rather than with reciprocation. An embarrassed response to joking is thus a signal of romantic interest. If a girl wishes to rebuff a boy who has displayed such interest, she may continue to joke at him, possibly even more so. If he has committed himself by sending a note, she may ridicule him directly, and make him the butt of public abuse by telling her friends.

For these reasons courtship develops into an enormously complex game based upon subtle signals and attempts to interpret barely perceptible cues. Since unrelated boys and girls are expected to be restrained with each other under any circumstances, it is difficult to tell who are lovers, except that perhaps in their anxiety to avoid suspicion, they are apt to be *too* shy with each other in public.

Boys learn about sex and courtship predominantly from their peers. Sex is not an appropriate subject for discussion between adults and children, including parents and their offspring. The boys, however, discuss it frequently among themselves, and the younger ones learn most of the "facts of life" by listening to their seniors relate their experiences, real and imagined. They also learn from listening to the older married men "yarn" about their sexual experiences. Boys generally confine their group discussions to sexual relations with *larrikin* girls; their affairs with others are kept secret, either because they have feelings for the girl and perhaps intend to marry her, or because it is strategic to do so. By publicizing an affair with a "respectable" girl, a boy risks public censure; he is apt to be quickly confronted with the alternatives of marrying or terminating the relationship. It is from these discussions that the younger boys learn most of what they need to know about the game of courtship and the strategies that are likely to be successful.

A boy's first coitus may be with one of three different kinds of women: an older woman, usually a widow or divorcee with previous sexual experience; a *larrikin* girl around his own age; or an inexperienced girl that he courts by himself. If it is with an older woman, she is likely to take the initiative in educating him to the delights of love-making. Older women are sometimes sufficiently successful in their pedagogical methods to induce youths to marry them. When the initial experience is with a *larrikin* girl, older boys may offer instruction and encouragement. Girls known for promiscuity usually live in households devoid of a dominant male; indeed, the absence of a father or older brother appears to be instrumental in the development of promiscuity, for they are the individuals who exercize the strongest controls over a girl's behavior in an attempt to maintain the dignity of their household. Households lacking a dominant male tend to become hangouts for young men, and several of them may spend the night from time to time. In exchange for sexual favors they help to support the family by bringing food and doing things that the men of a household generally do. This then becomes one of the vehicles for learning the adult male role. When both the boy and girl are inexperienced at first coitus they may be quite ignorant about the physiology of sex, with intercourse taking place only after a certain amount of experimentation. Young women in particular are likely to be ignorant about sex, for girls and women discuss it far less than men. In some cases a young girl's knowledge of her own anatomy may be so restricted that she can be induced to engage in coitus without realizing what is actually taking place.

Since contraception is not practiced, except among a few of the most acculturated persons, the risk of pregnancy is quite great for a couple whose romance has culminated in physical relations. An extensive analysis of demographic information indicated that approximately 20% of the young women become pregnant prior to marriage (i.e., give birth to a child within eight months of legal union). Considering the stereotype of Polynesian attitudes toward sex, this figure is remarkably low. Turning this figure around, we can estimate that four out of five girls do not engage in pre-marital sex relations sufficiently to become pregnant. Adolescent sterility accounts for some of this, and abortion is practiced to some degree, usually through the use of harsh purgatives or by rough massage, but one gets the impression that the strength of the social controls is the main factor accounting for this relatively low rate of pre-marital pregnancy.

When an unmarried girl discovers she is pregnant, she generally confronts her lover with the news and reminds him of his promises. If he has been sincere and is willing to marry, they then take the appropriate steps, but in some instances he has never seriously considered marriage and terminates the relationship. The girl is then regarded as having been "tricked," provided she is not already known as promiscuous and has not previously gotten into trouble; her family holds the boy in contempt. If he formally apologizes to the girl's parents through ceremonial gifts of kava or specially prepared food, and he accepts economic responsibility for the child's support, the situation is alleviated to some extent, but a young man who is a chronic philanderer becomes an object of scorn even to his own relatives, rather than a hero.

MARRIAGE

The golden years of youth come to an abrupt end at marriage. Even before the ceremony takes place a young couple is made to feel the solemnity of the action they are taking, or in some cases, that is being taken for them. A proper marriage brings into play all the intricacies of Rotuman social organization, and it is often during their own wedding preparations that a young couple first begin to learn about them. To understand the social intricacies that characterize a wedding one must begin with the fundamental concept that underlies the Rotuman social system—the concept of *kainaga*.

The Kainaga System

In its broadest sense the Rotuman word *kainaga* means "kind, sort, variety, species, class;"[3] in other words, belonging to the same category. It can be used to describe people of the same nationality, or in a more limited sense to designate persons "of the same blood," i.e., consanguinity. In this latter sense a person's *kainaga* constitutes his personal kindred, a grouping that becomes functionally operative during such life-crisis ceremonies as marriage, and when an individual becomes critically ill. The term is also used in a still more restricted sense, indicating common descent from an ancestor who has resided at, and held rights in, a given house-site, or *fūag ri*.[4] Every house-site is named and a person usually describes his affiliation by such a statement as, "I am a member of the Halafa *Kainaga*." Associated with each house-site are sections of garden land, presumably those over which an ancestor held rights, and to claim membership in a given *kainaga* is to claim rights in these lands. Ideally, the person who lives on a *fūag ri* has been granted control of the land by the *kainaga* members. He (or she) is known as the *pure* (one who decides) and is obliged to grant usufruct privileges to any member of the group. If a *pure* is unreasonable or overly stingy, the *kainaga* have a right to hold a meeting and depose him in favor of another person. If he dies, or otherwise leaves the ancestral house-site, the *kainaga* should hold a meeting to select a new man. At a *kainaga* meeting social relations are structured according to the principles of kinship, i.e., senior males are required to be the least restrained in expressing their opinions, and others are expected to acquiesce to the degree that they owe these men respect. The prescription for selecting a new *pure* is that the senior male of the *kainaga* should be chosen, seniority being based upon age in one's own generation and father's priority in the parental generation. Theoretically, then, succession goes from elder brother to younger brother, to elder son of elder brother, to younger son of elder brother, to elder son of younger brother, to younger son of younger brother. A woman may become *pure* only if there are no eligible males, and her oldest son is expected to succeed her (provided she has no brothers with sons). To avoid repetitive use of Rotuman terms, I shall hereafter refer to a person's "kindred" and "family branch" to correspond to the two kin-related meanings of *kainaga*.

Some house-sites carry with them chiefly titles, to which the men who become *pure* have claim. When titled a man is known as *as togi* (successor to the name) and given chiefly privileges and responsibilities. The assumption of a title is not automatic; it requires the performance of a ceremony in which the symbol of chiefly status, a short-legged eating table, is turned upright, after which kava is drunk, the candidate anointed with oil, and a feast eaten.

The Ho'aga System

Another important social unit in Rotuman society is called *ho'aga*. Historical evidence indicates that the term *ho'aga* was originally applied to discrete, localized kinship communities, but this has been altered as a result of changes following European contact.[5] Today *ho'aga* comprise three to seventeen households (the average is around ten) which are usually, but not necessarily, adjacent to one another. Each is under the direction of a sub-chief known as the *fa 'es ho'aga* (man of the *ho'aga*).

According to custom, sub-chiefs are supposed to be selected from specific family branches, i.e., from among the descendants of persons who owned rights in the proper house-sites. Associated with each of these house-sites is a family name to which the person chosen as *pure* is entitled, and when custom is being strictly adhered to, the man of senior rank within the family branch assumes the title following the death of a titleholder. Within some *ho'aga* there are additional titles belonging to other member households, allowing those who assume them the privileges (and responsibilities) of chiefly rank. The men holding these additional titles act as lieutenants for the sub-chiefs.

As with other customary rules, however, the Rotumans allow a great deal of latitude for manipulation. A number of the men who are acting as sub-chiefs do not, in fact, bear the appropriate titles. In some cases this is simply because a man who was entitled to succeed to the family name assumed the responsibilities of sub-chief without having taken the trouble to go through the ceremony required to assume the title. In other cases the title holder has moved to another location in Rotuma or to Fiji, and has handed over the duties of leadership to an untitled relative. As long as the substitute discharges his duties well and does not arouse the antagonism of *ho'aga* members, no one seems to mind the breech of custom.

Each household in a *ho'aga* has an obligation to the others, and whenever labor is needed for a special occasion *ho'aga* members can be relied upon for assistance. If a person dies, the bereaved survivors are relieved of many of the necessary funeral tasks by their *ho'aga* mates, and at births, weddings, or any other kind of ceremony, *ho'aga* members can be counted on to help and even to contribute food.

Sub-chiefs act as intermediaries for their subordinates with persons of higher rank. For instance, an individual wanting to leave Rotuma is obliged to obtain the permission of his district chief, but if he so desires, his sub-chief may enter the plea for him and act as his spokesman. Likewise, a sub-chief is expected to defend his group member's integrity against the anger of a district chief. On the other hand, he relays orders from the district chief to the people of his *ho'aga*, and he is held responsible for their subsequent behavior.

Interpersonal relations between members of the same *ho'aga* are characteristically warm and cordial. Neighborly contact is intensified by virtue of frequent working together, and their manner with one another approaches conditional or moderate license in all behavioral areas. *Ho'aga* members feel relatively free to ask for one another's labor or property, and they are relatively unrestrained in their joking, particularly between members of the same sex. This casualness may even extend to the sub-chief, although when serious tasks are being performed everyone is expected to show respect.

This does not mean that antagonisms never arise between *ho'aga* members. As a matter of record they do, and in some cases they are rather bitter. It sometimes happens that a member gets angry at his chief, and seeks to join another group. To do this requires the permission of the district chief, but most of the latter have preferred to allow changes rather than get embroiled in interpersonal squabbles. As a result, households belonging to the same *ho'aga* are now scattered in some districts, making co-operation more difficult. If a *ho'aga* chief is thoroughly unpopular, the members can usually generate sufficient pressure to have him deposed.

The various *ho'aga* are combined into seven districts, each under the leadership of a paramount chief (*gagaj 'es itu'u*). Table I shows the number of *ho'aga* and population of each district. *Gagaj 'es itu'u* are supposed to be chosen from one of the eligible family branches in each district. In most districts there are two or more eligible groups, but arguments as to which ones are eligible and which ones not frequently occur. According to custom, chiefs should be chosen exclusively by the family branch (*kainaga*) involved, in the same manner as a sub-chief, but in actual fact the rules of chiefly succession are not strictly followed. In large measure this is because various government administrators have exerted pressure for the democratic election of chiefs, and others have virtually appointed men whose qualities they have admired.

Districts form working units on occasion—when a new meeting house is being built or an old one is under repair, when the Government Officer orders that the roads be cleared of weeds, when a life-crisis ceremony involves a chief or one of his immediate descendants,

TABLE I. *Ho'aga* and Population by District

District	Population [a]	*Ho'aga*
Itutiu [b]	1088	13
Noatau	445	6
Oinafa	401	5
Juju	439	5
Malhaha	321	5
Itumuta	241	6
Pepjei	187	3

[a] The population figures used in this table are from MacArthur, *Report on the Census of the Population, 1956,* Conucil Paper No. 1 of 1958, Government Press.

[b] The population figures for Itutiu include several non-Rotuman families who are not members of any *ho'aga* and some Rotuman families, including those of government officers, who do not belong.

or when the district acts as host to large groups of visitors. Whenever labor is required on a district level, the usual procedure is for *ho'aga* to form work teams. Each sub-chief directs the male labor within his group, and his wife (or a substitute from his household) directs the female labor. They in turn are under the supervision of the district chief and his wife.

With this as background, we can now go on to describe what is involved in getting married.

Marital Arrangements

There are three principal types of marital arrangement. The first is the *sok faeag*, which is characterized by formal negotiations between the boy's and girl's families. The young man, or a member of his family that desires the match, initiates negotiations by sending a representative to the girl's family to speak in his behalf. A suitor often sends his father, or a fluent uncle, but if it is desired to add weight to the proposal a man of rank—a sub-chief, or even a district chief—might be implored to make the overture. According to custom, a girl's parents can make a decision without consulting her (although this is rare today), and marriages may thus be arranged between parties who have never spoken to one another. If the offer is accepted, the two families engage in a series of gift exchanges, culminating in an elaborate wedding ceremony. To have a marriage arranged by *sok faeag* is considered the proper way, and although it usually necessitates a large and expensive wedding, a girl's family generally prefers it since it brings no shame.

A second type of marital arrangement is called *fu'u* ("to stay"). This takes place when a boy goes to a girl's house and indicates to her parents his intention of assuming the role of her huband. *Fu'u* marriages are common arrangements between couples who have been having an affair; when their relationship is made known to the girl's family the proposal will almost certainly be accepted. If accepted, he remains in the house until a legal wedding is arranged. For a boy to go *fu'u* is a strategic move when a match has been opposed by either his or the girl's family. In other cases a boy may be encouraged to go *fu'u* as a means of avoiding the expense of a *sok faeag* wedding. This is particularly likely if it is common knowledge that the couple have "known" each other, since under such circumstances the most significant feature of a *sok faeag* wedding is eliminated—the absence of shame.

The third type of marital arrangement is called *taupiri* ("to follow"), and consists of the boy bringing the girl to his home. It is the rarest type of union and is considered the most shameful. If indeed a legal wedding ensues, its spirit is expressed in the phrase *Fitama a'ma'akia iria* (just to make them clean). Such a union is likely to take place only when a girl's family completely rejects her suitor, or when they have arranged a match for her in spite of her attachment to another boy. For a girl to go *taupiri* thus constitutes an act of outright defiance, for which she must formally apologize in order to regain her family's good graces.

Ceremonies

Marriage ceremonies are variable in character, but the variability is clearly patterned. There is an ideal pattern that represents a "proper" Rotuman wedding; the variations are essentially modifications, in the direction of increased simplicity, of this ideal form. The basic principles that determine the completeness of a particular wedding are (1) wealth, (2) prestige, and (3) the propriety of courtship.

Wealth is essential because a proper Rotuman wedding necessitates a large supply of food in order to feed the multitude of guests. A great many pigs and several cows are usually required, for all known relatives of the bride and groom, plus friends and neighbors, should be invited to a proper wedding. Although most relatives can be counted on to donate food, the ultimate responsibility for feeding guests falls on the immediate families of the couple, and their resources are apt to be severely taxed. A complete wedding may involve an expenditure equivalent to nearly $3000 in marketable supplies.

Prestige is a second consideration. The families of an engaged couple may have sufficient wealth to sponsor a large wedding, but if they are not of chiefly rank, their prestige will not suffer if they limit the extent of the ceremonies. By holding a lavish affair, however, they may gain prestige in the community. On the other hand, a chiefly family is *expected* to hold a grand affair, and its prestige may suffer if the feast is skimpy.

A third consideration affecting the elaboration of wedding ceremonies is the propriety of courtship. One of the basic assumptions implicit in a proper wedding is that the girl is a virgin. If the couple has had a publicly known romance and is suspected of having had sexual relations, the respective families are likely to avoid a full-scale ceremony, with its implicit assumption of virginity, as a matter of discretion.

The sequence of ceremonies that constitutes a proper marriage takes place over a period of time, initiated by a formal proposal to the girl's family by the boy's (*sok faeag*). This is followed by a ceremony known as *suf han ta* (to secure a wife). The prospective bride's parents fix a date for the ceremony; its purpose is to confirm the proposal. The *suf han ta* serves as a first public announcement of the marriage, and confirms the seriousness of intent. On this occasion the groom's party ideally includes a high ranking chief, preferably the *gagaj 'es itu'u* of the boy's district; two or more lesser ranking chiefs; the boy's namesake; and at least one relative. Collectively they present a gift of kava roots to the girl's family. The party need bring nothing other than kava, which is compulsory according to custom, but if desired, they may bring a *koua* (ceremonially prepared food; see below, pp. 91–92) in addition. At the conclusion of the presentation, the girl's family sets a date for the next step, registering an intention to marry at the Government Station. On this occasion, the bridegroom-to-be, accompanied by a chiefly representative and by his parents, goes to the girl's household. There they are greeted by the girl's parents and a female representative from each of the girl's family branches. The entire group then goes to the Government Station to post the marriage notice, after which they proceed to the boy's residence to partake in a small feast, and then to her residence for another meal.

The task of fixing a date for the wedding still remains, requiring yet another visit by the boy's representatives to the girl's family, this time with a ceremonial *koua*. A ceremonial *koua* must also be sent to the groom's district chief when informing him of the marriage date. All these presentations of kava and ceremonially prepared food border on the sacred. They serve to solemnize negotiations and to assure everyone that the participants are indeed commited to going through with the marriage.

The day before the wedding, all participating relatives gather to prepare food for the following day. Each ancestral *fūag ri* is a potential gathering place for the relatives of the bride and groom, with the *pure* of the associated family branch in charge of operations. On the wedding day the various family branches that make up a groom's kindred congregate at his household early in the morning and prepare to depart as a unit to the bride's home, where her relatives have assembled and are prepared to receive them. If the distance is far, they go by hired truck; otherwise, they go on foot. As the wedding scene is approached, they form a single line, led by a specially designated person known as the *'a'su,* who is appointed by the district chief. Next in line is the bridegroom. He is followed by women bearing mats; they in turn are followed by the men, bearing kava and food.

After a formal greeting is exchanged between the two sides, a series of ceremonies ensues, culminating in a grand feast. The ceremonies include a presentation of white mats, first by the groom's side, then by the bride's; a "dressing" of the bride and groom in white mats; a ceremonial cutting of the bridal couple's hair; and a Catholic or Methodist church ceremony. Throughout the day there is much singing and dancing, both in the traditional manner and in the modern (Pan-Polynesian popular) idiom.[6]

To ensure that the affair will be one of gaiety, a woman is appointed to act as a kind of clown. She is granted license to do as she pleases, provided it adds to the fun. She can walk over to a chief and force him to dance, make fun of him, or playfully strike him over the hand with a stick. Any of these actions would be a grave offense under ordinary conditions. If the woman appointed is skillful, the wedding party is likely to be an uproariously funny and entertaining event, and everyone appears to enjoy himself to the utmost. Everyone, that is, except the bride and groom! Throughout the day's events the bridal pair are highly restrained and subdued. One rarely sees them converse, even though they sit side by side; the seriousness of their countenances appears more fitting for a funeral than for a wedding by Western standards. There are probably several reasons for this. In part it may be a way of acknowledging the seriousness of the event—of communicating that they do not take lightly all the trouble and expense the wedding has caused their relatives. The magnitude of effort involved is brought home to them several times during the day in the speeches of their kinsmen. In part their restraint is an expression of humility. Being the center of attention, they are the subjects of everyone's scrutiny, and in Rotuma the safest way to avoid criticism and ridicule is to be inert. Also, both bride and groom are probably quite nervous, particularly if the marriage has been arranged by their parents and they do not know one another very well.

ESTABLISHING A HOUSEHOLD

Ideally, a married couple settles down with the bride's family, but during the first few months they often spend some time at the groom's home also. Although this is the ideal pattern, however, other considerations may enter in: the amount of land available to each family, the number of persons already living in each household, and various other practical matters. Most couples change their residence once or more during the course of their marriage, usually in attempts to gain control of more lucrative land holdings. The older a man gets the more senior is his claim in various *kainaga* lands, and the more opportunities present themselves for controlling them. His wife, too, has claims in family lands, and the couple may move to one of her ancestral homes in order to take advantage of an "opening."

Following their marriage, both partners are expected to assume a full share of social and economic responsibility, both within their household and within the community. By this time, however, they have learned the essentials of managing a household. The main new thing they have to learn, like newlyweds everyhere, is to adjust to each other. In Rotuma this is perhaps less difficult than in Western society, for the behavioral guidelines between spouses are relatively clear, but if they reside either with the bride's or the groom's parents, the one who has left his parental home has a more difficult adjustment. Relations between in-laws are governed by restraint, in sharp contrast to the atmosphere of warmth and intimacy an individual is apt to have experienced in his parental home. He (or she) also has to learn the routine of a different micro-culture, and to adjust to the intimate habits of several people at once. Although the clarity of behavioral rules aids transition, a visiting spouse's anxieties and discomforts may be overwhelming, and he may urge his partner to come to his parental home. If the request is urgent it may take the form of an ultimatum; refusal may lead to a separation or divorce. This is another manifestation of the Rotuman tendency to respond to frustration by withdrawing, but on the whole divorce is infrequent, and despite the fact that husband and wife are expected to manifest respectful behavior to one another in public, most couples develop a genuinely warm and affectionate attachment, whether or not their union had been the result of a romantic courtship.

When a man takes up residence at his wife's house, her father and brothers are obliged to socialize him into the household. They must teach him where they have land rights, what they have planted on each plot, which plots are left fallow, etc. They must also communicate to him their expectations of his role as a provider. If the groom has left his home village, he must also adjust to a new *ho'aga* work group and the expectations of a new set of leaders. The usual technique is for him to stay in the background and observe until he gains some confidence in what to expect from everyone. Rarely are questions asked; he simply relies on observing the models available to him and on absorbing advice when it is given. He slowly begins to assume more and more responsibilities, comes to relax his restraints, and slips into a full-fledged adult role in his new community.

If it is the bride who has left her home, her husband's mother and sisters take the responsibility of socializing her into their household. She, too, learns less by asking questions than by observing the models around her, imitating their behavior, and remaining sensitive to the cues that designate social approval or disapproval. "Good" parents-in-law are understanding and lenient, and strive to ease the transition to full responsibility, but many are impatient (particularly if the person was not of their choosing) and create friction. Confrontations between in-laws are rarely direct, however, and problems are likely to become serious only if they are aggravated by local gossip, or if parents encourage their children to take rash corrective measures.

Since birth control is not practiced, women begin to bear children almost immediately, and if a couple is healthy, child-bearing continues throughout a woman's reproductive cycle. Until 1930, when the first child welfare program began, infant mortality was very high, limiting the number of children to care for. Today, however, with much improved medical treatment available and a drastically lowered infant mortality rate, a high proportion of children survive, with the result that family size is rapidly increasing. The responsibility of caring for children is of paramount importance to most Rotuman parents, and the demands of feeding a family, providing them with clothes and perhaps a few luxuries, sending them through school (for which there is an annual fee), and getting them married place a heavy burden on parental shoulders.

Adapting to the traditional role of parent requires very little new knowledge or skill for either marital partner. Girls begin to perform maternal tasks from a very early age, as early as five or six years old. When only a little older they are given nearly full supervisory rights over their younger siblings or infant cousins. But since the child welfare program was inaugurated, expectant mothers receive instruction on modern baby care practices that were unknown to their parents.

They learn from a child welfare nurse about the nutritional requirements of infants, how to prepare baby foods, and how to prevent and
care for illnesses; they are even taught a few things about child
psychology. Fathers still have very little to learn; they are content to
leave most of the decisions concerning child-rearing to their wives.

During adulthood, life tends toward a settled routine, in which the
main pleasures come from seeing one's family prosper. Time is marked
by grand feasts and other dramatic occasions, but most of one's time
is spent performing the tasks of day-to-day subsistence. Within the
household, the division of labor between men and women is fairly well
marked, although not rigid. Men do the heavy work—planting and
caring for the family gardens, carrying firewood, and caring for the
animals kept in the deep bush. They also fish and take care of the
family's monetary needs by cutting copra. The women take care of
children, make pandanus mats, keep the family compound in order,
and fish on the reef. They may also care for some of the domestic
animals kept in the near bush, but they rarely venture into the deep
bush.

Almost every Rotuman man is basically an agriculturalist, at least
while living in Rotuma. Even those engaged in wage labor maintain
gardens to provide their families with food. Early in the morning,
Monday through Saturday, a little after dawn while the air is still
cool, the man of the house eats a few morsels left over from the previous evening's meal, drinks a cup of hot tea, picks up his bush knife
and carrying pole, and starts off for the bush. His son or son-in-law
may go along, but the most usual sight is a lone man disappearing into
the bush, carrying his knife as though it were an extension of his arm.
He is apt to be dressed in khaki shorts or an old lavalava [7] and a well-
worn undershirt. The distance a man has to go depends on whether he
has access to land near to his home. Most men do, and may have three
or four plots under cultivation within five or ten minutes' walk through
the bush. On reaching his destination he looks over the crops and
chooses some for picking—a few manioc roots, two or three taro, and
perhaps a few taro leaves that his wife will cook with coconut cream.
If he wishes to be considered a good provider, he is sure to take with
him a bit more than his family can consume. He may note the state of
his garden, pull a few weeds, and perhaps replant the taro tops after
removing their edible roots. If he is near other of his plots he may
take the time to have a look at them too, or on meeting a friend may
sit down for a while to have a smoke and chat. Generally he is back
home before noon, and has time to relax before the mid-day meal. He
may wander down to the local co-op store to buy a few things; while
there he can chat with friends about the price of copra, his gardens,

an upcoming feast, and local gossip. Or he may decide to stay around his house and do a few odd jobs, such as fix broken implements or sharpen his bush knife. During the heat of mid-day there is little activity around the household; a man is at his leisure. Late in the afternoon, when the air has begun to cool, he may decide to return to the bush for a few hours to weed a garden or do some planting, to move any horses or cows he might own to a new grazing location, to feed the pigs, and possibly to cut some copra. He returns home shortly before sundown, in time for a wash before the main meal of the day. During the evening his time is his own. If the moon and tide are right he may decide to fish on the reef with lantern and spear; otherwise he may sit around the house and play cards, talk, or just rest.

According to customary rules, the head man of a house is in charge of all male activities, and he may give orders to his sons and other men residing in his household. In fact, though, he rarely does so. Only if there is a special job to be done is he likely to request assistance, and even then the request is apt to be made in the form of a supplication. An adolescent son may accompany his father to the bush if he feels like it, but may stay home and do nothing without fear of chastisement. Fathers do not like to make their children work unless it is necessary, but at the same time they encourage it by showing appreciation. Married sons and other mature men in the household are expected to contribute to the family's support, but only if they are particularly lazy or neglectful is direct pressure applied to them. Thus, although the head man has the *right* to direct the activity of other males in his household, in fact decisions regarding use of time are usually left to the individual. When concerted actions are required, however, everyone looks to the head man for leadership.

If the reader gathers from this description of male activity that there is a lack of routine and strong central authority, he has gained a correct impression. Men frequently make a point of the fact that, "On Rotuma we are our own bosses. We can get up when we like, and don't have to go to work at all if we don't want to. Even without money we can eat, but in Fiji (or America), if you don't work you don't eat." Only the head of a household *must* work, for he is responsible for the people in his family, but the pressure on others is indirect. To be regarded as a "good" person a man must be a good worker, for this implies that he is a contributor and not merely a consumer. A lazy man is open to ridicule and derisive joking from anyone who knows his habits; after all, what has one to lose by alienating such a man?

Women get up at dawn with the men. Their first tasks are to start a fire over which a kettle is hung, and to prepare breakfast. They too have a great deal of latitude in organizing their activities. During the morning, while it is still cool, they sweep, rake leaves, tidy up, and take care of any arduous work that needs to be done. They also prepare the mid-day meal, but this is rarely very elaborate or difficult work. Women assist with the preparation of evening meals as well, but if it is cooked Rotuman style, the difficult work of preparing an earthen oven is left to the men of the household. Aside from caring for children, most women have a great deal of leisure time. This time may be spent in such economically productive pursuits as making mats, sewing, or fishing on the reef, or it may be spent loafing, a favorite pastime of many. As with men, a hard-working woman is praised, but there is less stigma attached to being a lazy woman than to being a lazy man, particularly since it is men who are expected to provide for a family's needs. The wife of a household head is in charge of female activities, but she, too, exercises her authority with discretion. Most women know their responsibilities well enough so that they need not be told what to do, and necessary tasks are absorbed as they arise by individuals who are otherwise unoccupied. Women enjoy visiting with neighbors and relatives; it is a common sight to see three or four of them sitting around weaving mats and talking incessantly. Much of the talk falls into the category of "gossip," and when a group of particularly acid-tongued women are seen together it is enough to make a strong man cringe.

Household property, with the exception of highly personal items, is freely used by everyone. The first person possessive, *'otou* (my), is rarely heard in a Rotuman house. Even between in-laws property is freely shared after they have lived together for a while. In other words, members of the same household usually come to exercise considerable license over one another's property regardless of how they are related. A lessening of restraint is also noticeable with regard to integrity. Interaction between individuals in a household is usually characterized by casual and easy-going permissiveness. Respect barriers remain strongest between in-laws of different generations, but between in-laws of the same age restraints are quick to relax. It must be emphasized, however, that permissiveness is a matter of consent (i.e., granted license) rather than a right, and when the privilege is abused outbursts of anger occur, sometimes resulting in one or more parties' moving elsewhere. Nevertheless, my overall observations lead me to feel quite safe in concluding that with few exceptions, Rotumans who interact frequently with one another come to like each other, and within a household this trend is most clearly evident.

PARTICIPATION IN THE COMMUNITY

Once a man assumes the responsibility for raising a family, he begins to take the affairs of his community more seriously. This is not always a matter of choice, for he is now subject to criticism in a much more focused manner than when he was an adolescent. Furthermore, his behavior now deeply implicates his wife and children, whereas his behavior as an unmarried youth only slightly implicated his parents and close kin. As a mature adult he is not only expected to work hard and to provide for his family, but also to contribute produce and labor to community functions on a regular basis. To be admired he must be generous, but not to the point of being foolish; he is expected to stand up for the interests of his family and kinsmen, but not to the point of disregarding the rights and feelings of others; and he is expected to be respectful to authority without being slavishly submissive. Above all, he and his wife are expected to maintain balanced relationships—balanced in the sense that they neither owe anyone an unreasonable amount in the way of goods or favors, nor allow anyone to become so indebted to them.

Economic Participation

Ceremonial Presentations. In order for adults to meet all their obligations, including maintaining a reasonable economic balance with relatives and associates, they must be thoroughly familiar with the value of commodities which are transacted. On ceremonial occasions in particular it is important that a person be aware of the worth of his gifts, for his presentation is on public display and he will be judged by it. The value of ceremonial presentations is standardized and easily learned. For men the essential commodities consist of foodstuff; for women they are mats. Following is a description of the items involved and their relative values:

I A. The smallest commodity a man may bring on a ceremonial occasion is an *'afa* (a basket woven from a palm leaf). A minimal *'afa* consists of two *tē la 'ā* (staples, such as taro roots or yams) and one *'i'ini* (meat or fish, such as a tin of corned beef, a chicken, or fish cooked in coconut cream and wrapped in taro leaves). Other items usually are included as well, such as native puddings and coconuts for drinking. If coconuts are included custom dictates that there should be at least four. If there are more than four they must be in even numbers; it is only considered appropriate for coconuts to be given in pairs.

An *'afa* is generally brought by each man attending a small, relatively intimate ceremonial event, such as the return of a neighbor's son or daughter from Fiji, or a small church affair. Men are also expected to donate an *'afa* when their community hosts a *tika* (spear throwing match). For some community events each man may be asked to bring two or three *'afa*.

A special instance when *'afa* are used as ceremonial presentations is after a person has been treated for an ailment by a native specialist. On the fifth day following treatment, the patient is expected to bring an *'afa* to the healer. He is also obliged to bring another, larger one on the tenth day. In some cases two *'afa* may be brought on the tenth day and none on the fifth, particularly if it is inconvenient for the patient to make two trips. After treatment has been terminated the patient is expected to make a final presentation; the nature of this gift is unspecified by custom and depends upon the patient's satisfaction with the treatment.

'Afa are also given when a person wishes to apologize for a minor offense.

I B. The next largest commodity is called *tē la 'ā mafa;* it consists of the uncooked equivalent of a *koua,* or earthen oven. If a person is invited to a relative's wedding, he may bring a *tē la 'ā mafa* in lieu of a *koua* (see below), allowing the contents to be cooked on location along with the host's foodstuff. There are two main advantages to bringing food in this form rather than cooking it at home. First, the donor does not have to go through all the work of preparing an earthen oven individually, but can do so in conjunction with others, thereby saving labor and making a public display of his efforts. Second, and possibly even more important, all animals that are slaughtered for human consumption must be inspected by the Assistant Medical Officer. If an animal is judged unfit it cannot be eaten. Thus if a donor slaughters an unfit animal at his own home, he would have to replace it, for he could not honorably go to the affair without including a pig or its equivalent; but if he brings the prospective animal with him to the host's home, even if it is then judged unfit he will have fulfilled his obligation. Precisely for these reasons, however, a *tē la 'ā mafa* is less valued than a *koua.*

I C. There are four types of *koua,* ranging from sparse to lavish.

    1. The first type has two versions:

        (a) A *koua* consisting of one case of tinned fish, such as

pilchards or salmon, and several baskets of *tē la 'ā* (taro, yams, or sweet potato). This is an absolutely minimal offering; a person would probably feel a bit ashamed if it were all he could afford.

(b) A *koua* consisting of one case of tinned meat, such as corned beef, plus several baskets of *tē la 'ā*. This would be acceptable on most occasions, but is not as valuable as the following types.

2. A *fekei moa*, which consists of ten chickens plus several baskets of *tē la 'ā*. It is customary for a small pig or six-pound tin of corned beef to be included in order to increase acceptability.

3. A *koua* consisting of one large pig plus several baskets of *tē la 'ā*. This was the standard ceremonial presentation in traditional times; the others are variations that have arisen as a result of acculturation. Traditionally, cooking a pig was a form of sacrifice to supernatural spirits, intended to insure protection against illness and to bring good fortune.

4. A *koua* consisting of one or more cows, and many baskets of *tē la 'ā*.

Included in any *koua* may be a number of other items such as native puddings, pineapples, watermelons, sugar cane, and bananas, to "dress it up." The number of baskets of *tē la 'ā* may also be increased to enhance the value of the offering; a minimal number would be four or five. Nevertheless, it is primarily the nature of the *'i'ini* (meat or fish) that determines basic value.

If a person wishes to solemnize his offering he may give, along with a *koua*, a bundle of *kava* roots. From this is made a drink that has a mild narcotic effect; in Rotuma it is only drunk ceremonially, by persons of high rank.

I D. The highest homage that can be paid on a ceremonial occasion is the presentation of a *koua puha*, in which the main ingredient is the sweet tuberous root of the dracaena. To prepare a *koua puha* properly requires the work of several men for three or four days. It must be done under the direction of a district chief, and considerable ceremony accompanies its production. Only on very special occasions, such as a visit by the Governor of Fiji, is such an offering made.

There are two types of mat that women bring on ceremonial occasions. One is an ordinary domestic type (*'epa*), which can be used around the house; the other is a fine white mat (*apei*), usually decorated with colorful wool designs, and of strictly ceremonial significance. Ordinary mats, which are of lesser value, come in three sizes; ceremonial mats come in two. The larger the mat, the greater its value.

II A. *'Epa* (regular mats)
1. *'eap hapa*—smallest size, about 6′ × 4′.
2. *'eap maunfaua*—medium size, about 12′ × 6′.
3. *'eap ag rua*—largest size, about 12′ × 12′.

II B. *Apei* (fine white mats)
1. *apei te hapa*—about 6′ × 4′.
2. *apei maunfaua*—about 12′ × 6′.

As a result of acculturation money has been introduced into the system of ceremonial exchange and people sometimes give money as a substitute for food or mats. The generally accepted equivalences, such that a person could give cash as substitute without feeling ashamed, are as follows:

'afa	10–15 shillings	($1.25–$1.63)
small *koua* (types 1 and 2) ...	2 pounds	($5)
regular *koua* (type 3)	3 pounds	($7.50)
large *koua* (type 4)	5–10 pounds	($12.50–$25)
'eap hapa	5 shillings	($.63)
'eap maunfaua	10 shillings	($1.25)
'eap ag rua	1 pound	($2.50)
apei te hapa	1 pound	($2.50)
apei maunfaua	2 pounds	($5.00)

The value of money in Rotuma, both as a substitute for ceremonial items and as purchase tender, varies with the price of copra. When copra prices are high the value of money relative to food and mats decreases accordingly. As items of ceremonial exchange, however, the Rotumans are not concerned with how much food or mats money can buy on the open market. In fact, the market value of the commodities is well above the ceremonial exchange equivalence; for example, when I was in Rotuma the cost of an *apei te hapa* was £3 or £4, an *apei maunfaua* £7 or £8. The Rotumans' primary consideration in evaluating ceremonial gifts is *the amount of time or effort required to produce the commodity;* the ceremonial value of money is therefore calculated in terms of the amount of effort required to cut and prepare enough copra to earn a given amount.

The fact that the amount of labor required to produce a ceremonial item determines its value has not been appreciated by European critics of Rotuman custom. At wedding ceremonies they see a bride and groom presented with great quantities of mats, only to have them redistributed, leaving the couple with just a few "souvenirs." "How unfortunate," these critics have commented, "that a young couple is forced to give away most of their wedding presents." They have missed the point, which is that to Rotumans the maintenance of interpersonal commitments is more important than the accumulation of wealth. In contrast to Westerners, Rotumans conceive of material goods as being in the service of relationships rather than the other way round. It is therefore not the utility of an item that counts, nor its market value, but the degree to which it represents the time and effort an individual is committing to a relationship. It is as if a person presenting a pile of mats or quantity of food is saying to the recipient, "This is how much I care about our relationship—enough to spend all the time required to produce and prepare what I place before you." The fact that a woman may not have actually made the mats with her own hands is not really important; by giving the gift she lessens her ability to give to someone else and has therefore made a social statement about her willingness to make a prior commitment to the recipient. The same is true of men when presenting their foodstuff.

The Strategy of Land Transactions. This does not mean, of course, that Rotumans are totally unconcerned with accumulating resources. They most certainly are, for only if a person has access to resources can he be sure of controlling interpersonal commitments to his satisfaction. The goals of different people may vary—some may want to gain prestige by being generous, others may want to establish a wide network of commitment in order to obtain political advantage, and still others may desire the security that comes from having people obligated to give assistance in times of need. But whatever his purpose, the more resources an individual controls the better able he is to achieve his ends, and unless a person is wage employed, to have control of resources in Rotuma is synonymous with having access to land.

It should therefore not be surprising that land matters are a focus of great concern and emotion. For an adult male, and often for a female as well, the surest path to success within the Rotuman system is the proper management of land transactions. In order to obtain land, individuals are willing to take exceptional risks, including engaging in disputes that rupture previously satisfactory relationships, but the real challenge is to obtain use of land without alienating others. To do this requires mastering the principles of strategy that are effective in Rotuma.

I have already described the "ideal" pattern by which family lands are managed. The senior man of the family branch ought to be selected as steward (*pure*), but in fact there is much room for individuals to maneuver to their own advantage. For example, a man in charge of family lands may hand over *pure's* rights to a junior relative when leaving for Fiji. In this way he can be assured of taking over again when he returns. Even when a *pure* dies a family meeting may not be held; often a mature son or daughter tacitly takes over unopposed. The fact that seniority is not always clear, especially if the people with claims do not know exactly how they are related to each other, also allows for some play within the system. This may lead to disputes, particularly if the land in question is valuable. Usually, though, individuals do not attempt to exercise rights in all the land for which they could legitimately make a claim. Instead they place their stakes in a few they can be sure of (e.g., those in the hands of close relatives), or in particularly lucrative lands. In general, therefore, large estates have many more claimants than less desirable lands. All this adds up to the fact that Rotumans, like people elsewhere, do not take their own formal rules so seriously that they ignore their own advantage when an opportunity presents itself.

It is not my intention to provide a detailed analysis of Rotuman land tenure for its own sake, although some might find the topic intrinsically interesting. My reason for describing the dynamics of land transactions is that nothing better illustrates the way in which Rotuman adults learn to operate in the economic sphere. By understanding how Rotumans handle their most valuable commodity—land—we can gain an appreciation of how their previous socialization affects their economic behavior.

Prior to European discovery, the Rotumans did not consider land a commodity that could be "owned" in the Western sense, or exchanged in a commercial transaction. Land was held in common by family communities; plots were allocated regularly by the chiefs according to rules of kinship and pragmatic circumstances related to the community's welfare. European traders and missionaries did not view things in the same way. They needed land for their stores and churches, and negotiated for it as private property. Although the chiefs had no cultural justification for bartering land, many were induced to do so, and thereby initiated a new principle into Rotuman concepts of land tenure (not, it might be added, without considerable resistance from family members). The growth of commerce also promoted the concept of individual ownership. In traditional times people were concerned with land for subsistence reasons, and one plot could do as well as another. Food surpluses were either shared or they deteriorated;

they could not be accumulated for future exchange as readily as money. Once the commercial value of copra was realized, however, people began to take a greater interest in the specific lands on which they worked. By the time Rotuma was subjected to British law the Rotumans were treating much of their land as private property, selling it and giving it as gifts.

Unlike some other Pacific Islanders, Rotumans do not distinguish rights over trees from rights over land; the *pure* of the land is automatically steward over the trees on the land as well; there is nevertheless considerable difference in the willingness of individuals to grant license over land on the one hand and coconut trees on the other. Many men are *pure* over lands with far more planting space than they personally need or can possibly use, and they freely grant usufruct privileges to friends and neighbors, as well as relatives. Often a request to use such land is based on no better reason than the fact that it is conveniently located. Granting usufruct privileges under such circumstances is in inexpensive way of raising one's prestige and bolstering status through a display of generosity, a primary Rotuman virtue. This same pattern of generosity and permissiveness extends to such fruit trees as orange, mango, and a number of other species. Fruit may be taken in moderation by anyone passing through the bush without asking permission from the owner. It is also regarded as permissible for an individual, in want of a drink, to climb a tree in order to obtain a few young coconuts to quench his thirst. The only exceptions to this free use of tree products for subsistence reasons occur when a tree has been made taboo, either by binding a coconut or coconut leaf to the trunk of the tree. When a tree is so marked, it is a warning to others not to take fruit from that particular tree—the implication being that the *pure* needs them for a special purpose himself. Violations are subject to sanction from the supernatural.

Granting license over coconuts for copra is treated in an entirely different manner. Since copra brings money, and money is a means to wealth, one person could not take another's copra without a conflict of interest. Money, unlike subsistence crops, can be accumulated, and each person can use all the copra he has. A *pure* may therefore be expected to grant usufruct privileges over coconut trees only with good reason. Thus, whereas the use of land for subsistence purposes is usually freely granted and no explanation demanded, requests for copra must be justified on the basis of legitimate cultural principles. Several strategic considerations enter into a request for copra, including relationship, need, previous obligation, relative wealth, and etiquette.

Relationship may be used to justify requests for copra cutting rights in two ways. In the first case a person makes his request on the basis of his membership in the family branch controlling the land. The logical basis for such a request may be stated in this way:

Formerly an ancester of mine was *pure* over this land. Since parents are expected to freely grant license over property to children, and to their children's children, and to their children's children's children, etc.; the original *pure* would have freely granted usufruct rights to me. So here I am.

A request based upon this principle involves a direct relationship to the land and only an indirect relationship to the *pure* of the land. The evidence leads me to believe, however, that this strategy is rarely used.

In the second instance a person makes his request on the basis of his relationship to the *pure* himself. When this is the case, the important consideration is social distance, that is, the degree of actual intimacy as opposed to genealogical reckoning. With intimate relatives it does not matter much whether the land involved is communally or individually held, since license is granted on the basis of the relationship of the parties to one another, rather than on an abstract conception of rights in the land. It is significant that under such circumstances gifts of money are often used as a substitute for granting copra rights.

A second principle required to justify a request for copra is need. The purpose for which a person requesting rights wants money is taken into account by the *pure*, and if he does not regard the reason as legitimate, he may feel justified in refusing. The supplicant would also be expected to have exploited all more readily accessible resources, including his own lands and those of more intimate relatives. Not only absolute need is taken into account in this reckoning, but the relative needs of the two parties involved. If the *pure* has a legitimate need for money himself, or if he has a previous commitment to a more intimate relative, he is entitled to refuse.

Previous obligations are also taken into account in determining the legitimacy of a person's request for copra. On innumerable occasions relatives exchange gifts, give aid, and do favors for one another. A careful, though informal account is kept of favors owed, and there is little reluctance to base requests on obligations so incurred. A request for a cutting of copra that is backed up by a remainder of a previous gift or favor carries much more weight than one made without such backing.

Relative wealth is a fourth factor. One of the prominent Rotuman values is that the rich should give to the poor. Underlying this value, of course, is the strategic awareness that a wealthy man is more likely to have a surplus to invest in establishing a reputation as a "good man." A *pure* with especially large land holdings is a more likely target for copra cutting privileges than one with meager holdings, and the refusal of a reasonable request by a wealthy man is much more difficult to defend than a refusal by one with lesser resources.

Still another consideration may enter into the picture—the question of etiquette. The attitude displayed by an applicant is of primary concern in such matters. Rotuman custom requires a supplicant to be humble, and even though the *pure* may be indebted to him, culturally-approved tactics call for disguising what may in fact be a demand as a plea. It is very awkward for a Rotuman to refuse a man who employs tactical humility in the customary manner, and to do so requires great delicacy. On the other hand, if a man were to make his request in the form of a demand or without a show of humility, he would almost certainly be refused, for by implication it would be a challenge to the *pure's* decision-making rights in the matter.

It is difficult to say exactly how such strategies and tactics are learned. To a considerable extent they are implicit in the entire fabric of Rotuman culture; what I have done is merely to state analytically a mode of behavior that has been shaped from infancy. Still, not every Rotuman utilizes these principles to optimal effect. As in every society, some men are masters at obtaining their goals by using culturally-sanctioned strategies with subtle precision and tact, whereas others are obvious and awkward, and hence ineffective. Using strategic principles to optimal effect requires a profound sensitivity to the cues emitted by others, a precise sense of timing, and a good deal of control of one's own expressive behavior; not everyone develops these characteristics to the same degree.

Political Participation

As a man matures he is apt to begin taking a more active role in the political affairs of his community. This means voicing his opinions more frequently at meetings and perhaps serving as an opinion leader among a group of his kin and neighbors. Age alone increases a man's prerogative to express his viewpoint, but if he is socially and economically successful his advice is more likely to be accepted. If he is especially well regarded he might be elected to a chiefly position. This generally requires a wholesale readjustment of interpersonal relations, for chieftainship involves a good deal of tension between the requirements of leadership and the pressures of egalitarianism. For district chiefs in particular this often creates a situation calling for extremely delicate maneuvering.

Not surprisingly, increased democratization in selecting chiefs, resulting from pressures exerted by government officials, has aggravated rather than abated the problem. When freedom of choice can be exercised, chiefs are selected on the basis of their being "good men" according to basic Rotuman values. The necessary attributes are generosity, humility, and consideration for others. To choose such a man is, of course, a most expedient move on the part of the selectors. Such a chief's generosity may be tapped in times of need, his humility opens him to persuasion, and his considerateness constitutes an assurance that no harsh demands will be made. These same expectations, however, make chieftainship a very difficult role to play, particularly since the functions of district chief include arbitrating quarrels and making decisions on controversial matters. It is almost inevitable that delicate decisions will antagonize someone, and in return the disgruntled parties may do their utmost to make the chief's life miserable. Accusations are continually made that the chiefs favor their relatives, that they are acting to benefit themselves and not the district, or simply that they are incompetent. Sometimes these accusations are true, but often they are the result of an inability to satisfy conflicting demands. It is not uncommon for a chief's orders to be ignored, or flouted outright, when they are considered to be unjust or contrary to one's interests. In such circumstances a chief has no recourse except to complain to the District Officer, an action no chief likes to take because it amounts to an admission of ineffectiveness.

The strains inherent in the role of district chief can perhaps best be illustrated autobiographically. A man who had served for many years gave the following account of his experiences:

After my wife and I had our first two children, the problem of choosing a new chief arose in our district. To my surprise I was chosen and I had no idea how I was going to lead my people. I felt so strange and nervous sitting in front of so many people: old people, young men and women, and children. How would I speak to them? I knew that being their chief I was their servant at the same time. I took my place as chief and because my wife was a good woman my task was made easier. Everybody seemed to like her. At the beginning my father helped me, telling me how to act and how to make the people like me. Unfortunately he died two years after my election, leaving me alone to lead my people. Not long after that my poor wife became seriously ill and died, leaving me with five children to take care of. How sad I was to lose two people in so short a time. My mother was too old and feeble and couldn't care for the children properly. For a whole year I led my people alone, and my sister took my wife's place as leader of the women's activities.

I then re-married, taking for my wife a woman from my district. How different I found the people this time. They seemed to hate my new wife and began to disobey my words. Even my own children did not like this woman, and I, too, noticed that she was not as nice as my first wife; there was really a great difference.

Now we have stayed together for many years without a child, but since she's my wife I love her. Many times people have refused to show her the respect that's due to a chief's wife, but she is my wife and I must support her position. It's not all her fault; she has something to say, too. I noticed that many people did not like me because of my wife, but I would not leave her for them. Many of them grumble and say that they should have someone new in my place because I was not doing the right things at times, but none of them had the courage to air their views at the district meeting. Sometimes I knew I was doing the wrong thing, but if my wife wanted the things done a certain way I did not like to oppose her. Sometimes my wife has caused my people to be angry with me, but I care more about her than I do about them; she is still the one who takes care of me.

I am now still chief of my district and am trying my best to look after the people. Many of them like me, but many hate me. They think I am getting old and am no longer suited for this kind of work.

This particular case illustrates the conflicts that may develop between kinship obligations and the requirements of good chieftainship, although in this instance the problem is no doubt aggravated by the fact that the offending relative, the chief's wife, occupies a position of leadership over the women in the district. The tone of the chief's comments should be noted, for it typifies the reciprocal passive defiance that often characterizes the relationship between a district chief and his subjects.

The reluctance of people to obey commands regarded as unjust is reported in the autobiography of an ex-chief:

I was chosen to take over as chief of a district with the approval of all the people, and I ruled over them. Even the adults were like children; sometimes they were so naughty that I had to speak to them like children. I made them cut copra for me, or do any work I wanted done. My wife did her very best and the women in the district all liked her. Whatever she wanted done, they were ready to help. But for my part, whenever I called my men to do my work only a few came, out of more than a hundred who lived in the district. My people built a house for me and cut my copra, but they were not satisfied with what I had done for them. One day I received a letter from the District Officer telling me that another man had been appointed in my place, because the people were no longer willing to let me be their chief. I felt sorry, because whenever I had difficult work to do they would come and do it for me in a short while. Now I had to do the work myself. I can remember how glad the people were when I was told I was no longer to be chief.

The authoritarian attitude of this informant contrasts markedly with the attitude of the previous one who, despite his limitations, has been eminently more successful as a chief. It is apparent that the subjects of this ex-chief felt themselves intolerably oppressed, and indeed, his use of their labor for private ends and overall selfishness is entirely contradictory to the spirit of chieftainship on Rotuma. In traditional times such a chief might have been able to maintain his position by force, but under British administration this possibility is absent; by complaining *en masse* to the District Officer, his subjects were able to depose him.

This man's failure as chief has some interesting corollaries. He was chosen not long after he had returned from receiving secondary education in Fiji. His selection was thus an experiment on the people's part with an educated chief; he was chosen on the presumption that the skills gained through formal education would suit him for chieftainship. As is apparent from his account, the experiment was a failure.

Still one more example is instructive. During my stay on the island a new chief was chosen in Itumuta, the district in which I was living. He was a young man, thirty-two years old, and following his election [8] he voiced these apprehensions in an interview:

Now I am a chief and it is the first time in my life I feel really bad. Being a chief is very difficult and I am very unhappy. From the night that I found out I was the new chief, for about four days, I could not think properly or remember what I was doing—just like I had no brain. One day I went to the bush to weed my garden and I left my knife stuck in a tree. I didn't feel like working so I just prepared my food and when I finished, I couldn't remember where my knife was.

Now I've been chief for three weeks and I still have trouble thinking and worry a lot. It would be better to live like I did before than to be chief. If you're a good chief the people will all like you, but if you are a bad chief they will hate you. I'm worried about whether I'll be a good chief or not. A worried life is no good.

An obvious impression one gets from reading this man's comments is his lack of psychological preparedness for assuming the role he has been selected to fill. It will be recalled that the first informant reflected upon similar apprehensions when he was called upon to assume office some years before. A lack of psychological preparedness for assertive leadership seems to be characteristic of men about to become chief, the second informant being a rare exception.

Why should this be so, when in other parts of Polynesia, such as in Hawaii, Tahiti, and Tonga, chiefs held great authority and often were powerful personal leaders? The answer, in part at least, lies in the fact that in Rotuma the differential probability of one man rather than another becoming a chief is quite small. There are over one hundred titles of one kind or another available, and since a man is eligible to succeed to a title held by any of his ancestors, traced either through his mother or his father, the chances of his being eligible for a title are considerable. Thus, as some Rotumans are fond of saying, usually with a tinge of irony, "Everybody thinks himself a chief." The important point is that differential privilege does not begin in childhood as it does in systems with more clearly defined succession rules, such as primogeniture. Under the latter circumstances, which prevailed in the other Polynesian societies mentioned, everyone knows who is the legitimate successor to a chief from the time he is born, and they treat him accordingly. Leaders are thus conditioned over many years and are psychologically groomed to accept a superordinate position. In Rotuma, however, no one knows who will eventually become a chief; consequently interpersonal relations tend to be stabilized on an egalitarian basis. When a man is finally selected he suddenly finds himself chief over people who only yesterday were his friends, and who may have been taking joking license with him. Some perhaps were even his social seniors. One can hardly expect a man under such circumstances to be a self-confident, assertive leader. If the personal attributes of humility, generosity, and consideration for others that are the criteria of selection are also taken into account, it is easy to understand why chiefs feel more like servants than leaders.

In return for playing the difficult role of leader, chiefs receive several privileges. They are shown respect on all public occasions, and although a chief may be joked about in private, it would be considered a gross breach of etiquette to do so in front of him. People rarely contradict a chief, although they may refuse to carry out his orders by passive resistance. It is on ceremonial occasions, however, that being a chief really pays off. Chiefs are sheltered under lean-to sheds for protection from the sun and rain while others are exposed, are fed the best food while others may have to be content with left-overs, and are generally given special treatment. If kava is ceremonially served only titled men and other dignitaries partake. Chiefs are also excluded from manual labor on these occasions, although they may be involved in directing the work of their subjects. Chiefs are obliged to give speeches at the conclusion of ceremonies, both in appreciation on behalf of their group and in apology for any grievances caused, willingly or otherwise, to others.

Homage is also paid to chiefs in other ways. The custom of *äfe* is but one example. The term *äfe* literally means one thousand; it is applied to the custom of bringing one thousand taro or yams to a district chief. This may be done by a group of youths who are working together on the same land, or by the men of one *ho'aga*. It could conceivably be done by one man or household. A chief so honored rewards the donors with a light meal and distributes the tubers among the families in his district. An *äfe* is not given merely to pay homage, of course; the donors gain prestige for their productivity and generosity (and perhaps some extra consideration when the chief has to settle one of their disputes).

A more elaborate activity of the same order is the *kiu* (ten thousand). Ordinarily an entire district is required to prepare a *kiu*. A round of *kiu* began during the 1920's when one of the districts made a gift of 2,000 taro roots to each of the other six districts. In the next few years three other districts followed suit, each producing more than the previous one and holding a more elaborate distribution ceremony. The last one to be held prior to my arrival on the island was in 1949. It involved ten thousand taro and ten thousand yams, plus valuable white mats, cows, and pigs. These were divided into twelve shares: one for each of the other six districts, one for each of the two Catholic mission stations, one for the Methodist mission, one for the District Officer, one for the European firm managers, and another for anyone not otherwise included. Each share included one cow, one pig, and two white mats in addition to a share of taro and yams. Finally, the men of the district fed the entire island for the day on which the event was held. The impressiveness of the event was enhanced by the fact that it was put on by the district with the smallest population on the island! On such an occasion a chief is in his glory, for he acts as the principal distributor and is a focus for the prestige to which the members of his district are entitled.

Another occasion for paying homage to chiefs is the annual presentation known as *tokag'omoe*. In traditional times this event was marked by a presentation of "first fruits" to the district chief, in recognition of supernatural blessings brought about by his influence with the gods. Today this ceremony is performed during the Christmas season. In some districts, gifts of money have replaced traditional offerings of food, a shift in custom favored by many chiefs since they can pocket the money but would be expected to distribute food. In either case the chief is required to make a speech thanking his donors and supplicating the supernatural (including the Christian God) for continued blessings in the year to come.

Being the wife of a chief involves a similar change in status and similar problems, since her responsibilities parallel those of her husband. The wife of a recently-elected district chief described her feelings as follows:

When my husband became chief I felt very bad, right up until now. I'm afraid, because I know I have to be kind to the people all the time and have to lead them in the right way. I always worry about what I should do to lead them properly and make them happy. This is the first time in my life that I've always had to worry about what I'm going to do and whether my husband and I will be able to do the right things. I feel anxious because we are poor people and it will be very hard for my husband and I to get the things that the people will need to make them happy. If the people like you they will do what you say, but if they are angry at you they won't want to do what you want them to do. This is the first time in my life that I am really worried and live unhappily, because my husband has become a chief and we are poor people. It's better for a rich man to be chief.

OLD AGE AND DEATH

As individuals approach old age they decrease their participation in community affairs, and yield authority within their household to their mature children. They are generally respected, but not revered. Although some old people remain economically productive until their ultimate illness, for most it is a period of increased dependence; Rotumans often characterize this stage of life as a return to childhood helplessness. It is a difficult period for some, both socially and psychologically. Old people frequently express exasperation over their failing capabilities and their inability to do their share in maintaining a household. They feel themselves a burden and indeed are sometimes treated as such. As a result of being less productive, and hence less capable of making contributions to the economy of the household, they often come to rely on such manipulative strategies as helplessness in an effort to evoke nurturant responses in others. Whether this strategy is successful depends on their skill in presenting themselves as legitimately helpless, the degree to which they are able to avoid irritating those upon whom they rely for support, and whether their providers are kindly disposed toward them. Some old people, particularly those without grandchildren around them, express a feeling of loneliness. A few have been completely neglected by children immersed in their own affairs. Nevertheless, the majority of the elderly are able to maintain an adequate network of relations as long as they live.

The following are some typical comments by a sixty-three year old man:

Now my wife and I are old and there is only one of my daughters and her children taking care of us. Most of the days I have to stay in bed, and only my grandsons are supplying us with food. I can see that they are doing their best, but it is so pitiful for me to watch them working so hard to supply our whole family with their needs.

I loved all my children, but I think my twin sons were closest to me. One of them died when he was about six years old, and the other just died at the beginning of this year. I really felt very sad when he died because he was working very hard with my grandsons to help me, and I felt at ease when I stayed at home because I knew I could trust him to supervise them in the gardens. Now I am very weak and in ill health, so that only my grandsons are left to supply our family with what we need.

A sixty-five year old woman described her situation this way:

Now my youngest daughter has a husband and I am living with them and my grandchildren. My son-in-law is a very kind man. He works very hard every day and since my husband and I are very old and feeble we are counted to be children. But he takes good care of us—like we were his own parents. He does everything we want him to do for us. The only thing I can do now is look after the children when they are asleep, but I am unable to do any hard work. I just sleep and eat like other children do.

Death, like birth and marriage, is likely to affect many people in the community, and it too is an occasion for elaborate ceremony. As soon as a death occurs, the body is prepared by close relatives and laid in state. The dead person's sub-chief is then notified, and he in turn informs everyone in the vicinity by means of a wooden drum. The slow, irregular beating of the drum summons everyone to the village; the men return from their plantations, the women from fishing. All approach the chief's house silently in answer to the sad call.

A number of considerations determine the size of a funeral, and hence the labor required to prepare it. The most important criterion is the extensiveness of the deceased's circle of relatives, friends, and other associates. For this reason an adult's funeral tends to be more elaborate than a child's, and a chief's more elaborate than a non-chief's.

If the funeral is elaborate, several chiefs may be involved, and as on other occasions, the highest ranking one is responsible for directing operations. Work parties are formed along *ho'aga* lines within the district in which the death took place. One group prepares the grave, another is responsible for preparing the funeral feast, and others are assigned to look after the needs of the deceased's family. The latter are not required to do anything, so that they can be free to mourn.

Shortly after this basic organization has been determined, messengers are sent to inform concerned persons in other districts; those who decide to attend form parties, usually in the form of family branches after the fashion of weddings, and proceed to the funeral location. When a group arrives, they enter through the front door of the house if they have an *apei* (white mat) to present; if not, they enter through the back door. Usually a prominent chief leads each procession; before his party enters he engages in a ceremonial exchange of greetings with a woman inside the house who has been selected to represent the family of the deceased. He introduces his party by announcing the name of a famous *'atua* (ancestral ghost) from his district. Implied in this announcement is that this *'atua* will protect everyone from any evil that might be afoot.

At the time of death, female relatives begin to wail; this occurs at sporadic intervals until the body is buried. Religious hymns may also be sung periodically by the mourners. If the deceased is Catholic, his body is brought to the church, where funeral rites are performed by the priest, before it is taken to the cemetery. Methodists are brought directly from the house to the grave, where a minister performs the appropriate ceremony. Following burial the entire funeral party returns to the house of the deceased, where they eat the funeral feast. Funeral feasts are neither as elaborate nor as festive as wedding feasts. The tasty puddings and fruits, indeed all the embellishments that make a feast something to look forward to, are conspicuously missing. The purpose is merely to feed the participants.

SUMMARY

The sequence of life stages described in this chapter represents only one modality—that associated with individuals whose basic education takes place entirely in Rotuma. Many people who fit this modality have been to Fiji or abroad and have learned things there, but they are likely to be cast into a separate memory compartment as alien experiences. They may provide an individual with something to talk about, but play little role in ordering his behavior when he returns to Rotuma. Another modality, involving effective learning outside the island, will be discussed in Chapter VII.

NOTES

[1] There was some evidence of homosexual play among children and episodic homosexual encounters among adolescents, but no one was cast into a homosexual role and all adult males appeared to be actively heterosexual.

[2] Excerpt from my field notes.

3 C. M. Churchward, *Rotuman Grammar and Dictionary* (Sydney: Australasian Medical Publishing Company, 1940), p. 235.

4 It is the custom for houses to be built upon raised platforms of stone and earth.

5 See Alan Howard, "Land Tenure and Social Change in Rotuma," *The Journal of the Polynesian Society,* LXXIII (1964), pp. 26–52.

6 This includes Hawaiian and Tahitian songs played on guitar and ukulele, and Rotuman adaptations of American popular music.

7 A cloth worn around the waist and extending below the knees.

8 The election was carried out in a thoroughly democratic fashion with all the men in the district participating. Nominations were taken by the acting District Officer (a Rotuman), who urged that traditional considerations be put aside and the best man chosen. A secret ballot was held, but in fact the man chosen belonged to an eligible *kainaga.*

Life Style, Education, and Rotuman Character

THE ROTUMAN WORLD VIEW

Now that the central attributes of Rotuman society and culture have been described, we can consider the relationships among the style of life on the island, the educational practices that nurture it, and the psychological character of the people. Let us begin with the basic premise that underlies Rotuman culture: *social life should be harmonious and free of conflict.* Achieving economic success, being able to support a family comfortably, having friends, and being free from inner conflict are also valued, but they are subordinate to this more central theme. To fail to understand this is to fail to understand Rotuman culture, for almost everything important about the islanders' style of life follows from this premise. It is toward this goal that Rotuman socialization practices are aimed and it is within this framework that they must be understood.

That does not mean, of course, that conflict is nonexistent. On such a small island, where people are in face-to-face contact year after year, conflict is inevitable, but for precisely that reason its management is given high priority in the Rotuman hierarchy of values. Covert conflict is considered less threatening than open confrontation, for the latter forces individuals to take sides, creating social schisms between groups of people and endangering the harmony of the entire community. Many Rotuman cultural practices can best be understood as a means of reducing the possibility of interpersonal conflict to a minimum, and keeping it socially contained when it does occur. Perhaps the most far-reaching example is the body of custom that governs interpersonal relations.

Interpersonal Relations

By providing clear-cut guidelines for behavior, the rules governing interpersonal relations are an aid to avoiding embrassassment and insult. With individuals of higher rank, including senior kinsmen, one is expected to be restrained and compliant. If the person is of especially high rank, a Rotuman is likely to restrain himself to the point of complete silence until asked for an opinion, in which case compliance is expressed by agreeing with the other's view. This has led some European officials to label the Rotumans as "yes men" who offer no ideas of their own. They fail to realize that agreement is a mark of respect rather than an expression of a concurring belief. Especially when a European official expresses a strong opinion, as many are prone to do, Rotumans are reluctant to contradict him publicly; to respond with argumentation would be viewed as an attempt at humiliation. Reservations can be expressed, but they are subtle enough to be missed by persons unfamiliar with the expressive code within which they are embedded. Thus, whereas another Rotuman is able to *sense* the difference between "ritual" and personally motivated agreement, an outsider may not be able to make the necessary discrimination.

With persons of lesser rank one can be less restrained and more freely expressive. Nevertheless, Rotuman ethics require that authority be tempered by consideration. It is nearly as bad for a person of senior rank to be publicly disrespectful of someone of lesser rank as the other way around, unless the latter has committed such a blatant offense that the entire community has been offended.

The rules governing relations between persons of equivalent rank are less explicit, but there are guiding principles that are understood by everyone. Most important of these is reciprocity. In Rotuma this requires that individuals exchange goods and favors as an expression of mutual concern. The balance of exchange should never fall too heavily on one side or the other, but it should also never be equalized, for to pay off all obligations would be to eliminate the social fabric that binds a relationship together. Here again is a point of frequent misunderstanding between Westerners and people from cultures not thoroughly dominated by a market economy. For us, reciprocity implies equal payment for a gift or service. Thus we are apt to respond to a gift by quickly giving one of equivalent value; to give one of lesser value is to risk being accused of stinginess, to give one of greater value is to risk embarrassing the recipient. I believe the reason we feel most comfortable when our balance of obligations is equal is because this allows us to disengage at will. For us, reciprocity is a means to non-commitment; for Rotumans, in contrast, it is the very essence of commitment. That is why Rotumans are actually *offended* at times by Europeans who insist on responding to a gift by giving one immediately in return. It is perceived as a sign that the relationship is being rejected; the return gift changes what might have been a commitment to friendship into a contractual bargain. If one waits a while, however, tries to determine the other's needs and desires, and gives a gift or provides a service without reference to the initial overture, he is perceived as affirming the relationship.

There is a difference in the link between goods and people here that is subtle but quite profound. I would maintain that for middle-class Westerners human relationships outside the immediate family are subordinated to a concern for obtaining and accumulating goods (including money), whereas for Rotumans goods are primarily in the service of maintaining relationships between people. This difference is reflected in attitudes toward wedding gifts reported in the preceding chapter. We evaluate wedding gifts in terms of their utility for the betrothed couple; the Rotumans give presents in order to affirm relationships. An even more subtle example is embedded in contrasting forms of hospitality. In America it is regarded as appropriate for a host to ask his guest if he would like something to drink or eat, and we expect an "honest" reply. If the person refuses, we assume that he is neither thirsty nor hungry. In Rotuma, however, such an overture by a host would almost certainly be refused, no matter how hungry or thirsty the person might be. If the host really wants to supply his guests he simply gives food and drink without asking. This contrast in custom is consistent with the difference in values. Our asking a guest implies that if we were to provide food and drink and he did not want it, then something valuable would be wasted. The Rotuman host is communicating, "Let us not worry about the food and drink, it is my relationship to you that is important. I give to you freely; if you want it, fine, if you do not, it doesn't make any difference." This, then, is the essence of Rotuman generosity. It is not giving for the sake of living up to an inner belief or to nurture a particular self-image; rather, it is a social phenomenon that is intended to establish and affirm interpersonal relationships.

More generally, the cultural approach Rotumans take toward interpersonal relations can be characterized as one of pragmatic immediacy. This contrasts with the approach of Westerners, particularly middle-class Americans, who tend to give a great deal of weight to an individual's intentions. It is as if to middle-class Americans the primary question at issue when behaving toward others is, "How do I have to act in order to be true to myself (i.e., my beliefs, my conception of correct behavior, etc.)?" The concern is one of living up to a self-imposed standard. It is true that we act contrary to our beliefs and feelings from time to time, particularly if there is a high payoff, but we have been trained to feel guilty about doing so and admire men who refuse to deviate from their ideals regardless of the social cost. The behavior of an honorable person should be consistent through time, in different places and with different people. The term "integrity," which denotes what is perhaps the most highly valued personal attribute for Americans and Europeans, implies just such consistency. Rotumans, however, tend to focus upon overt behavior, particularly upon the immediate social consequences of an act. For them for primary question might be phrased "How do I have to act in order to get along harmoniously with others?" When this is a focus of concern, an individual is best guided by being sensitive to others rather than by following internal dicta.

I should like to make it clear that I regard this distinction between middle-class American and Rotuman culture as one of emphasis rather than kind. To be sure, Americans are concerned with maintaining social harmony, just as Rotumans cannot easily be persuaded to do things they really believe to be wrong. Still, the contrast in emphasis is sufficiently pronounced to give a noticeably different flavor to human relations.

For Europeans, encounters with such people as the Rotumans are often disconcerting. They find an individual expressing one opinion at one time and the opposite opinion a short while afterward. They are offended when a Rotuman agrees to do something in what appears to be perfectly good faith, then does not do it. From our cultural viewpoint such behavior is easily interpreted as willful deceit or dishonesty, but such judgments are almost always unjustified. They merely highlight our preoccupation with internal consistency at the expense of external harmony. The apparent contradictions in Rotuman behavior dissolve as soon as one understands the situational ethic that provides the guidelines. The things it is suitable to do and say in one social circumstance may not be suitable in another, and a promise or commitment is always contingent upon subsequent events. For example, a man may agree to lend someone a horse on a certain day, but the district chief might subsequently ask for the use of the animal in order to carry foodstuff from the bush in preparation for an upcoming feast. The prospective borrower arrives only to find the horse gone. The explanation that a district chief enjoys priority, and that his request was unforeseen, is sufficient to justify the broken agreement. Furthermore, the requirement of avoiding overt conflict also makes it difficult for Rotumans to deny a request, even when they have no intention of complying with it. If one understands that it is a lesser offense to fail to abide by a promise than to reject the validity of a request, this kind of behavior makes sense. After all, to reject an overture for assistance is to deny flatly the significance of a relationship, whereas the failure to comply can generally be attributed to external conditions.

The Concept of Time

This lack of emphasis on keeping appointments and compulsiveness in adhering to verbal commitments has led some observers to suggest that Rotumans "have no sense of time," that they are only concerned with the present. Here again are the roots of a misunderstanding. We are so used to thinking of time as being divided up into units of hours, minutes, and seconds that we think of it as natural, and we organize our lives accordingly. Since these units are as applicable to the future as they are to the past, we have come to think of time blocks as precise periods that can be reserved. When we make an appointment to meet someone on Friday at ten o'clock for an hour, we are promising to set aside a particular segment. Other commitments are then allocated to the remaining segments. We also treat time as a commodity—"Time is money"—and workers are paid more by the time they put in than by any other consideration. To fail to appear busy during "work time" is to risk being accused of laziness, even if it means making work when there is none.

Rotumans think of time somewhat differently. For them time is the interval between events—for the most part, human events. The past is marked by a sequence of weddings, funerals, births, visits from relatives, etc., and the future anticipated in terms of similar events. But future events can be delayed, moved up, or even cancelled. Whereas for us future time is rigidly segmented, for Rotumans it is quite flexible. Future time can only be reserved provisionally, since unanticipated intervening events may infringe on the time period that had been set. Inherent in any Rotuman's promise to do something tomorrow is the qualification that what happens between now and then may negate the agreement. When everyone understands this there are likely to be few diffiiculties; only when a European administrator or businessman takes someone's word to be sacred do serious conflicts arise. The idea that time can be sold or purchased is foreign to the Rotuman viewpoint. When there is a job to do one works. That work should be scheduled by anything other than pragmatic considerations, such as the heat of the day, the tide, availability of labor, etc., makes no sense to them. From a European viewpoint Rotumans sometimes appear lazy because they do not "keep busy" when there is no compelling work to be done; to the Rotumans, Europeans appear irrational because they set aside time to work quite irrespective of the amount of work or the suitability of conditions.

One should not construe from this that Rotumans do not plan for the future. They do look ahead and lay plans. They encourage their children to get a good education so that someday they will have good jobs, and they are willing to make sacrifices toward that end. They also save money in order to make future purchases and effectively plan such events as marriage ceremonies well ahead of time. The difference is that they see the future as fluid and beyond individual control; it is therefore somewhat foolish to plan things too precisely, and wiser to wait until events unfold before committing one's energy and efforts.

Man and his Environment. Related to this orientation toward time is a view of man's relationship to his environment. We tend to see ourselves separately from our environment. For us nature presents a challenge, its forces to be controlled and harnessed to our advantage. Man's goal is to conquer nature, even if it means climbing mountains just "because they are there." Rotumans, on the other hand, see themselves as being part of their island environment. Man's goal is not to conquer nature, but to live in harmony with it. We prefer that nature react to us in accordance with our whims. The Rotumans are quite willing to be the reactors and to grant to nature her vicissitudes.

Social Behavior. Another aspect of the Rotuman world view related to their orientation toward time is the priority they give to an individual's *current* social behavior in judging him. In part this follows from the emphasis on interpersonal behavior and the situational ethic that accompanies it, just as our holding a person responsible for his cumulative behavior follows from our focus on individual motivational and belief systems. For us any offense, even if it is against another person, is basically an ethical or moral offense. A person who has committed a serious misdeed is forever suspect, for his very nature as a social being is called into question. Everything a person has done in the past is seen as useful for diagnosing his "true" motives; hence the more we know about his past the better we are able to judge him and the safer we feel about anticipating his future behavior. A "bad" person is one whose accumulated unacceptable behavior is not sufficiently balanced by proper behavior.

For the Rotumans, an act of behavior is reprehensible only if it violates the terms of a relationship. All offenses, even those that are conceived as being against God or other supernatural beings, are ultimately interpersonal offenses. Even the Rotumans' commitment to

Christianity, and it is very strong, is much less an adherence to a code of morality than a personal commitment to God and his church representatives. But God, too, is bound by the Rotuman ethic of reciprocity. If he fails to live up to his part of the relationship by not tangibly rewarding individuals for their ritual investments and adherence to church rules, then deviation is justified. When the relationship is working properly, God rewards "moral" behavior with good fortune, just as Rotuman parents reward compliance with material indulgence. When a relationship has soured, for whatever reason, steps ought to be taken to restore harmony, with the burden of initiative placed on the shoulders of the offender. The restoration of harmony is served by the custom of *faksoro*, which is a form of ritual apology. No matter how egregious an offense a person may have committed against another, it is always possible to balance the slate by offering recompense and going *faksoro*. Thus the "bad" person in Rotuma is one who is too proud to apologize and make up for his offenses; when he does so the stigma is removed.

CHILD REARING—A SECOND LOOK

Let us now re-examine Rotuman child-rearing practices in the light of this world view. There are two points to keep in mind. One is that the behavior of Rotuman parents toward their children is affected by the dominant concern for minimizing social conflict; it is therefore regulated by the situational ethic that accompanies that concern. The other is that parents want their children to be good citizens of Rotuman society and educate them accordingly. The extensive indulgence, for example, with its physical displays of affection and emphasis on material giving, can now be understood as the culturally-approved strategy for establishing and affirming a relationship. One of the consequences of parental indulgence is that a child incurs an enormous social debt that his parents can use for control and influence purposes. A constant theme in Rotuman life history accounts is the report of parents who were so kind and generous that the person felt a profound obligation to comply with their wishes, even to the extent of marrying someone he did not want because his parents desired it. The power of this parental tactic was dramatized to me recently when I asked a Rotuman girl attending the University of Hawaii about the forms of punishment her parents used with her. After thinking for a few moments she declared that she could not remember being punished at all. When I inquired how her parents got her to comply with their wishes, she replied: "They were always so

*Motusa isthmus from the air. At upper left is the Upu
Catholic Mission Station, at lower left the village of
Mofmanu.*

*Donations of food (in coconut leaf baskets) being publicly
announced prior to a feast.*

Above: A wedding party leaves the Methodist Church following the ceremony. The bride is the granddaughter of the chief of Oinafa; the groom is
a schoolteacher.
Below: The bride and groom at the wedding feast.

Left: A daily chore—grating coconuts.

Below: Preparing a pig for the earthen oven. Hot stones are put inside the carcass to cook it from the inside as well as outside.

Grandmother and grandchild.

A funeral procession.

Above: A first grade class at the Upu Mission School.

Below: Learning to recite a lesson.

Above: A third grade classroom. Note the case on the wall to the right of the teacher; it contains toothbrushes.

Below: A seventh grade classroom.

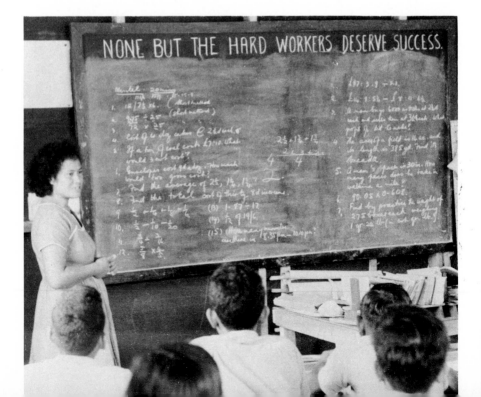

wonderful to me—they never denied me anything they could give. How can I do anything *but* comply with their wishes!"

One reason she could not remember being punished is probably because the main control technique, shaming by ridicule, is a somewhat disguised form of punishment. When a child does something of which his parents disapprove, they are likely to make very pointed remarks, but usually under a cloak of humor. They are therefore able to communicate to the child that his behavior is offensive without disrupting the relationship. It is significant, too, that parents are not the only ones who use shaming to control a child's actions; virtually everyone does. The child's behavior is thus shaped by an expanded social universe as contrasted with the far more focused parental shaping that is characteristic of the American middle class.

Another important characteristic of the Rotuman socialization pattern is that children are punished for the consequences of their actions rather than for committing the acts themselves. This follows from the interpresonal emphasis described above; it is not what the child *intends* that counts, but how his behavior affects others. One never hears a Rotuman parent ask a child, "Why did you do that?" The question is irrelevant, and the answer would not alter the situation. Accidental offenses are just as likely to be punished as intentional ones. Likewise, an attempt to cause harm that fails is likely to be ignored or laughed at rather than punished.

Related to this emphasis on social consequences is the timing of punishment. Rotuman children are usually punished only after the interpersonal effects of their misdeeds become apparent. They are rarely punished for an act at the point of initiation, the pattern favored by American parents. Thus we communicate to a child that certain acts, such as sexual play and the destruction of property, are inherently wrong, and punish them whenever they occur, in public or private, at their very inception. In contrast, by waiting until the social consequences of an act are realized before inaugurating punishment, the Rotuman parent communicates to his child that right and wrong are a matter of how one's behavior affects others. Since the child's behavior may be offensive only to particular categories of people and in particular circumstances, the same behavior may be punished on one occasion and ignored on the next. The net effect of these contrastive patterns is that American children, when properly socialized, learn generally to inhibit certain classes of behavior, whereas Rotuman children learn that certain acts must be inhibited in certain situations and with certain people, but that it is quite all right to exhibit the same behavior with other people in other situations.

The entire socialization pattern in Rotuma is geared toward producing a child who is sensitive to models; it should therefore not be surprising that personal demonstration is the preferred educational technique. Since children are so frequently in the company of adults while the latter are working, they have a great many opportunities to observe how essential tasks are performed. Children's efforts at imitation are encouraged with subtle praise or non-verbal expressions of approval, unless, of course, they start to "show off." If a child experiences difficulty in performing an action, an adult might physically manipulate the child's body in order to correct an error or refine a movement, but explicit verbal instruction is rarely offered and children rarely ask for it. If they do, they are likely to be told to watch a skillful adult in action.

We might reflect for a moment on the way in which this approach to education contrasts with ours. For most middle-class Americans, education is virtually synonymous with verbal instruction. This is true not only with regard to formal education, but within the confines of the household as well. As soon as a child learns to speak and understand, by far the predominant technique for teaching him is through the use of language. I have heard middle-class parents frequently express the viewpoint that you really cannot teach a child anything important until after he learns to speak. Furthermore, our emphasis is heavily upon the denotative aspects of language, i.e., the literal meaning of the words used. Thus we urge a child who relies upon expressive cues to verbalize his message, even if it is otherwise perfectly clear. As soon as the child is able, reading becomes a major source of knowledge. Reading permits the child to educate himself, and this perhaps is the ultimate educational goal in our society. At the same time, reading depersonalizes the educational process, and places an even more pronounced emphasis on the denotative aspects of language.

This difference in educational strategies is clearly related to the different functional requirements of Rotuman and American society. In Rotuma, the essential tasks a person must learn are not technically complicated, and once learned need not be continually altered. They are tasks that can be learned *in situ*, directly from a competent performer, and the skills involved can be practiced and perfected long before they are needed. For this kind of learning, demonstration by a competent model is an optimal tactic. In our technologically complex society, on the other hand, learning occupational tasks often requires a great deal of foreknowledge. Job functions frequently involve a series of operations disconnected in time and place, and efficient planning and record-keeping are required to run the large-scale organizations involved. Change rather than continuity is the rule, requiring individuals skilled in the manipulation of verbal and other symbols, so that innovative plans can be formed and evaluated without resorting to costly trial-and-error procedures. For transmitting this kind of knowledge, teaching by personal demonstration is less adequate; reliance on a highly elaborated denotative code is a virtual necessity.

A PSYCHOLOGICAL VIEW OF
ROTUMAN CHARACTER

The socialization practices that prevail in Rotuma produce individuals who share a number of psychological traits, which can be considered the basic attributes of Rotuman "character." The premise underlying this statement is that individuals who share similar social learning histories are likely to be predisposed to respond similarly to the same social stimuli. Other social scientists have employed such constructs as "basic personality structure" and "modal personality" to summarize such commonalities, with each concept embedded in a well-defined theoretical and methodological framework. Even under the best conditions, however, descriptions of the psychological attributes of a group of people can come perilously close to the stereotypes and glib generalizations carried home by the casual traveler. To do a truly adequate job, an investigator would have to conduct extensive observation of many individuals, carefully select for examination a wide array of variables, both individual and situational, and devise reliable operational measurements. It was outside the scope of my interests to do this in Rotuma. The best I can do, therefore, is to present my subjective interpretation of what Rotumans are like as people. The strongest defense I am able to make is that by the time I left the island, the way in which they did things seemed logical and orderly to me, and I was able to anticipate wih a high degree of certainty how they would respond in various situations. In short, I felt as though I understood them. Undoubtedly other observers would arrive at somewhat different characterizations. If I am biased, it is in the direction of evaluating the Rotumans favorably, for I derived so much pleasure from being with them that I have been unable to shed my devotion to the island and its inhabitants in favor of scientific objectivity.

Perhaps the trait that is most central to Rotuman character might be called "acute social sensitivity." On the one hand this sensitivity is expressed in a careful reading of other people's feelings and a constant adjustment of one's own behavior to promote interpersonal harmony; on the other hand it is reflected in personal touchiness and susceptibility to being hurt. As a consequence, Rotumans are motivated to be cautious in any interpersonal encounter with persons they do not know well. Unlike some other South Sea islanders, the Rotumans do not greet strangers with broad smiles and overwhelming cordiality. Quite the contrary—they have been described by many visitors as having a sullen disposition. I think a more correct interpretation would be that they are highly restrained until they get to know something about a person and his attitudes. By quietly observing someone for a while it is possible to get a feeling for what he is like; also by restricting one's own actions it is possible to avoid saying or doing something that might prove offensive. A sensitive person is vulnerable, hence he is unwise to lower his guard before he is sure that a person with whom he interacts is kindly disposed.

In encounters with strangers or persons of unknown disposition, Rotumans focus much more upon the expressive aspects of communication than do Europeans. Being primarily interested in whether a person is safe or not, they have learned that the best information upon which to make such a judgment is not the denotative content of messages, but upon such cues as tone of voice, facial expressions, subtle body movements, and the like. This is often confusing to the European administrator, who is focused upon what is being said rather than how it is said. He thinks a message has been understood for what he intended and is distraught when the response appears inconsistent or bizarre. He often fails to recognize the cues by which Rotumans communicate their dismay, anger, or hurt because he is only "tuned in" to the manifest content of their speech, which is limited to respectful prescriptions when one is talking to a person of higher rank. The European teachers on the island are confronted with the same problem when trying to communicate to Rotuman children within the classroom, unless they have learned to identify the system of expressive cues.

This is not to suggest that Rotumans are motivated to avoid interpersonal involvements; whereas we generally rely on internalized defense mechanisms to cope with interpersonal conflict, however, the Rotumans learn to rely on avoidance. For them the establishment of an enduring relationship depends upon continual assurances that each party will respect the other's integrity. When assurances are continually given, a relationship may develop into a profound commitment, but it still may be brittle; a single breach by one of the parties may void the previous assurances and shatter the relationship. Even marriages that have endured for many years without conflict often buckle under the weight of a single, apparently trivial, incident. My initial temptation when confronted with this evidence was to interpret it as an indication of repressed or suppressed hostility, bursting to the surface when an opportunity to express it occurs, but as I came to know the culture better I changed my mind. It is just that the cultural significance of a hostile confrontation, even a single one, is so great that it can alter the entire substance of a relationship. Once hurt, a person is reluctant to expose himself again, although if the offender formally apologizes, admitting his error and humbly asking forgiveness, the relationship may be re-established.

Given this background, it should not be surprising that the most powerfully expressed emotion is jealousy. It has its roots in the continual reassurance that is required to maintain a relationship; when a person who has been trusted appears to be favoring a commitment to someone else, not clearly entitled to preferential treatment, Rotumans feel highly threatened. Violent outbursts are quite rare among these people, but when they do occur it is usually the result of jealousy.

One effect of this acute sensitivity is to limit explorations into new behaviors. Take, for example, learning a new language. If a person makes a mistake of pronounciation while speaking English or Fijian in front of others who can speak the language, they may latch onto the error and turn it into a riproaring joke. To illustrate: If a person mispronounces a word like "calendar," by saying something like "culundah," the group may begin to call him "culundah" in mockery. Even this form of ridicule is sufficiently painful to cause most Rotumans to say things in the new language only if they are sure of themselves. The use of mockery is sufficiently institutionalized to constitute a custom, called *sapa*. A mistake or absurdity may even become classical and be transmitted through generations, being applied to the descendants of the person who made the spectacular error. The people of one district are still called "biscuit planters" in reference to a woman who, shortly after the island was discovered by the Europeans, planted some biscuits obtained in trade in order to grow her own supply.

Paradoxically, the strong sense of social awareness that characterizes Rotumans also lies behind the almost unbelievable capacity of the islanders to adapt to new social environments. I can still recall the utter amazement I experienced in seeing people I had known on Rotuma behaving in urban contexts in Fiji. They seemed like social chameleons. Within a very short period of time they had learned a whole new code of conduct and appeared to be entirely different kinds of persons. This was not only true of Rotumans coming to Fiji, but also of the majority of educated Rotumans, who were equally adept at switching when they returned to their home island.

Thus the general sensitivity of the people acts on the one hand as a force for conservatism, and on the other as a force for culture change. Any effort by a person to act in a Europeanized fashion in the company of other Rotumans is apt to be interpreted as a form of showing off and becomes the object of ridicule. I was told by some in-

formants that there was quite a bit of resistance to the introduction
of tooth brushes into Rotuma because it was felt that people using
such instruments were doing so in imitation of the Europeans. The
same attribute, however, leads Rotumans to be very concerned with
the way in which outsiders, including Europeans, view them. They do
not want to be looked upon as primitive or backward and are therefore motivated as a group to make changes that will tangibly enhance
their status in the eyes of others. The vigor with which they have
engaged in the Government-sponsored co-operative movement is an
outstanding example of such group change. Conservatism therefore is
most closely exercised over individualized changes, or changes that
might affect differential status between persons, whereas cultural
change is encouraged in areas that affect all of Rotuma or a substantial group within it.

The resistance to status differentiation does not mean that
Rotumans are not competitive with each other. As I have already reported, children and adolescents are highly competitive, and this
motive carries on into maturity. Men strive to produce larger taro,
yams, and other foodstuffs than their fellows, and women strive to
make finer and more beautiful mats. What they do not do is brag about
their achievements or demand recognition. Instead, to the extent that a
person *is* outstanding, he is required to belittle his achievements. The
excellent farmer suggests that his large crops are the result of unusually fertile soil and the excellent mat-maker asserts that her skill
is no more than a gift from her teachers. Indeed, the consequence of
conspicuously drawing attention to one's accomplishments would be
to lose all the prestige gained by the achievement. In most areas of
behavior the goal is to present oneself as competent but not outstanding. At social affairs, for instance, Rotuman women try to dress prettily,
but scrupulously avoid gaudiness; a family may furnish their home
comfortably, but never lavishly.

Rotuman character can therefore be characterized as being essentially "other-directed." They look for guidance from the people
around them rather than from an internalized code or belief system. In
the words of some theorists, they are shame-oriented rather than guilt-
oriented. Indeed, the Rotumans appear to suffer very little from the
pangs of conscience that make Westerners psychologically uncomfortable after having performed a socially disapproved act. This was
most tangibly demonstrated to me on those Sundays when I attended
the Catholic Church at Upu. On every occasion nearly the entire congregation took Communion, which presumably requires a clear conscience. This contrasts markedly with my observations in the United
States, where only a small proportion of the congregation goes to the

rail. In further confirmation, one of the priests, whose former parish was in New Zealand, remarked that Rotumans confessed less often than his New Zealand parishioners. They also confess to very few "trivial" sins. "When they do confess they're generally dealing with pretty big things," he remarked.

This is not to say that Rotumans exhibit no anxiety after having done something wrong. They sometimes do, but it appears that a fear of discovery lies behind it. The practical consequence of this kind of anxiety is to motivate violators to avoid blame, whereas the guilt-oriented person may feel compelled to "turn himself in" in order to alleviate the pangs of conscience. Also consistent with this distinction is a lack of motivation to inflict self-punishment to ease one's conscience, whereas guilt-oriented persons are frequently driven to do so. If a Rotuman does confess to a misdeed it is likely to be because he feels that discovery is imminent, or because he is having such bad "luck" that he feels the consequences have already been realized. Under either circumstance confession is a prelude to a request for forgiveness, which is the major technique for mitigating undesirable pragmatic consequences of an act.

The roots of this external control orientation can be traced to the way in which Rotuman parents respond to the social transgressions of their children. Since the parents themselves are not primarily concerned with "good" or "bad" acts in an abstract moral sense, but with the consequences of their children's behavior, punishment, as previously noted, is ordinarily inflicted well after the offense has been committed. The children therefore learn to associate punishment more with the punishing agent than with the act itself, and come to feel more anxiety about avoiding potentially punishing agents than about prohibited acts. Consistent with this is the lack of anxiety Rotumans express with regard to impulse control. For them the practical problem is seeking an appropriate situation in which to express their impulses rather than striving to suppress them.

For the sake of contrast, let us reflect on the treatment of auto-erotic stimulation among middle-class Americans and Rotumans. Unless I am mistaken, the American pattern is for parents to scold or punish a child as soon as they discover a child masturbating. They make such comments as, "Don't do that, it's bad (or disgusting, or sinful)," and demand of the child explicit expressions of regret. As a result the child is conditioned to be anxious and feel guilty in response to his own sexual arousals. The socialization goal implicit in this pattern is the establishment of an internally cued, generalized inhibition. The problems that arise from this type of training have to do with over-bearing guilt over unexpressed impulses, the difficulty of unlearning inhibitions at the proper time (i.e., when one marries), and the socially indiscriminate expression of impulses when controls fail. Rotuman parents, true to the situational ethic, are permissive of their children's auto-erotic activity as long as it remains out of public view. If a child should continue in the presence of visitors, however, he is likely to be reprimanded with such comments as, "Shame on you, doing that in front of everyone." With this training the child does not come to feel anxious about sexual arousal *per se*, but only about the potential consequences of sexual behavior. Thus unmarried adolescent girls fear pregnancy for its social consequences, and are reluctant to become engaged in affairs they feel may become public knowledge, but they do not appear to experience guilt over sexual involvement once these matters are settled. The main problem inherent in this socialization approach is that when external sources of control are removed (e.g., as when a girl is left alone with a seductive male), internal restraints are insufficient to suppress an act that one or both parties would rationally prefer to avoid.

The Rotumans also rely upon shame controls to restrain physical aggression within the community. The large majority of Rotumans will do almost anything to avoid a fight, although a few of the young men are known to be "hot headed" and are easily provoked. Jealousy and frustration during competitive events were the chief motivations behind the few incidents that occurred during my stay on the island, but most of them were quickly stopped by mediators. On a few occasions liquor was involved, but even under the influence of alcohol most Rotumans are strikingly unaggressive. The low tone of physical aggressiveness can be traced to the social cohesiveness of the community on the one hand and to the child-rearing pattern on the other. Parents use very little corporal punishment and are rarely severe when using it. Children are encouraged to avoid physical confrontations and are punished for fighting, particularly with neighbors, as this would create strain on inter-familial relations. From a social learning point of view, therefore, Rotuman children are presented with very few aggressive models and are not reinforced when they act aggressively.

In contrast, verbal aggression, particularly in the form of gossip, is prevalent. The acrid tongues of the old women are legendary, and it is said (usually by men) that most of the trouble on Rotuma "starts over the weaving of mats," when the women get together. That people in such a community are quick to criticize one another's shortcomings should not be very surprising. Since an individual cannot enhance his own status by the display of achievement, it is tempting to find fault with others as a way of improving one's own status relative to theirs. Gossip is nevertheless an important form of social control, and because

Rotumans are so sensitive it is indeed very effective in limiting deviation.

Although many Rotumans revealed what I felt to be a remarkable
insight into their own individual personalities, they did not appear to
be preoccupied with the processes of self-analysis and thoughtful con-
templation. Until I returned to America I was unaware of just how
much time and energy we devote to the analysis of our own and other
people's psyche, and more generally, to a consideration of ideological
concerns. It is as if we each walk around with a highly developed com-
puter program in our heads to process the incredibly complex messages
we are continually being bombarded with; in order to keep the machine
running efficiently the "program" must be under constant scrutiny and
continual readjustment. Our great reliance on verbalization during the
socialization process provides the technical means for developing the
elaborate programs we build into our children. In Rotuma there is less
need for such elaborate programming. The mastery that most of the
islanders come to exercise over their somewhat limited and benign
environment does not require a great deal of analytical thought, or
complicated and innovative planning. Life in Rotuma is not without
hardship, but the customary techniques of problem solving are both
universally available and efficient. This is not to imply that every act is
a matter of habit or dictated by custom, or that behavior is mechanical.
Rather, I am suggesting that since the complexity of problems faced by
the people in Rotuma is less great, and their solvability more assured
than the problems faced by urbanized peoples, complex analytical
thinking is only rarely strategically required. I also do not mean to
imply that Rotumans are incapable of abstract or contemplative thought
—only that it is not a requirement for success within their cultural
system nor is it selectively reinforced for any other reason.

The Rotuman attitude toward religion is indicative of this difference in style. Although many islanders have learned the dogma
of their respective churches, they rarely become embroiled in genuine
ideological discussions or arguments. Their commitment to a particular
church, which may indeed be very strong in the sense that ritual is
scrupulously followed, is not primarily a matter of ideological conviction. It is in the nature of an interpersonal commitment to the leaders
of the church, particularly to the priests and ministers, and is subject
to the same principles as any other human relationship. If church
leaders are overly harsh or otherwise do things that members of the
congregation construe as a breach, they may cease to practice their
religion. Likewise, if other interpersonal commitments taking priority
require a person to change his religion, he will readily do so. It is
common practice for one partner in a mixed marriage to change to

the religion of the other, with the change dependent upon whose home or village they decide to reside in. I was startled at first to find that a person who had been a model Catholic throughout his youth, upon marriage converted and became a model Wesleyan within a remarkably short time.

One of the interesting ramifications of the Rotuman socialization process is that many of the psychological conflicts engendered by our middle-class pattern are eliminated. Thus we are continually confronted with the problem of reconciling our motives and beliefs with the demands of social life. We value honesty, but how honest can one be and still get along adequately? Many young children insist that it is wrong even to tell a "white lie"—one calculated to avoid an insult or injury—but they soon learn that absolute honesty is incongruous with viable social relations. A sense of guilt, however, tends to persist. The Rotumans do not have this problem. The question of "lying" is irrelevant; it is right and proper to say appropriate things irrespective of the "truth" of the statement. Since we focus on intent, we hold a person responsible for his words as well as his deeds, and if as children we learn our cultural lesson well, we come to hold ourselves responsible for our thoughts, too. At the ultimate extreme, we even assume responsibility for our emotions! We experience guilt and anxiety when we *feel* hostile or sexually aroused, or when we fail to *feel* love for our children, grief for a deceased relative, or compassion for someone who is suffering. We surely stretch the logical extremes of rationality with such dicta as, "A mother *should* love her child." Even within our own cultural framework this is an absurdity *par excellence*. Emotions are responses; they cannot be turned on and off like a water tap. They cannot be controlled by intent. One does not always feel love for anyone. In any interpersonal relationship emotions constantly shift. Sometimes we may feel love, at other times anger or disgust, jealousy or resentment, and much of the time, no emotion at all. The notion that feelings can be made subservient to intent is as irrational as the most bizarre primitive customs recorded in the anthropological literature. It is logical only from the standpoint that it is consistent with our cultural focus. We endeavor to control our emotions as we try to control everything else. If one wants to confirm for oneself the problems this creates, all one has to do is reflect upon the response of Americans to funerals. Even if the deceased meant nothing to us we do our best to act sad because that's the way we're *supposed* to feel. For Rotumans this quandry is nonexistent. Feelings belong to the private world of the individual. A person is held no more responsible for his emotions than he is for his biochemical processes (which, of course, lie behind emotion). It is how one *acts* that counts. When a Rotuman mother acknowledges that she should love (*hanisi*) her child she is referring to affectionate, indulgent *behavior*. You can dislike someone and still have *hanisi* for him.

The behavior of Rotumans at funerals fascinated me at first. I saw people on their way to a house where the body was lying in state, and they appeared as casual and unconcerned as if going to a wedding. They were joking and engaging in light banter. Then, upon entering the house and being confronted with the corpse surrounded by his immediate bereaving family, they would burst into a fit of unrestrained crying, or even wailing, that seemed to come from the depths of their inner beings. After engaging in this display of emotional behavior for a half an hour or so, they would emerge and within a few minutes be back with their friends, again joking and otherwise showing no evidence of sadness. My first response was like that of many other Occidentals—the emotion can't be real; they have got to be putting it on. People aren't happy one moment and agonizingly sad the next, then just as happy a few moments later. But the more I thought about it the more I came to see our emotional style as strange. There is no reason why emotions should persist when the stimuli that trigger them are removed. Again, our great concern for internal consistency leads us to think it natural that such emotions as grief should persist for some time. Upon reflection, however, the Rotuman response began to appear more "natural." Their emotions were congruent with the social circumstances in which they were behaving; ours often are not. I think what happens is that these people do not feel compelled to assume an emotional state, but that they genuinely respond to the sight of the deceased and the bereaved with grief, which they freely express. When removed from this stimulus, they begin to feel such other emotions as the pleasure of being with friends, which they also freely express. When finally I was able to shed the compulsion to feel things, I experienced an enormous sense of relief and freedom—freedom from "the tyranny of the should."

Thus Rotumans did not appear to experience all those inner conflicts we associate with neurosis, but this does not mean they are free from emotional pain. It is just that the locus of torment is different. For a people as sensitive as they are, to be shamed is agonizing, and even the threat of shame can make an individual feel extremely uncomfortable. Furthermore, the Rotuman cultural option provides little insulation from external hurt, for shaming depends on what others do, whereas we are skilled at developing defenses against the outside world; instead, we are our own most ardent tormentors.

The sense of mastery that most Rotumans display within their familiar environment is reflected in an absence of a sense of impending danger, as reported in Chapter II. For me, at least, watching a three-year-old child playing with a razor-sharp machete is an anxiety-producing experience. Yet it is a common sight in Rotuman villages and adults usually do not interfere if the child appears to be handling the instrument satisfactorily. Eight- and nine-year-old children are permitted to climb forty-foot coconut trees, which they do with ease; they also scale precipitous cliffs like mountain goats and swim in the deep sea like fishes, all without parental disapproval. Accidents do occur, of course, but they are far less frequent than one would suspect. It seems that lack of punishment for experimental behavior leads to the development of a sense of mastery and self-confidence. I came to the conclusion that American children would probably injure themselves more frequently doing these same things precisely because we communicate our own anxiety to the child and weaken his confidence in his own physical dexterity. Whereas the Rotuman parent is apt to respond to a near accident with a joke, an American parent is likely to call the child's attention to the terrible consequences that would have resulted had an accident actually occurred, thereby increasing his anxiety the next time he attempts to perform the same or a similar feat.

In marked contrast to the self-confidence displayed by Rotumans in familiar circumstances, however, is the apprehension they show when confronted with an unfamiliar challenge. In school, as has been noted, each new task tends to provoke anxiety, and if it is not readily mastered, children quickly stop trying. This reaction to frustration is indicative of a strong passivity streak, a characteristic that some European administrators have interpreted as either laziness or willful stubbornness. Such criticisms have usually followed attempts to pressure the people to do things in an unaccustomed way, but both interpretations are misleading. Rotumans are neither lazy nor stubborn when confronting problems in a familiar context, or in new circumstances in which they have a reasonable expectation of success. Indeed, they delight in displaying their competence in tasks they can perform well. When preparing a feast they work extremely diligently, and at a pace most Europeans would find exhausting. Under such circumstances they may put in extremely long hours, working around the clock. On the other hand, Rotumans do not feel *compelled* to work in order to validate their feelings of self-worth.

I think this contrast with American middle-class character can be neatly related to the difference in socialization techniques. Thus, middle-class American parents tend to offer rewards to their children on a contingent basis—the more a child performs to his parents' satisfaction the more likely he is to be rewarded. If he fails to perform, or is inactive, rewards are diminished. He may even be punished. This tends to produce individuals who are unhappy unless they are active. Not only do we come to feel it important to work to reassure ourselves of our worth, we also feel compelled to fill our leisure time with activity in order to avoid depression. Rotuman parents, in contrast, reward children on a non-contingent basis. A child does not have to perform to be indulged, and the amount of increased reward for an outstanding performance is usually not very much. Furthermore, by being passive he reduces the possibility of offending others. Rotuman parents therefore often directly encourage their children to be passive, just as middle-class American parents do what they can to stimulate their children to action—almost any kind of action.

This contrast is clearly reflected in our respective theories of illness. Rotuman parents blame over-activity as the cause of many childhood diseases and have strongly opposed their children's participation in such vigorous sports as rugby and soccer, claiming it increases their chances of contracting tuberculosis. They also try to keep children from engaging in hard physical work for the same reason. When an individual becomes ill, he is encouraged to rest as long as possible. We reverse this prescription. Vigorous exercise is seen as the path to health, and we encourage a sick person to resume his normal activities as soon as possible.

For Rotumans, therefore, work and achievement are valued, but not because of the satisfactions provided by living up to a self-imposed standard of excellence (as is inherent in the concept of *achievement motive*). They are valued as paths to public approval. The payoff is praise or recognition, rather than a feeling of self-satisfaction. In other words, it would seem that Rotumans are motivated to optimal performance by a need for approval rather than a need for achievement. As a motivating force, the need for approval is somewhat offset, however, by a fear of disapproval, which acts as an inhibiting force in uncertain situations. This would appear to explain why Rotuman children stop trying when they encounter problems in schoolwork that they cannot readily master. From their point of view it is better not to try, and hence not to become vulnerable, than it is to try and fail. It also explains why adults prefer a passive strategy when confronted with a new situation. Rather than try out random forms of behavior by trial-and-error to discover which are acceptable and which are not, thereby risking disapproval, they prefer to wait and watch until they feel they have caught on to the game. They then proceed cautiously, encouraged by signs of acceptance and approval, discouraged and motivated to disengage by criticism or disapproval. Thus, although industriousness has its rewards, work is regarded as a necessary evil to the Rotumans—something one must do to survive. It is also a source of approval, but not a good in and of itself. As far as values are concerned, inactivity is considered a more desirable condition than activity. A favorite way of spending leisure time is to "rest," a pastime very much in evidence on ceremonial occasions. (And remember, this is a pre-television society!) The majority of people at a wedding, for example, spend the entire day sitting in one place. They eat, talk with friends, eat some more, talk some more, and so on throughout the day. There is no felt need to organize activities or to find ways to keep the guests busy. To feed one's guests to satiation without their having to work is a satisfactory formula for a successful party.

The ability to remain inactive and unagitated is an important ingredient of a related attribute—patience. This is best illustrated by an example. One of my first encounters with Rotumans was in a back yard in Suva. The family I was visiting lived in a duplex apartment, and their neighbors owned a large dog. Several young men and women had gathered together and were playing guitars and singing Rotuman songs that I was recording, much to their pleasure. In the middle of a tune the dog began to bark. The musicians stopped playing and I was asked to shut off the recorder. The dog continued to bark for nearly ten minutes without anyone getting angry or even showing much annoyance. A few jokes were made, but that was all. No one made any effort either to pacify the animal or to threaten him. When he finally stopped of his own accord, the musicians began playing again and the recording session resumed.

To the educated Occidental, life on Rotuma might seem monotonous and dull, and there is no question that it lacks variety in comparison with an American or European city. Nevertheless, when one is involved in such a culture as this, life can be rich and fulfilling. People have time to enjoy fully the pleasures that are available; they come to care, often quite ardently, about the events that do take place —the feasts, the marriages, a visit from a relative in Fiji, or even a sojourn to the other side of the island. Leisure time is plentiful and is spent in the company of comrades and relatives. The payoff for a successful life is the sense of contentment that comes from being a member of a community in which one enjoys full acceptance.

SUMMARY

Rotumans are a pragmatic people whose major concern is the maintenance of harmonious social relations. They are extremely sensitive to social approval and disapproval, and their behavior can best be understood as an attempt to maximize the former and minimize the latter. In those circumstances in which mastery is within reach and approval is expected, they display a remarkable competence; in other circumstances, in which success is doubtful and disapproval expected, they tend to disengage themselves.

Advanced Western Education and the Bicultural Dilemma

ADJUSTMENT TO A NEW ENVIRONMENT

Those students who leave Rotuma to continue their schooling in Fiji have many new adjustments to make. Besides leaving the social and emotional support of their families, they are cast into a multi-ethnic community in which the main colloquial language is Fijian rather than Rotuman. They therefore have to become tri-lingual, adding Fijian and improving their English, in order to communicate with the people around them. In Fiji most secondary students are obliged to attend boarding schools, and in some cases they are required to do farm work in addition to studying. Within this new milieu an entire new set of coping strategies has to be learned at the same time that academic learning is supposed to be taking place, and it is common for first-year students to fare poorly while making an adjustment. Some become discouraged and return to Rotuma or look for a job in town, but others struggle through and many are extremely successful. These problems are clearly reflected in the autobiographical accounts of individuals who have had to make the transition.

Samuela

"I started to go to school when I was six years old. I went to the Paptea school. There were only about two teachers in the school at that time. I liked it then, I think most of the boys and girls in Rotuma like school when they first go. You have a chance to play around with your friends. There were only a few teachers, so you had plenty of freedom. I came in first in class two, a class of about thirty something.

The schools then were giving out better prizes than they are nowadays. I can remember that I got one shirt and a pair of pants for coming in first.

"I liked school when I was little, but when I got to class three or four they began to give corporal punishment, cracking you on the head for just about anything. At that point I dreaded going to school just about every morning. James Tipo was my teacher then. He was very hard, but was also the best teacher in Rotuma. I stayed in the Paptea school for about seven years, going through class six. In 1945 three of us sat for the entrance exam for the Queen Victoria School (QVS) in Fiji. Two of us passed and went to Fiji at the end of 1945 and started the QVS in the beginning of 1946.

"Going to QVS was totally different than anything I had known. I was one of the smallest boys in the school. You can imagine how I felt looking at the older fellows. My first year was horrible—being an outsider the older boys always used to bully you. I made some very good friends, though. Some of the big boys used to give me a hand with things. Besides school, we had to cut firewood and do an hour's work every morning—before school, from 6 to 7.

"It was a boarding school. The food wasn't very good; we had meat only about once a week. We had to wash our clothes and iron them. This was the first time I ever had to do this kind of thing and I found it tough. The big boys used to help sometimes, though. The washing wasn't too bad, although you can imagine how clean the clothes got, but the ironing was difficult, and sometimes you would spend 15 minutes with a shirt and get nowhere.

"During the first week at the school I got the measles and was sent to the hospital. I felt awful, and missed my parents very much, and the care they used to give me. I'd say I really missed home for about the first three months, but once you know the boys you tend to forget them. In the first exam I came last, mostly because I came back from the hospital only about three weeks before the exam.

"The first year was preparatory and once we passed that we went into Form I. After failing that first exam I felt like chucking Suva altogether and going back home. Some of the boys encouraged me to carry on. It was worse because they arranged us in class according to the way we did on the exam—the person who did best in the back and the one who did worst right up in front. On the next exam I did better, though, and in the final exam at the end of the year I came in tenth out of about 35 pupils.

"I spent seven years in the QVS, through Form VI. During the later years in the school I liked it very much and did quite well. I got through the Junior and Senior Cambridge exams all right, and during the fifth year I became one of the three house captains and head boys of the school."

Viliama

"I went to school at Upu. I didn't find school very difficult. I was very studious. One year we had an exhibition of handwriting and I took first prize in my group. I boarded there for three years. We had to do work in the bush as well. At that time we were building the church at Upu and we helped there sometimes.

"When I was thirteen years old I went to Cawaci, near Levuka, on Ovalau. I went to the minor seminary; a brother (Rotuman) suggested that I become a priest. I was a bit more intelligent than the other boys. I liked the idea, but my mother didn't like it. She wasn't sternly opposed to it but she wasn't very happy. She thought something might happen and I'd have to leave the priesthood later on. That happened to some of the lay brothers. That kind of thing is more shameful I think to the Rotumans than to the Europeans. She also said that by the time I come back she'll be dead, and she was right.

"When I got to Fiji I was sorry that I had gone. I felt terribly homesick. I thought I was better off in Rotuma; the food was more plentiful and the clothes were better. The Fijians went around without a shirt. In Fiji you had to be independent—wash your own clothes. We had practically no *'i'ini* (meat, fish, eggs)—mostly just *vati* (leafy vegetable), but it was a mysterious thing to me that I became fat. I was very thankful to my parents—every time they sent a letter they sent me cash, 10 shillings or so. One peculiar thing—in the 10 years that I was away while my mother lived, she never sent me a single letter, but my father told me that every letter he sent she would read first. Another thing in school, I didn't know what my future would be. It was very unsettled, but I was living among the Fijians, and I reckon the Fijians are a very kind hearted people. I stayed in this school for seven years. We had to pass the Leaving School Certificate and the Qualifying examinations, which permitted me to go to the training college, but since I was going to become a priest I stayed at the seminary and continued studying Latin, theology, and catechism. I still found school easy for me. After seven years I had to move to Namosau, in Mba. I spent two and a half years there. Life was even tougher there. They didn't grow any food there, so we had to buy everything. For *'i'ini* we had to go to the river and search for shellfish. Still at that time nothing was settled. But at the end of time I was told that I was going to be sent to St. Patrick's college in Silverstream, near Wellington, in New Zealand. I was about 24 years old then. When I was told that I was delighted. I came to Rotuma for about two weeks after hearing that. Only once during my seven years at Cawaci did I return to Rotuma for a holiday. My mother had died in the meantime."

Jione

"One reason I was never happy in school in the early grades was because I was always in the bottom of the class. I was a year younger than the other kids, and besides I was very naughty. I was one of those little bullies. My uncle lived right next to the school and he was a sub-chief; I could run to his house and if I wanted to I could swear at everyone and they couldn't touch me. Besides being at the bottom of the class my elder siblings used to say that I wasn't any good and wasn't getting anywhere. In the fourth grade I repeated the year and that gave me a chance to catch up and from then on I held my own. I had two years in the fifth grade because that was the top grade in the schools in Rotuma and I was too young to leave school—only ten years old—so I had to stay in school.

"During my second year in the fifth grade—it was 1941—one of the teachers left to join the service in Fiji, so the other teacher asked me to take a class. For three months I taught class three. I was only 11 years old at the time. My pay was 12 shillings a month.

"In 1942 Wilson Inia came to Rotuma and took about six of the best students, including myself, to coach for the Queen Victoria School examination. I was the youngest of them. At the end of 1942 we sat for the examination and myself and two others passed. But they said that I was too young to be accepted, so in 1943 I went to the Paptea school for about a month. Then I was having severe headaches every morning about 9 o'clock for about 3 weeks. I would cry out loud until school was over about 3 o'clock without any inhibitions at all. The Assistant Medical Officer recommended that I leave school, so I did. After I left school the headaches stopped completely. Later on in that year another teacher came to the Malhaha school and I went back for the third term."

(What caused the headaches?) "I had ear trouble at that time too, and maybe it was the wind in Paptea—that's the windy part of the island, or maybe it was a fear of the school teacher. Tipo was a rough teacher. He used to walk all over the class, hitting the students over the head with a stick if they didn't know their lessons. Sometimes he would hardly give you time to answer.

"At the end of the year I sat for the entrance examination again and passed, but I didn't come top and missed getting the Rotuman scholarship. The next year, in 1944, I went to Fiji, but I didn't go to Queen Victoria School. I went to Lelean Memorial School at Davuilevu and they placed me in class 5. This was my fifth year in class 5, but it was a more advanced school. I was 14 years old at the time. In the first year I was not very happy because I didn't know English well enough, and I knew no Fijian. For the first few weeks I knew nothing about what the teacher said. Then gradually I got to know some Fijian and my English got better and I got to know some boys. This was the first time that I was absolutely separated from home. Many of the things you did at home you couldn't do at the boarding school. We had to wash our own clothes and look after our own things. We had to learn to be completely independent. The first two years were spent getting on my feet and adjusting to the new life. I didn't do badly those first two years. I came in 2nd in my class both years. The third year I was well adjusted and did well. I came in top in the end of the year examination."

THE ROLE OF MODELS

One of the key variables that seems to make a difference is the availability of a significant model, particularly a model who exercises some form of control over the struggling student. As I have pointed out in the previous chapter, Rotuman socialization practices produce individuals who are extremely sensitive to the approval of others, and they readily model persons who are themselves successful and receiving social rewards. On the other hand, they are not trained to acquire a strong measure of self-discipline, and are easily led astray from prolonged work efforts if external controls are absent. The experience of Jimione with a cousin-teacher is indicative.

Jimione's Experience

"I started going to school when I was six years old. I think I was probably the worst boy in the school. One reason for that is probably because my adopted father—Fatafisi—was the chief of Malhaha and I was used to having my own way. So I didn't listen to the teachers and if they would say anything to me I would just go home and they couldn't touch me. At that time I know the people of Malhaha didn't like me much. The children my own age hated me because I was such a bully at the time.

"I stayed in the Malhaha School until I was twelve years old and had reached Class 4. I wasn't very interested in the work and only did things because I was told to do them, so I didn't do very well in school in Rotuma.

"I went to Fiji with Fatafisi to a Methodist Synod meeting when I was 12 years old (1934). While we were in Fiji he put me to school at the Suva Methodist Boy's School for the three months period he planned to stay, but when it came time for him to go back to Rotuma he asked me if I would like to stay on at the school and learn some more, and I agreed.

"While I was going to school there I stayed with a cousin of mine who was a teacher in the compound. I found life at this school different than any thing I'd ever known. The boys didn't waste time there as much as they did in Rotuma. They studied seriously and I had to study hard too if I wanted to keep up with the class. My cousin also did me a lot of good. He taught me many things, not by the third degree, but by logical methods that made me interested and eager to learn. I began to change my ways then and became interested in school. I began to pick up in school very well. During the first year I was in Class 5 and barely passed, coming in about 64th among about 70. Part of my trouble was with the language, because most of the teaching was in Fijian and English. The next year, though, in class six, I came in eighth in the class and earned the progressive prize for greatest advancement."

Tomasi's Experience

Without doubt the man who has done most to serve as a model for Rotuman youngsters has been Wilson Inia, the current headmaster of the Malhaha School and guiding light of the Rotuma Cooperative Association. Not only has he personally coached dozens of promising students, like Jione, and encouraged them to go on to secondary education; he has also been a source of inspiration to an entire generation. The power of his impact is difficult to overestimate, but it is reflected in the account of Tomasi when he tells of life in a hostel at the Methodist Missionary School at Davuilevu, not far from Suva. Tomasi's parents had brought him to Fiji a few years before while his father took a course in technology. When they returned to Rotuma they left him at Davuilevu to obtain further schooling.

"At the end of 1939 my parents returned to Rotuma, after my father completed his course. I was left to live with Rotuman boys. They had a separate hostel there, more or less organized by Wilson Inia. Then I realized the change. I suppose my life seemed empty with both my parents gone. But since the boys were all Rotumans, and Wilson was there to look after us, it didn't take me long to adjust— about a month or two. The new "family" was quite an interesting one. There were 21 of us. We had a head boy (prefect) and we had to plan to feed ourselves, apart from the money our parents used to send over. This money was kept by Inia. Organization was very good at that time. We were well looked after. He was very careful about how our money was used and he made sure that none of the boys ran out of money; once a boy would run out he would inform his parents and get them to send more. We looked upon him as someone who represented our parents, especially in a far away country.

"Life in that little dormitory was as I said before, very well organized. We used to work on the plantation very early in the morning —six to half-past seven, and then go to school after that. After school at three o'clock we would go back home and again go to the plantation from 4 to 5 o'clock. After that we could shower and have our dinner. In the evening we had study time, compulsory, from around 7 to 9 o'clock. That was the schedule on Mondays through Fridays. On Saturdays we washed our clothes and maybe went to the movies if we had funds. On Sunday we went to church and Sunday school. I liked going to church and Sunday schools then. I lived with these boys for two years like this.

"At the end of 1940, Wilson went to a conference in India, and we were left on our own. Things became very badly disorganized then, particularly on the financial side. There was no one to look after it; each boy had to look after his own. He returned in 1941, but unfortunately he got sick and was laid up in the hospital. When he recovered he went to Rotuma for a holiday, and because of the disorganization, most of the boys left, but I stayed, along with three others. Eighteen of the boys left and went to look for jobs."

Tomasi was more fortunate than some of the others because he was too young to take a job at the time. It was his plan to wait a year and then go to Suva to look for work, but in the meantime two of his uncles came to Fiji and exerted an influence on him.

"I was too young to go and look for a job then. I was thinking that I would wait until the following year—1942—and would go to Suva then and try to see what I could do about a job. But in 1942, fortunately, one of my uncles came to Davuilevu to take the theological course, and my parents suggested that I stayed with him and his wife. I noticed a great change in life from the hostel to this family. He was rather harsh in his ways, and I found life very hard living with him, because I had to work hard, doing planting and hard jobs to please him. I stayed with them for the whole of 1942, and in 1943 another uncle of mine, who was a schoolteacher, came over to Fiji to teach in a nearby school, so my parents suggested that I go and stay with him. Although I found it hard, life was more or less organized living with this uncle. I had to travel three miles to school every day. One thing I liked about staying with him was that I was back again into an organized life, more or less like when Wilson was at the hostel. Besides, there were two other chaps of my age living with them. Although he was a strict disciplinarian, there were three of us to share the punishment, so it was not so bad. In fact I was quite happy living with them."

THE "HAZARDS" OF BOARDING SCHOOL

City Life

The lure of the city is an additional hazard for the teen-age scholar. Compared to Rotuma, a place like Suva is exciting indeed. Not only does it provide the promise of new experiences, but it also offers the freedom from restraint that goes with urban anonymity. Tomasi relates the effect his acquaintance with town life had on his scholarship.

"Towards the end of 1943, when I was in Class 7B, my uncle suggested that I go and board at the school. At first I wasn't very keen on the idea, because I would be the only Rotuman there. The others were mostly Fijian. I would have been the first Rotuman to board there, but my uncle thought it would be better for my studies. I was doing quite well in school, but the traveling tired me out and I often went to bed early without doing any reading, so in 1944 I left to board in this school.

"In spite of the previous experience I had had living with the Rotuman boys, I found this very different, and much to my dislike. There were several reasons. First, I suppose, because of the complete Fijian society, and the hard manual labor we had to do. Most important of all was because by then I had an attraction for Suva, and I realized I had a few very close relations in Suva whom I could live with. I was about 15 years old at the time. Another thing that drew me to Suva was the fact that the Rotuman labor corps was doing war work there at the time, so there was a large Rotuman community there, most of whom were boys roughly about my age or a little older.

"During that year of boarding, I began to spend quite a bit of my time in Suva, especially during the weekends. I very much wanted to go to Suva then, but I stayed on in school for the remainder of the year. During one period though, for about two weeks, I went away from school and tried to get a job, but I couldn't find one. I even tried to enter the army, but was told I was too young, so I had to go back to school. In spite of all this leaving school and going to Suva, I came in second in my class in 1944, and the headmaster was holding me as sort of a prospect for the Fijian Qualifying Examination, which I would take after the following year. I wanted to leave school, but the headmaster talked me into staying for the next year—after Class 8—in order to sit for the exam. At that time the Fijian Qualifying Examination was very highly regarded in Fiji because it was the only exam they had. After passing that you could become a trainee for almost any job in Fiji—go to the medical school, get a government job, etc. So I stayed in boarding school for the next year.

"I didn't do much that year by way of school work. I spent most of my time in Suva and created so much of a problem—staying out of school for weeks at a time—that the headmaster finally decided not to let me sit for the examination. I was almost on the point of leaving school of my own accord, when towards the end of 1945, my uncle— the teacher—was transferred to my school. He had heard of all the reports and threatened to send me back to Rotuma if I was to leave school. I dreaded that, and decided to stay in school for another year. I had to stay back in Class 8 for another year. I concentrated on my work and was selected to sit the Qualifying Examination. I passed the exam at the end of 1946. After I passed the exam I went right to Suva, before school closed down, and got a job. I didn't know I had passed and was awaiting the result. I got a job sorting mail in the post office. I worked there for two weeks and quit because I didn't like it, so I got a job as an office boy in a legal firm. I didn't like that job much, either. I would have stayed there, but three weeks after I had joined that firm I learned that I had passed the exam, and I decided to go into the Nasinu Training College and become a teacher."

Visits to Rotuma

Perhaps even more hazardous than the lure of the city is a return visit to Rotuma after some time away. The key problem for the youth who returns for a holiday is coping with the seductiveness of family and friends. A returnee is treated with, if anything, an increased magnitude of indulgence over his childhood experience, and after having gone through a period of boarding school austerity, the youth finds this indulgence gratifying indeed. He becomes a center of attention; his parents are proud of his successes and his friends admire his knowledge and wealth of new experience. The situation is often made more acute by the fact that most students return during the Christmas holidays, which is mane'a (play) season on the island, a time of much fun, little work, and considerable freedom for the young unmarrieds. Many students have their first love affairs during such a return visit. It is no wonder that some do not go back to school, and others do so only reluctantly. Jimione's experience is typical.

Jimione. "After the fourth year I sat for the Fijian Qualifying Examinations after coming in top of my class. I got through and was selected to go to medical school, but at the time I didn't know what I wanted to do, so I went back to secondary school at Davuilevu. Then

I went into Form III. At the end of that year I came back to Rotuma for a holiday at Christmas. That was my first taste of adult life. My friends had all finished school and some of them were already married. I was 18 years old at the time. I learned to smoke and drink at that time. My mom was still alive then and she still treated me like a pet.

"When I came back I was shy at first, but soon I got my feet, and realized that I wasn't so bad after all. I had been away and had learned something, and the girls looked up to me, and I was able to take advantage of them quite easily. My emotions were very intense. I really went for it. It was new and I certainly enjoyed it. To break it off was very painful.

"At one of the beach games I met a girl who I really thought I liked. I told my mother that I didn't want to go back to school the next year. She said it was up to me. Just before the boat came, my elder brother, who was the money earner in the family—cutting copra —sent over my school fees and paid for my passage on the boat. It was he who supported me through school when my father was getting too old to work. He learned what had happened but he flatly refused to accept it. He said that this would be one time that he would have his way after all he had done—that I had to go back to school, so I went back. I went, but I didn't intend to go to school. I planned to collect the money my brother had sent and go to Suva to work. My very close friend was with me and we decided to do this together. We were a month late to school. We went to the headmaster and asked for the money our respective brothers had sent, telling him our intentions, and also asked him for testimonials. I don't mean to boast, but we were the two best brains in the school. He looked at us and flatly refused. He said he would send the money back to our brothers and wouldn't give us a testimonial—for one thing it was past the time for us to apply for government jobs. So that ended our job hunting so we went back to school. That was a tough year for us, because we had had a taste of outside life. We were real smokers by then, and we weren't permitted to smoke in school, so we had to smoke in secret. As a matter of fact we were caught once, and were given four hours of hard labor."

Vamarasi. For Vamarasi, a young woman whose ambition it was to become a secretary, a holiday visit to Rotuma was more costly.

"I spent four years in the secondary school. I tried very hard and did well, especially in typing and shorthand. I consistently got over 90% in both those subjects. In the second year I never failed an examination and ended up first in the class. The next two years I studied so that I could sit for the Junior Cambridge Examination, but the Christmas before I was to sit for the exam my father asked me to come home to Rotuma to spend the holiday season at home. He hadn't seen me for four years and he wanted me to spend some time at home before going back to school. Not only that, but he had heard of how well I was doing in school, and was proud of me.

"I thought it would be a good idea to take a holiday because I had been studying very hard and felt it would be good to have a rest before beginning to study again. So I left the secondary school and returned to Rotuma in December of 1953. But I still liked school and intended to return after the holiday.

"When I got home my parents were very glad to see me, and were very kind to me. The other people in Juju treated me well, too. I really spent a good Christmas holiday that year and had plenty of fun. Nearly every night I went out with the boys and girls. It was the first Christmas holiday I had ever spent in which I had such good fun. My mother and father let me go with the boys and girls every night. They didn't mind because they trusted me. They said I had learned everything in school and should know how to protect myself from the sins of the world.

"Unluckily, I didn't know how the Rotuman boys trick the girls, because I had been at school and didn't have any boyfriends. So I didn't know the ways of the Rotuman boys. One night during that Christmas holiday I met a boy and he talked to me. He told me that he loved me from the first time he saw me. I believed him because from the first time we had met he always acted good to me and talked sweet. On that night he told me all about his feeling for me. I thought that he was telling the truth—that he really wanted to keep me—so I trusted him, but when he knew I was going to have a baby he left me.

"When my parents and close relatives knew that I was going to have a baby they got very angry with me. At that time I didn't know what to do and cried myself to sleep nearly every night. I said that it was my father's fault, because he was the one who wanted me to come to Rotuma in the first place. My father got really angry with me and sent me to my mother's brother's house in Maftoa. I stayed in Maftoa and got married in 1955. This time I knew how to make a man keep me for his wife. We have two children now. I don't really like married life, but I have no choice because I've already spoiled my life."

FURTHER EDUCATION IN NEW ZEALAND

A few students do sufficiently well to obtain scholarships to New Zealand, Australia, and, more recently, the United States. Once again they are exposed to "culture shock." After coming from a colonial environment with all its restrictions and limitations, the opportunities for divergent behavior afforded by metropolitan areas in these countries may be difficult to cope with. There are a wide variety of new models available and much depends upon with whom students accidentally become acquainted during their first few weeks in the new country. If they get to know supportive individuals who are serious students, they generally settle down to the student's role, but if their initial acquaintances are hedonistic, they are easily drawn into a diffuse social life at the expense of academics. In general most of the Rotumans who have spent some time in one of the more urbanized countries find it to their liking.

Tomasi

"I left for New Zealand in 1956. It took me almost six months to adapt myself—particularly to the social life there. The college I went to was co-educational and residential. Social life there was very high —very advanced in comparison to what I had experienced in Rotuma. Over here there are a lot of restrictions between boys and girls, but there there was almost complete freedom. I liked it from the beginning, but several things kept me out of the scene. One was that I was conscious all the time that I had been sent by the Rotuman people and I felt obliged to accomplish something and bring it back to them. My main aim was to succeed in my studies. The other thing that kept me out of the social life for the first six months was the attitudes of the Europeans in Fiji and Rotuma for the natives. I felt inferior and was very reluctant to take an active part in the social life. But this inferior feeling gradually wore off and I began to make friends and got to know most of the students. I found that there was in fact very little feeling of color superiority among the European students and the faculty. After the first six months I was very well adapted—too well adapted in fact. I think that one of the things that made me popular there was the part I played in college sports. They're not quite like the Americans, but they're quite keen in sports. I played rugby as one of the first fifteen (first team varsity) and participated in track and field—I threw the shotput, javelin, and discus; I also played soccer on the first eleven, and finally became a representative player for South Auckland County—the provincial team. I began to take a very lively part in most of the social functions there. I went to nearly all the social dances, and joined several college groups. At first I was very reluctant to partake in dating. But it was more or less encouraged by the friendly response of the girls. To be honest, although I was dating I was still conscious of the fact that I was different. When I started dating I was always sure that a boyfriend of mine and his date were along. Soon I got used to dating on my own and my self-consciousness died out.

In fact I got really used to dating, and perhaps I overdid it. I felt that it was an honor and a privilege to go around with European girls, since it was something that was not practiced here in Fiji. But even then I felt that it was just a temporary sort of thing. I was never convinced that any of these girls would ever be willing to lead an island life, so I felt that there was no sense proceeding with a romantic affair where one finds it hard to turn back. For me it was just like playing a game. There were times when girls got infatuated, and mistook it for love. Maybe it's because they were young—only around 19 or 20. I made sure to tell them the facts about island life and made it clear to them that it was hopeless—that they could never be happy in an island life. I considered staying in New Zealand to get an advanced teacher's certificate, but I never considered staying there permanently.

"In school, those subjects concerned with education I found to my liking from the beginning and I did well in them. I also took courses in art, science, and English during the first year. The only thing I really found tough was English. I finished the two-year program and received the certificate."

Samuela

Samuela also found his experience in New Zealand to his liking.

"I went to New Zealand early in 1954. At first I found it a bit strange. The first thing I noticed was the amount of cars. After being there for a week I started Ardmore Teacher's College about 18 miles from Auckland. I found it easy to adjust to the life there, it was very good. I didn't feel strange at all being with Europeans. There were many Maoris, Cook Islanders, Samoans there. Besides I had many European friends in Suva and had lived on and off with a New Zealand couple—he was a teacher. I spent three holidays with them. The only thing that really seemed strange to me was the size of the place.

"I didn't find the school work itself very hard. Most of it was just educational courses. I had some difficulty with physical education theory, because some of the terms were new, and I hadn't any experience with some of the activities that were included.

"I wasn't used to the social activities at the start. I wasn't used to the idea of courting. At first I was rather embarrassed to ask a girl to go the pictures, but I was lucky because on the boat to New Zealand I met two part-Maori women who had a niece in the college, and they wrote me a letter of introduction to her. I got to know her and she introduced me to a lot of other girls. There were about 800 girls and about 200 boys, so the girls would try to get the boys to date them. So about four or five months after I started I began to date. I dated throughout the two years, but I never had any intention of having any serious affairs. For one thing it was against regulations for me to get married in New Zealand, and secondly I didn't want to get a wife I couldn't support. Someone who was used to living in New Zealand would be apt to demand more than I could give her in life here.

"I stayed in New Zealand until the middle of 1956. I got out of college at the end of 1955, but spent the last six months roaming around New Zealand—taking different jobs. My first job was on a sheep farm. I worked for a building contractor, on a wharf, in the freezing works, as a delivery boy. I enjoyed that period very much. I saw a lot of people and a lot of places. I spent most of my other holidays visiting with people who had invited me to their homes. One time I hitchhiked around with my friend about 390 miles."

THE EDUCATED ELITE

The Emerging Leadership

Many of the individuals who obtain an advanced education in Fiji or abroad never return to Rotuma. The island has been producing highly trained persons at a rate well beyond its capacity to absorb them; it has, in effect, been exporting brains to Fiji. Those who do return to fill the available positions form the nucleus of a new elite. Their special skills, including a command of English, their comparatively high salaries, and their knowledge of European ways, gained from extended residence in urban areas, all tend to bestow upon them high prestige.

This nucleus has a responsibility to guide the Rotuman people into the mainstream of the modern world. Medical personnel have the responsibility to educate the people in such subjects as sanitation, personal hygiene, diet, care of children, and the proper treatment of patients. The Assistant Medical Officer holds a weekly pre-natal clinic at the dispensary on the Government Station, in which he not only examines expectant mothers, but advises them about proper care as well. The nurses hold child welfare clinics in each district and meet with mothers to answer their questions and to explain proper child care. Medical and sanitation information is also disseminated through pamphlets published in Suva in the Rotuman language.

The managers of business firms are storehouses of information on business affairs. It is mainly from them that news of business trends in Fiji reaches interested parties, and they act as informal advisors to those who seek advice.

The ministers and priests also contribute to change by introducing church activities that are popular in Western society. The Methodist Church has youth clubs that meet regularly. The members have learned to play such games as ping-pong, checkers, and various card games; in one case they have been taught to sing American folk spirituals by an educated catechist. The Catholic Churches hold bazaars, bingo games, and European dances in order to raise money and entertain the people.

But it is the teachers, perhaps more than any of the others, who are concerned with the transmission of "modern" ideas. In response to questioning about goals and reasons for entering the teaching profession, a second grade teacher responded:

My aims are: (a) To make children realize that they are lucky to have what their parents missed, and it is up to them to try to do better, while they have the chance to do so. (b) To teach them to be able to cope with everyday life's problems, e.g., buying things from the shops, telling the time, etc. (c) Through stories of important or good people, to encourage them to want to do something useful in their life. (d) To prepare them for the upper class work.

As a teacher I would like all my children to be good and useful people, here in Rotuma or wherever they go. The reasons why I chose teaching are: (a) I love children, (b) I want to be useful to my people and country, by helping children to become good citizens in their communities.

A seventh grade teacher answered the questions in the following methodical way:

I would like the children to achieve from my teaching all the requirements for the welfare and happiness of the Rotumans, e.g.: (a) The enjoyment of good health. That is why I teach hygiene and mother craft. (b) Ability and opportunity to earn a living. Gardening, native craft, agriculture, sewing, cooking, woodwork, etc., help the children to earn a living. (c) Opportunity to enjoy satisfactory social relations. I teach them English so that they can talk to non-Rotumans in that language. Co-education helps both boys and girls to have a better attitude towards one another; "houses" (team divisions) in sports and well-supervised concerts are good. History and geography help the children to adapt themselves to changing conditions. (d) Opportunity to exercise political rights. History, civics, debates, groups may fit the children for democracy. (e) Freedom to enjoy leisure. Reading, handwork, sewing, gardening, fishing, etc., lead to good leisure occupations.

Conflict between Old and New

But the emergent leaders are not unequivocal about the effects of European influence; they express a good deal of ambivalence about the changes that have taken place in Rotuma. The assistant manager of one of the firms, for example, had this to say:

European influence has done a lot of good and a lot of bad. To an educated person you can see some progress—education, for example. Some of the old people probably resent it. They feel that when a child gets educated he tries to throw his weight around and ignore old customs. The standard of living is better. One bad part of it is, say the films. Youngsters are exposed to gangster films. They come to think that a man should be respected only because of his strength. They overlook the intellectual part. They think to act like a gentleman is to be a sissy.

If it were up to me I'd try to give them as much as I know is good. Whether they take it or not is up to them. That's one reason I've started this sports club. To teach the boys sportsmanship. I believe this—you can do what you like to a country—build houses and all—but you can't change it without changing the people.

A minister offered this evaluation:

There are some good things and some bad things. Conditions of living are much better. We're learning from the Europeans a better way of living. Also education in the church. The bad things—they brought over here strong drinks.

If it were up to me I would teach the Rotumans to live happily and to use their belongings properly instead of spending their money on things that are useless. They would spend their money on things like getting a good education for their children and building decent homes, instead of wasting it on things like feasting, etc. For example, they run short of water, but they don't know enough to spend money on building proper tanks.

A teacher said:

I think to a certain extent the European influence has done Rotuma a lot of good socially, as far as sports is concerned, for example. One thing that has been spoiled is the relationship between relatives. Nowadays people think mainly in terms of wealth. If a man is rich he will have plenty of friends and relatives.

If it were up to me, I would try to improve education and sanitation—especially getting rid of flies and mosquitoes. I'd put better roads through the bush. Another thing I'd like to do is to introduce more money crops to the Rotumans. Coffee and cocoa would grow quite well here. It's only a financial problem to get started. Also I would like to improve the banana trade, and I would like to improve the water supply.

The majority of these educated leaders have been put under strain as the result of the clash of cultures. Perhaps the main area of conflict is that of social prerogatives. As part of their education in the urban milieu, they have become used to such activities as beer parties, mixed socials, and casual dating—activities that they could freely enjoy in the cities and towns. But in Rotuma these activities are severely frowned upon by the majority of the people. It is particularly difficult for an unmarried person to enjoy a satisfactory social life because relations between boys and girls are highly restricted. For those who are caught in such a position, the conflict between progressiveness and conservatism is immediate and real. The forces of conservatism in this area are steadfast, however, and show few signs of changing. The frustration experienced by some of the young leaders in this situation is reflected in the statement of a young teacher in his life history:

The older generations are holding fast to customs and culture—very reluctant to depart from them. And the younger generation's lives are sped up by modern influences. They are eager to disregard the old and adopt the new. In my opinion there is a conflict between the two. Then comes the question, who is going to win? As an answer to that I feel that the younger generation is always aware of the older customs, and will never really oppose the beliefs and attitudes of the older generation. The people who belong to the younger generation gradually give way to the older folks. The only way a person can really stay progressive is to leave Rotuma. That is something that shouldn't happen. These old people should give in to the younger ones in some ways. An example is the religious attitudes of the old folks. They cling to this notion that you shouldn't play sports on Sunday, or that you shouldn't go to dances. They tend to look down on us if we do these things. If they asked us, we would have something to say, and what we have to say would have been largely influenced by modern society.

In response to a question regarding his role as a teacher, he said:

To begin with I'm quite happy as a teacher, but I feel that to become a teacher in Rotuma places additional burdens on a person. In Rotuma people expect too much from a teacher with regard to his personal life. People expect you to be a moral leader as well, and if you don't work up to their expectations, they have a disregard for you. At the moment I don't take too much notice of what they say, on the assumption that I have a private life to lead. But I think the longer I stay in Rotuma, the more I'll be influenced by Rotuman attitudes toward life, and will tend to fall back towards Rotuman ways.

Another conflict area is that of personal obligation in the social sphere. By the rules of Rotuman ethics the rich should give to the poor and the strong should help the weak. For a man who is well off to deprive his own relatives in times of need is almost unthinkable, and since the island is so small and kinship reckoned bilaterally, one is apt to be related to almost everyone. It is a Rotuman maxim that if you are poor, you will have few relatives, but if you are rich you will have plenty, and people certainly seem to go through considerably more pains to trace their relationship to the wealthy. For an individual who has gone through a long period of training so that he could enhance his own and his immediate family's standard of living, being in Rotuma creates a bind. If he tries to save his money, he will be despised and ridiculed; if he submits to the pressures, he will save nothing and may even go into debt. One person interviewed who was caught in these circumstances asserted that if he were to stay in Rotuma, he would be unable to afford to educate his own children, so heavy was the drain on his finances.

The majority of Rotumans who return to their home island nevertheless accept the community's social conservatism, and they direct their efforts toward the common goal of raising the standard of living. In many instances it is they rather than the chiefs who are the most staunch supporters of Rotuman custom. It is not unusual at a meeting to hear a chief speak out against maintaining a custom he regards as inexpedient, whereas it is given ardent support by teachers or government officers. In one instance, when the traditional custom of offering ceremonial food to district chiefs was raised, it was attacked by an elderly chief who suggested that the ceremony be eliminated and a cash payment be substituted in its stead. His stand was strongly opposed by a university-educated teacher who pointed out that the chiefs would lose the respect people still paid to them if such ceremonies were eliminated. Largely on the strength of his argument, the chief's motion was defeated. Also, whereas the chiefs tend to be somewhat haphazard about their dress, often wearing trousers instead of the traditional *lavalava*, the two most prominent educated leaders on the island, the District Officer and headmaster of the main school, both wear well-tailored *lavalava* on all public occasions. The former is a recognized expert on Rotuman custom and has been known to get quite upset when custom is ignored, or when ceremonies are improperly carried out.

To be sure, not all educated leaders hold such attitudes nor exert conservative pressures, but enough do to ensure that the community as a whole maintains a markedly conservative social climate. Those who dissent do so in the face of strong social pressure, and are likely to leave the island after a minimal stay.

To uneducated persons, being Rotuman is simply a fact of life. Sometimes it is regarded as a fact that can hinder social and economic advancement in the modern world. Rotumans are pragmatic people, little concerned with ideological reflections on the significance of group identity. The majority are concerned that Rotumans do not get a bad name in Fiji and elsewhere, but this follows from the fact that they are identified by others as being a group; it is not a result of their own efforts to sustain group identity. In short, for the uneducated Rotuman, pragmatic expediency rather than a set of abstract principles is of primary consideration. If following custom is expedient, then fine, let it be followed; if it is not, dispense with it. There is little reverence of custom for its own sake among the uneducated, whether or not they hold a chiefly title.

The educated leaders, on the other hand, have more to gain from the perpetuation of Rotuman culture than do the chiefs. Their high status depends to a considerable extent on the existence of a distinctly Rotuman community. They are leaders because they are educated Rotumans among uneducated Rotumans. If they were among non-Rotumans, their pervasive leadership would be much less readily accepted. It is the fact that they are "insiders" that matters most to their followers.

It should not be presumed, however, that the educated leaders' conservatism is motivated simply by its expediency for supporting their status. A genuine idealism seems to be involved and appears to be of greater consequence. Each of these persons has passed through a process of European schooling and their success attests to a mastery of at least a portion of the content of Western culture. At one level they have been taught the "mechanics" of European culture, usually with a good deal of ethnocentrism when the teachers were Europeans. But covertly a secondary learning process takes place that ultimately can be of far greater significance—learning to evaluate phenomena in terms of abstract concepts and relationships, as these are expressed in systematic models of law and social organization (e.g., the government of Great Britain). This kind of cognitive activity, although it has correlates in traditional Rotuman society, was much less significant in a tradition distinguished by a present-oriented concreteness. Some Rotumans who go through this educational process turn away from their childhood culture and direct their efforts toward successful participation in the modern Europeanized world. Others, however, intensify their self-identification as Rotumans and derive from their educational experience an idealism that they direct at Rotuman society. Very often they are struck by the inconsistencies between ideology and behavior in Western society, and they see in their own Rotuman culture a far greater consistency, not only between Rotuman values and Rotuman behavior, but between Western (particularly Christian) ideology and Rotuman behavior. Rotuma then becomes a model community for them, and they add an ideological justification for the culture that was not inherent in the traditional society.

The significance of this alteration can be better understood in historical perspective. When only one way of life was known, there was no need to idealize culture and to justify it with an abstract ideology. Most things were done in a prescribed manner, not because they were abstractly regarded as being "right," but because it was the way of the land. The myths used to justify custom implied that this is why, in the historical sense, things are done as they are, not that this is the reason that they are the right things to do. The distinction is perhaps subtle, but is important. Formal sanctions were not applied to breaches of abstract "moral" principles, but to behavior that infringed on the rights of others. A person could use a wide variety of possible precepts to justify what he had already done on the basis of personal expediency, but there was no explicit overriding model or abstractly conceived system of law or ethics.

European contact exposed Rotumans to a completely different culture, one that held many contrasts to the "Rotuman way." There followed an expansion of the socio-cultural milieu; the number of alternative behavior patterns multiplied and a great many new precepts were found to justify them. Tendencies toward Westernization were fostered by a recognition of European superiority in the technological sphere, and those who could master technical skills gained prestige rapidly. Along with technological competence and earning power often went initiation into European social ways, and for most Rotumans the ability to participate in Western social functions became a source of pride. This is reflected in the romantically colored tales and songs composed by Rotuman sailors during the last century, describing their experiences. It is true that some berated this Europeanization and criticized European ways, but they did so in "sour grapes" fashion. It was asserted that European ways may be all right for Europeans, but for Rotumans it was better to stick to known ways. During this stage virtually all Rotumans attributed to Western culture an outright superiority and they tended to look upon their own as backward.

A large proportion of the Rotuman people, including the majority of the chiefs, still manifest such attitudes. Their behavioral conservatism, as distinct from ideological conservatism, is rooted in a felt inability to participate successfully in European society, rather than in a conviction that Rotuman culture is valuable for its own sake. They follow the Rotuman way because it is the way they know best and because they feel inadequate in the face of modern society. Their sensitivity to ridicule is a reinforcing factor, for if they were to try to act in a European fashion and fail, ridicule would surely follow.

The conservatism of the recently emergent non-traditional leaders is a different kind of phenomenon. They have become thoroughly acquainted with Western society and have demonstrated their ability to participate in it successfully. They are not awed by it and can compare European and Rotuman culture more objectively. The roots of their conservatism lie in the ideological sphere; they recognize the value of Rotuman custom for its own sake, from a moral-ethical point of view. They can also recognize its significance as a source of common identity and make efforts to endow custom with dignity. To paraphrase the statements of one such leader:

I want to be able to help the Rotumans to make a good adjustment to the modern world. To do this they will have to learn many European ways, especially in the field of economics. They need Western education. But we should not accept everything from Western society without regard to whether it is good or bad. Many Western customs are bad, and some of our Rotuman ways are good. I think we should take from Western society those things which can benefit us, and we should keep what is good in our own, and should never stop being Rotumans.

The sentiments expressed by Viliama after having been ordained a priest and returned to Rotuma are also indicative:

"I felt great about being sent to Rotuma. I have no desire to be posted any place else but here. When I came back they had a big *katoaga* [public celebration] for me. I felt especially grateful to the Wesleyans—to go to all that trouble. I don't think the Catholic people would do that for a Wesleyan minister who was returning.

"I like being in Rotuma, but now I feel somewhat deficient. If I had another chance to study in New Zealand I think I would do better. There are so many things I don't know—music, for instance. I'm very interested in music. The most important thing for a priest is to be able to deal with the people. I still think I have a lot to learn about that. I think most of the time I'm too easy. But it's better to have charity for the people. I really should keep a certain distance, but I find it difficult to do it. Maybe it's harder for a young fellow. The old people don't like the priest to be easy going—they like him to be a priest. It's because they're used to the French fathers I think. The only trouble is if you're too strict the people will be scared of you and stay away from you. However I think the Rotuman children respect you even if you are familiar with them, unlike the Fijian children.

"As a priest you can't be perfectly happy, but when you come back from talking to people as a priest, you feel good because you've done something worthwhile. One shouldn't be surprised if he isn't perfectly happy, because God doesn't intend you to be perfectly happy in this life.

"In Rotuma we have two denominations, and in order to be successful you should treat them both equally. If the Wesleyans see that the priest is kind to them they may feel more sympathetic to the Catholic Church.

"I also think that the priest should be respectful to the chiefs. I think the French fathers were wrong in the way they treated the chiefs. After all, the people look up to the chiefs and if you want to get their cooperation it's better if the chiefs are favorably disposed towards you. Otherwise they just try to stay away.

"I think a man goes on learning until he dies. I've done some things seriously wrong—about Rotuman custom—since I've returned to Rotuma. Like one time when I was riding on my bicycle past a *mamasa* [celebration upon returning to Rotuma from abroad] given for Tanu in Pepjei. I went right past without slowing down. I felt very bad about that. It's respectful to at least slow down, if not get off your bicycle and walk until you are past. That shows that you feel something about what's happening; not like it doesn't mean anything to you. The worst thing was they stopped me near the end of the road and asked me to join them and eat. I really felt ashamed. In New Zealand they might say that is silly, but in Rotuma it's the accepted thing and I think it's proper to follow the custom. I wouldn't do anything like that again. I think that some of the Rotumans who get educated ignore the proper customs of etiquette and I think the old Rotuman customs should be kept."

Education, Employment, and Mobility

The degree to which Rotuman culture survives over the long run will probably depend on the extent to which it interferes with the attainment of a satisfactory standard of material and social well-being. We might therefore ask at this junction, just how much does their traditional world view and the values associated with it interfere with this goal? This is not an easy question to answer, either for the Rotumans or for Western observers, but we can begin by attempting to assesss the success of European education in Rotuma to date. Let us start with some statistics. Using information which I collected from a household census involving 1,280 adults, I found that 471 (36.8%) reported having either no education or only basic education; 712 (55.6%) reported having completed between five and eight years of schooling; 54 (4.1%) reported having completed between nine and twelve years of schooling; and 44 (3.4%) reported having received professional or semi-professional training. If these statistics are broken down by age categories, they reveal that a significantly higher proportion of Rotumans are now receiving at least an intermediate education than previously (see Table II). If one uses as a basis for comparison the level of education attained in the United States, these figures are not very impressive; indeed the majority of the population at all age levels would be considered "dropouts." This would be an unfair basis for comparison, however. By world standards, and particularly in the perspective of developing countries, Rotumans are progressing very well. Their relative success becomes clear when the adaptations of Rotumans and Fijians to the urban market economy of Fiji are compared.

Although precise employment statistics by ethnic group for Fiji are unavailable, what information there is suggests that Rotumans have fared much better than Fijians both in obtaining employment and in upward mobility. The situation at the Vatukoula gold mines on Viti Levu provides an example. As compared to most other industries in Fiji, employment at the gold mines is considered desirable. Wages are high and housing is available to the workers at a nominal rate. In addition, supplementary income can be earned in the form of incentive bonuses and overtime wages. There are invariably a number of applicants for each vacancy. Despite the fact that in the Colony of Fiji the ratio of male Fijians to male Rotumans of working age is about 35 to 1, the ratio of Fijians to Rotumans employed at the gold mines is less than 4 to 1. This apparent favoritism reflects expressed satisfaction on the part of the mine managers with Rotuman workers. In interviews the managers were unrestrained in their praise of the responsibility displayed by Rotumans and the quickness with which they learned to carry out tasks. In virtually every instance when comparisons were made with Fijians, Rotumans were favored. One mine official summed up his feelings with the statement, "I just wish there were more of them to employ." Such attitudes are by no means unique to the mine management. Employers all over Fiji are nearly unanimous in their praise of Rotumans. As a result Rotumans have little difficulty in obtaining employment despite job shortages.

TABLE II.   Rotuman Educational Attainment, By Age

Education	Age 20–29		Age 30–49		Age 50 and above		Total	
Basic, or none	45	9.7%	258	44.0%	168	73.4%	471	36.8%
5–8 years	366	78.9%	293	49.9%	53	23.1%	712	55.6%
9–12 years	35	7.5%	15	2.6%	3	1.3%	53	4.1%
Advanced, or special	18	3.9%	21	3.6%	5	2.2%	44	3.4%
Total	464	100.0%	587	100.0%	229	100.0%	1280	99.9% *

* Due to rounding of figures.

The ability to obtain employment and please employers is only one part of the competition. At the mines, jobs are ranked in a hierarchy and mobility up to the level of sub-foreman is possible on a merit basis. Here too the Rotumans enjoy an advantage: 6.3% have risen to supervisory positions, whereas only 3.2% of the Fijians are supervisors, in spite of a shorter history of Rotuman employment. In addition, although exact figures are lacking, Rotumans are more mobile at the sub-supervisory level and make up the majority of leading land miners (i.e., those in charge of work teams).

An even more dramatic indicator of occupational mobility can be seen in the relatively high proportion of Rotumans who have achieved professional status. The 1956 census of Fiji showed that the proportion of the male population in professional and allied roles was 84 per 1,000 for Rotumans compared to 48 per 1,000 for Fijians in the 30 to 44 age category, and 102 to 36 per 1,000 for the 45 to 59 age category.

Still another indication of Rotuman success is their ability to accumulate capital resources. The Rotuma Co-operative Association, with a membership in 1961 of 485, listed their subscribed capital at £23,754, an average subscription of £49 per capita. The combined Fijian societies for the same year had a membership of 1,293 and listed a capital of £5,797, an average per capita subscription of £4.5. Furthermore, the Rotuman Development Fund, which is supplied by a self-imposed tax on copra earning, has accumulated well over £150,000. The Rotumans have invested the money and seem so enamored with the idea of making a profit that the Administration is having a difficult time getting them to use the capital for its avowed purpose of development. Finally, whereas the Fijians are notorious for their inability to succeed in private business ventures, the few Rotumans who have tried their hand at private enterprise have been moderately successful.

CULTURE AND ACHIEVEMENT: SOME OBSERVATIONS

It would appear, then, that the Rotumans have been making a steady advance toward successfully coping with the modern world, particularly when contrasted with the Fijians. Still, this does not answer the question concerning the degree to which Rotuman values interfere with a positive adaptation. After all, it is quite possible that factors other than cultural ones have given the Rotumans an advantage over their Fijian competitors. For example, some people might be tempted to seek an explanation in racial terms. Although both populations manifest a range of physical types, the Rotuman mode more closely approximates the Polynesian type, whereas the Fijians are generally classified as Melanesians. Recognition of this difference constitutes the primary European "folk" explanation of Rotuman superiority. Whether race has anything to do with biologically inherent capabilities, local definitions of race may therefore have provided Rotumans with a social advantage. Is it not possible that the darker-skinned Fijians are sufficiently discriminated against to block their social mobility, whereas their Polynesian neighbors are favored because they appear more Caucasian? This possibility alone cannot account for the facts presented here. Racial discrimination does not seem to account for the superiority that Rotumans have exhibited in accumulating capital resources, for example. Furthermore, if there is discrimination against the Fijians, it is not extreme; it is certainly not institutionalized in the economic sphere. The Europeans regard the country as belonging to the Fijians and their major prejudices are directed toward the East Indian segment of the population. The Rotumans enjoy no legal advantages; until recently, in fact, they were not even represented in the Fiji Legislature. As for the biological capabilities associated with race, it can only be asserted that the explanatory power of race has not yet been adequately tested, although the bulk of accumulated evidence appears not to lend this factor much support.

Others might try to look to historical factors for an explanation; but Rotuma has had, if anything, a less favorable history for promoting individual and group achievement than the rest of Fiji. Although most of Fiji has experienced long and intensive contact with Europeans, Rotuma has remained relatively isolated. All the major industries and sources of large-scale employment are in Fiji; there is none in Rotuma. Except for a handful of missionaries, a few traders, and government officials, there have been virtually no resident Europeans in Rotuma to serve as appropriate models. From the standpoint of opportunity, then, Rotumans have certainly not been favored.

Another possibility is that Rotumans have enjoyed educational advantages. In a study carried out by Mamao Managreve, comparing a sample of Rotuman children in Rotuma with a matched group in Fiji, it was found that the Rotuman children being educated in Fiji consistently scored higher on achievement tests than those being educated in Rotuma. Managreve, himself a Rotuman, interprets the data as indicating the inferiority of Rotuman schools. His analysis of the deficiencies in Rotuman schools and recommendations for their alleviation are of some interest and have been included in Appendix C.

If neither race nor opportunity nor superior schooling is responsible for the Rotuman success in comparison with that of Fijians, where might we look for an explanation? One possibility is that Rotuma's isolation has had a beneficial effect. If colonialism has negative effects upon the ability of an indigenous population to achieve, as numerous scholars assert, then the advantages of isolation may have outweighed the lack of opportunity. Isolation slowed the pace of change on Rotuma to the point that innovations have been absorbed without creating undue stress. The result has been a strong sense of conservatism on the one hand and a sense of integrity and control on the other. What may be important is that Rotumans have not been overwhelmed by European culture; they do not seem to feel that being Rotuman is an insurmountable barrier to success within the Western urban market complex, an attitude that contrasts with those expressed by the Fijians.

A more compelling argument, however, is that Rotuman culture does more to foster achievement and less to hinder it than Fijian culture. In most parts of Fiji social relationships are highly ritualized and prescribed. Status differences are marked and breaches of etiquette are strongly sanctioned. Writing about the Southern Lau portion of the Fiji group, Laura Thompson states:

> Social life in Lau conforms to strict rules of etiquette based on rank. The same pattern of behavior, with variations in degree of elaboration according to rank, is used on the whole social scale. Each individual observes the main rules of the polite . . . etiquette towards persons, whether related or not, of higher rank or toward persons who stand in the avoidance relationship. The rules are learned by children before the age of seven or eight, and the infringement of them causes a loss of social prestige.[1]

The severity of sanctions is indicated by Thompson's statement that in the past "infringement of chiefly etiquette was punished by clubbing or death, depending upon the rank of the chief and upon the offense."

In Rotuma rank is less important and the rules governing social relations are less ritualized. Restraint is appropriate in the presence of a chief and with certain relatives such as in-laws, but relationships are not *prescribed* in the same way as in Fiji. Correspondingly, breaches of etiquette are only weakly sanctioned; they are generally regarded as interpersonal affronts rather than affronts against society. In other words, in Fiji social relations are sanctioned by tradition whereas in Rotuma they are sanctioned by public opinion; the Fijians are "tradition-directed," the Rotumans are "other-directed." In general the ethos of Rotuman society is secular and egalitarian; in Fiji it is sacred and hierarchical.

A corollary of the hierarchical emphasis in Fiji is that obedience to authority is stressed in the child-rearing process. Marshall Sahlins describes parent-child relations on Moala, a Fijian island approximately ninety-five miles southeast of Suva:

> Obedience and respect are demanded of the child by the father. After infancy the child is constantly taking orders, doing tasks relegated by his

parents, from whose command there is no recourse save fleeing from the house.

Punishment by the father is the outstanding disciplinary mechanism in the family. The father's anger is proverbial; younger children he whips, older children he lectures harshly . . . The child should accept either punishment stoically.

The mother is more indulgent toward the child than is the father. Particularly for boys and men, the relationship with the mother is freer than with the father. After infancy intense social relationships with sons and mothers are confined primarily to mealtimes where the mother appears as giver and server, and it is this image that becomes characteristic.[2]

From this description it seems that in Moala, the family is father-dominated. There is little overt affection expressed by parents for children, especially after the period of infancy, and dependence rather than independence is encouraged. This is in marked contrast to Rotuma, where parents and parent surrogates of both sexes are extraordinarily warm and indulgent, not only during infancy but throughout childhood. Fathers are not domineering. Discipline is usually carried out by the mother, and independence is encouraged in children, particularly with regard to task performance.

A good deal of evidence has accumulated in the psychological and sociological literature indicating that socialization of the Fijian type, i.e., socialization characterized by strong demands for obedience to authority and a predominance of punishment over reward, produces individuals who are cognitively rigid and more concerned with avoiding failure than achieving success. On the other hand, the Rotuman style of socialization is more closely associated with cognitive plasticity and a concern for eliciting approval by displaying situationally appropriate behavior. This would appear to give the Rotumans a considerable advantage in learning the social and technical skills that are prerequisites to success within the culturally alien Western market economy.

We have not answered the question of how much cultural integrity the Rotumans are going to have to sacrifice as a price for achieving economic success. It is clear that certain customs, such as those associated with traditional medical practices, will have to be altered or replaced if progress is to be made, and other aspects of the formal culture will inevitably disappear as a new technology replaces the old. Many customs will atrophy and dissappear as their functions cease to have relevance. But there is much more to being a Rotuman than simple adherence to custom. Being a Rotuman involves a distinctive expressive style and set of interpersonal strategies. It implies a commitment to the underlying premise of Rotuman culture, that social life should be harmonious and free of conflict. It implies a commitment to interpersonal relations rather than to the accumulation of goods, a concern for the consequences of behavior rather than intentions and motives, and a situational ethic as opposed to an inner-directed adherence to abstract moral principles. This is the area in which Rotuman cultural identity is most deeply imbedded, and the critical question is, must these things also be changed? As an anthropologist I fervently hope that the answer to this question is no, but I am apprehensive. We are living in a period of increasing cultural homogenization, a period in which "modernization" has not yet been disentangled from "Westernization." We still are unable to differentiate aspects of non-industrial culture that actually hinder development, and hence will have to change, from those that do not. The unfortunate result is that our current "missionaries" of industrial development too often attempt to sell the whole undifferentiated package. All too frequently their models for development require the scrapping of everything distinctive of the original way of life. To become successful in the modern world, they say, other people must share our values and world-view. They must become "achievement-oriented" and learn to be competitive. In its most succinct form, it is argued that they must become *motivated.* What a marvelously Western ethnocentrism!

But ethnocentrism aside, are these single-minded developmentalists correct? I think not, and I believe that the Rotuman case offers evidence to the contrary. The Rotumans seem to be adapting very well, and I would argue that their overall conservatism has been an asset rather than a hindrance. Their cultural identity is a source of dignity and self-respect, and it is perhaps these qualities that are the most vital universal "requirements" for achieving competency in the public culture of the modern world. Furthermore, there is no reason why people cannot learn two styles of behavior simultaneously, one that is appropriate in one set of circumstances and a second that is appropriate in another. The very idea that a person's behavior should be consistent across all situations is itself a distinctly Western cultural assumption. As we have seen, the Rotumans are not concerned by such inconsistencies within their own culture. To them behavior is primarily situationally determined, and their integrity rests on behaving appropriately in each social context. That a person should exhibit one style of behavior and profess adherence to a given set of values in one situation, and another style with a different accompanying set of values in another situation, does not distress Rotumans in the way it does culture-bound Westerners. To me this is an indication that Rotumans, in a very basic sense, understand the concept of culture much better than we do, for the concept of culture implies just this: In different places with different people different kinds of behavior are appropriate.

The significance of this—an appreciation of cultural diversity—for education within both Western nations and developing societies is necessarily profound, for it raises the issue of just how much we must strive to alter the personal world of children who are culturally different if we are to prepare them for a productive life. Until recently we have been rather unimaginative in confronting this issue. The model we have developed for educating our young presumes that everyone learns in the same way, that they are motivated by the same rewards, that they fear the same punishments, and that they value the same achievements. In short we presume cultural uniformity, and we have labelled children whose experiences do not conform "culturally disadvantaged."

In the next and concluding chapter of this book we shall consider the concepts of culture and cultural transmission as they relate to the events that take place within school classrooms. My thoughts on this matter have been stimulated in part by recent attempts to diagnose and remedy the American school system's failure to educate so-called "culturally disadvantaged" children adequately.

NOTES

[1] Laura Thompson, *Southern Lau, Fiji: An Ethnography* (Honolulu: Bernice P. Bishop Museum, Bulletin No. 162, 1940), p. 64.

[2] Marshall Sahlins, *Moala* (Ann Arbor: University of Michigan Press, 1962), p. 114.

—VIII————————

Culture and the Classroom

Is there anything to be learned from the Rotuman case that is relevant to our problems in educating American children? One might be tempted to answer "no"—that the Rotumans still have a coherent culture from which they come and to which they may return; that even if they fail in school they can still become successful Rotumans; and that the problem with so many American children is that they do not come from a coherent culture, but rather are "culturally disadvantaged" or "deprived."

I can think of no more unfortunate label for children who do not respond to our middle-class model for education than "culturally disadvantaged." It is a phrase that I find both misleading and irritating. It is misleading because it implies an absence of cultural experience rather than a different set of cultural experiences. This leads many teachers to presume that their task with these youngsters is to fill a void with more and earlier educational experience of the same type they provide for "advantaged" children, a strategy that is insufficient at best and a contribution to failure at worst. The phrase "culturally disadvantaged" is irritating because it is so ethnocentric; it presumes that the model we have selected as a basis for formal education is inherently correct and that those children who do not respond to it are somehow in error. I have the distinct impression, after extensive discussions with American teachers, that a great many of them have found the phrase attractive because it provides a means for externalizing responsibility for the school's failure. Previous generations were able to find comfort in notions of racial inferiority and differential intelligence quotients, but social scientists have stripped such explanations of their respectability. With the concept of "cultural disadvantage" came the opportunity to blame the sub-culture of the home and the nature of early experience. As an anthropologist, however, I must register an objection; this is a misuse of the culture concept.

If we are going to bring the concept of culture into the domain of education, let us begin by becoming cognizant of cultural *differences.* I grant that it is necessary to transmit a basic repertoire of knowledge and skills to anyone who is going to participate productively in our broader American social system. It is also true that some segments of our population do not train their children in a way that is consistent with the attitudinal and motivational model that we have found associated with success. But then let us speak of educating the *culturally different child.* Let *us,* the educators, assume responsibility for getting the job done rather than requiring every parent to conform to the middle-class child-rearing protocol. Let us explore ways to modify the culture of the classroom to accommodate the culturally different, so that their strengths can be tapped in the learning process.

Each classroom evolves into a socio-cultural system of it own—a small society with two main categories of personnel, teacher and students. During the school year this may become elaborated, as the students are divided into permanent or temporary groups, and as such positions as monitors, group leaders, etc., are established. The structure may vary from highly authoritarian, with the teacher making all the decisions, to very democratic, with considerable reliance upon group decision-making procedures.

Two cultural factors are of interest in discussing the classroom situation. One is the cultural background that the students and teacher bring with them into the classroom; the other is the pattern of behavior that develops over time as a result of day-to-day interactions. I should like to suggest a three-fold classification scheme as a framework for analyzing the classroom environment: (1) classrooms in which the teacher and all her students share the same cultural background to a high degree (e.g., teacher and students are middle-class Caucasians); (2) classrooms in which the teacher is of one cultural background and the students of another (e.g., the teacher is a middle-class Caucasian and the students are working-class Mexican-Americans); and (3) classrooms in which the teacher is of a cultural background that she shares to a high degree with some students in her class, but not with others (e.g., the teacher is a middle-class Caucasian and the students are mixed, some being middle-class Caucasians, others being working-class Afro-Americans).

I want to re-emphasize at this juncture a point that I made in the introductory chapter—that people do not "belong" to cultures in the way they have membership in a club. When we say people are of different cultural backgrounds, we are not suggesting that they are unalike in all ways or that they do not share any of the same attitudes, beliefs, and feelings. Rather we are drawing attention to those differences in experience that create problems in communication within a particular social system, in this case the schoolroom. For our purposes, therefore, social class differences are equivalent to cultural differences.

Our main concern with regard to the culture that develops in a classroom as a result of day-to-day interaction focuses on the communication process, and particularly the problems raised when a teacher and her students are from culturally divergent backgrounds. Communication channels have to be open for effective transmission of knowledge to take place. When they are blocked, the intended goals of education are frustrated. Channels are "open" in a communication system in which there is a high degree of correspondence between a message and its interpretation. With this understanding, let us examine classroom communication from a cultural perspective.

By far the most significant vehicle for the transmission of knowledge in the formal classroom is language. Most usually the teacher does a good deal of talking—telling, describing, explaining—and the students do most of the listening. The teacher uses the children's communications as feedback by which she can judge how much information they have absorbed. Since most school curricula deal with the transmission of formal information (as opposed to expressive or strategic information), there is a marked tendency for teachers to focus their attention upon the denotative aspect of language. This corresponds, I believe, to the middle-class cultural norm. That is, middle-class individuals tend to rely upon an elaborated denotative code, which emphasizes highly standardized grammar and finely differentiated vocabulary, for communicating with one another. With children who have learned to place a similar emphasis on speech, teachers generally feel quite comfortable, even if the children speak a different language, as long as translation is possible.

Problems dramatically arise when children come from a cultural background (including much of working-class culture in the United States) that relies less upon an elaborated denotative code, and more upon the connotative, or expressive, aspects of interpersonal interaction. Very often these children speak a dialect that is considered crude, vulgar, and "sub-standard" within a middle-class person's frame of reference. What this judgment often reflects is that the denotative aspects of their language do not, and would not even if elaborated, communicate the kind of information that is the teacher's focus of concern. In many of these children's cultures and sub-cultures, the most important information one can obtain from an encounter is information about the relationship. Each person wants to know whether the other person is benevolent or malevolent, whether he is serious or playing, whether he is powerful or weak, whether he is active or passive, etc. Such information is much more readily obtained by reading such expressive cues as tone of voice, gestures, body posture, and tensions, than by decoding denotative messages. It is therefore very often the expressive code that is elaborated in these culures. From this perspective, the middle-class person often appears stilted and incompetent; in the domain of communicating about relationships, it is he who might be called "disadvantaged."

When a teacher is from the same cultural background as a group of students who are strongly tuned in to the expressive aspects of communication, he enjoys some distinct advantages. He is likely to have a much clearer picture of what is expected in relationships between himself and the students, and among the students. If he knows the expressive code, he can accurately calculate the moods of his students—when they can be approached and when they are best left alone; when they are hurt, angry, and upset and when they are happy; when they require pacification and when they need a firm admonishment. If he is sufficiently conscious of the expressive code, he can with some efficiency elicit the kinds of responses he wants from the students. He can, in short, employ effective strategies. Rotuma is an example of a culture in which both students and teachers share these sensitivities and the educational results are surprisingly good, given all the limitations of an island environment.

When the students are from an expressive culture and the teacher does not understand the code, some major problems usually develop. One frequently observed phenomenon under such conditions is that the teacher is unaware of the emotional loadings contained in his own messages; he therefore generates unpredictable responses from his students. A complaint often heard from teachers of culturally different children is that they are "moody," but what this usually means is that the teacher has produced emotional responses without being aware of it. He has emitted highly meaningful expressive cues, turning the children on and off, so to speak, without knowing it. From the teacher's standpoint, the children's behavior is unpredictable and erratic, but although he may not realize it, the children are having the same problem with his behavior. In such situations, a teacher whose cultural background emphasizes the expressive aspects of communication is better off than one whose cultural heritage strongly emphasizes the denotative content of messages. It is easier for the former to learn a new code than for the latter to learn to focus on expressive content when his own socialization has not prepared him for it. We sometimes call attention to this distinction by contrasting "sensitive" teachers to those who are "insensitive." It may take time, but a sensitive teacher stands a good chance of learning a new code and putting it to educational advantage.

In classrooms in which the teacher shares a common cultural background with some students and not with others, an additional complicating factor is present. An obvious expectation is that regardless of the sincerity of his motivation the teacher is likely to feel more comfortable in his relationship with culturally similar students. He is able to anticipate their responses more easily and they his, and he feels that he is getting through to them, whereas the culturally different students' behavior appears more erratic. I suspect the usual result under such circumstances is that the teacher unknowingly begins to direct more and more positive communication (i.e., information transmission and approval) to the culturally similar group and more and more negative communication (i.e., disapproval) to the culturally different group. If this is in fact the case, it requires that we rethink the implications of "integrated" education.

The point I want to make is that for education to take place properly, a classroom must develop into a sub-cultural system in which everyone, teacher and pupil alike, learns to use the same language, not only denotatively but connotatively as well. If the teacher and students are from different cultural backgrounds, it may be necessary to work out a unique communication code within the classroom before the business of transmitting information is seriously undertaken. That is, the teacher and students must come to some kind of mutual understanding of what is going to be meant by what, of what are meaningful cues and what potential cues shall be ignored. To do this may take quite a bit of time away from what most teachers think of as teaching, but it will not only prove to be a good long-term investment, it will provide an extremely valuable learning experience in its own right. Of course, to do this, the teacher must also be willing to be a student; he must be willing to discard or temporarily set aside his own culturally conditioned interpretations of interpersonal events in favor of interpretations that are more meaningful in the newly formed cultural system. He must recognize that within such a sub-culture he can be as deviant as one of the students.

This brings us directly to the problem of teaching a language such as standard formal English. A vast literature is emerging on this topic and I do not pretend to be an expert in the area, but there are a few points that have become clear to me, partly as a result of my Rotuman experience and partly as a result of research into the education of Hawaiian children. First, I would accept the anthropological cliché that there are no inherently inferior or superior languages. Every human language known is capable of communicating anything that human beings wish to communicate. It is true, of course, that languages vary in the degree to which their vocabularies have been elaborated, but that is a matter of culture content rather than a measure of linguistic superiority. People elaborate language in areas that are culturally important—e.g., European languages have an elaborate vocabulary related to technology, the Subanun of the Philippines have an elaborate disease vocabulary, and the Eskimos have an extraordinary number of words pertaining to snow-covered landscapes. But any language can develop a technical vocabulary, just as English did over a period of time following the industrial revolution. Likewise, we can translate Subanun concepts of disease and Eskimo snow words into English if we wish. All this might seem somewhat trite; not many teachers really believe that English is superior to Spanish or French, or even to Eskimo or Subanun. The issue becomes confused, however, when they are dealing with the language spoken by slum children, whether their first language is Spanish or a colloquial English dialect. Their language is usually labelled something like "broken English," "substandard English," or "Pidgin," with the implication that it is inadequate as a vehicle for communication. I strongly agree with those who hold that such languages are not merely deficient forms of English, but are fully adequate languages in their own right. It is true that they may not be adequate for use in our public culture (i.e., the culture of our business and legal world), but they are well suited to the cultures in which they were learned and are used. They are languages in which the expressive code is usually elaborated while the denotative code is left somewhat undeveloped.

I am not suggesting that these children do not have to learn standard English. They obviously do if they are to be able to adapt to our public culture, and nearly everyone will agree that this is a desirable goal. The issue is one of assumptions about learning and appropriate methods. If a teacher starts with the premise that the language a child brings into the classroom is deficient, rather than different, he is prone to assume that his job is one of merely filling partially empty vessels with the right kinds of material. He may remark to a child who has said something in his colloquial dialect, "No, that's not the right way to say that. You should say. . . ." What he will have done is tell the child that the way he has learned to say something for some five or ten years, the way he *must* talk if he is to communicate with his parents and peers, is wrong! But if the child tries to speak as the teacher wants, he has difficulty communicating with the people who are important to him. If he is confronted with two ways of saying things, one that his teachers approve and one that everyone important to him favors, what option does he really have? Once a teacher accepts the legitimacy of a child's colloquial language, however, his approach is likely to change. Instead of correcting the child he can say, "Yes, I know what you mean, but there is another way to say that, and you must learn it because that's the way we speak in school." The principle is that of teaching English as a second language. The goal is to develop bilingualism, so the child can communicate effectively in both the private culture of his home and neighborhood, and the public culture of the business and legal worlds.

Another aspect of language learning that has come to my attention has to do with familiarity with concepts. One of the propositions derived from the deficiency model that has prevailed in recent attempts to educate slum children is that since they lack sufficient cultural experience, many of the concepts used in the school are strange and unfamiliar; this, it is believed, seriously impedes learning. A highly valued remedial technique has been to "enrich" the children's experience by taking them on excursions, field trips, etc. Although I do not think such measures are harmful, I suspect their remedial effects are quite negligible, in part because they are based on false assumptions. There are few places in the world where formal education is institutionalized that are as remote as Rotuma. Nevertheless, the curriculum these children are confronted with places a heavy emphasis on European, particularly English, cultural content, most of which is sensually inaccessible. Rotuman teachers recognize this fact, and strive to explain concepts orally, visually, and by demonstration. For the most part they are successful—not because they provide the actual experience, for they obviously cannot, but because they do not make false assumptions about the children's knowledge, and because they make use of "open" channels of communication. They can start from the vernacular if need be, and build meaningful imagery for the children. The point I am trying to make is that language can provide an adequate substitute for experience if the teacher understands the culture of his children, but when this is lacking, I doubt that gaining first-hand experience really makes much difference in the educational development of the child. Experience is made meaningful through a cultural filter; as long as the instiutions of formal education remain alien to the children who attend them, the experience that takes place within them will be both distorted and of low interest.

Language and cognition are only two of the areas that are vastly complicated when education takes place within a multi-cultural setting. Another important area is motivation. From the standpoint of a middle-class teacher, children from other cultures or sub-cultures often seem to be lazy and uninterested. I have heard many teachers say that these children "are not motivated," implying some kind of character defect. In part this view is a reflection of our middle-class assumption that normal people are internally driven to strive for achievement, and that the failure to show this spontaneously is an indication of deficiency. Such an assumption is really quite unjustified; the fact is that everyone is motivated to perform certain kinds of acts when expecting meaningful rewards, but the rewards we offer in school are not equally meaningful to everyone. Middle-class children learn to value delayed, symbolic rewards, and that is what is offered to them in school. Children from other sub-cultures learn to value other forms of reward. They may place little value on such offerings as grades, but are strongly stimulated by other things—food, money, leisure, companionship, or the social approval of their peers. Unfortunately, our assumptions about achievement are such that we regard immediate, tangible rewards as "bribes," and hold them in low esteem. Let's face it. There are not many middle-class students, even at the university level, who will work hard without any promise of reward. Grades are bribes too!

To claim that certain kinds of rewards are better than others irrespective of their motivating capabilities is sheer ethnocentrism. From the standpoint of learning, the important thing is to use rewards that increase the probability of desired responses. That is what psychologists mean when they refer to rewards as "reinforcers." The value of a reward, and hence its strength as a reinforcer, depends upon a subject's experience, in large part, his cultural experience.

One of the most fundamental assumptions underlying the middle-class view of education is that competition stimulates motivation to learn. This is quite understandable. After all, our country's massive technological development was forged in the crucible of intense individual competition, and we are justifiably proud of the material accomplishments it has wrought. We therefore consider it rather natural that accomplishment is stimulated by competition. There are many cultures, however, Rotuma being one of them, that emphasize co-operation rather than competition. In Rotuma an individual who publicly demonstrates the desire to be better than his fellows is strongly ostracized. The competitive spirit is not absent, but its expression is confined to group activities; it is therefore always moderated by loyalty to one's teammates or peers. This is also true for many of the sub-cultures in the United States, most notably for the Hawaiians and certain American Indian groups. When children from such a background are placed in the individually competitive framework characteristic of the American classroom, they are confronted with a serious dilemma. The teacher is tacitly asking them to place a higher value on the rewards that he is offering them than on the approval of peers, an option most middle-class children are willing to take; for Rotuman children, and others like them, however, the loss of peer approval is too high a price to pay. Rotuman teachers are well aware of this and make much use of work groups, in which the children cooperate in performing learning tasks, although the groups may be competing against each other. This makes use of both cooperative and competitive motivations; the children reward each other for contributing to a team effort. Most American teachers I have talked to have found it easy enough to accept this idea when it comes to reading, which is not ordinarily very competitive, but they have found it difficult to comprehend when it comes to doing problems in mathematics. That children should get together to come up with a group answer seems too much like cheating, but this of course represents a cultural bias. The goal is to get children to learn, and some children learn better from other children than they do from teachers.

Related to this same individualistic bias is the assumption that children learn better when they are quiet. The focus of attention is supposed to be on the teacher, and a high degree of interaction with fellow students is presumed to interfere with the proper transmission of information from teacher to student. For many culturally different children, however, the teacher is not a very important model, whereas certain of their classmates are. Among these peer-oriented groups, it is other children who control important approval rewards, and it is they who are the *effective* teachers. Interaction often focuses upon leaders of the peer group and they may be seen as classroom nuisances. If a teacher recognizes such a situation, and is shrewd enough to form an alliance with influential students, he may be able to enhance his teaching capabilities immeasurably. Again, many American teachers are opposed to this strategy on moral or ethical grounds; they regard it as unnatural and manipulative. What they fail to realize is that what may seem "natural" in their culture is "unnatural" in other cultures, and that successful teaching *is* manipulation. Much of the content of university education courses has to do with manipulating students in order to facilitate learning. Unfortunately, most of the techniques suggested are culturally biased and do not work with culturally different children, so we have to explore new techniques. The fact that we may be acutely aware of these new strategies does not make them any more manipulative.

Our cultural lenses also may contribute to social control problems in classrooms containing culturally different children. Largely as a result of the teachings of psychiatry and clinical psychology, we have come to see certain control techniques as harmful to children's psychological development. Our emphasis is upon positive rewards and the withdrawal of love and approval. The two most harmful techniques are considered to be physical punishment and shaming; in fact, they are strictly forbidden in the vast majority of American schools. If we look at the Rotuman example, however, we find that these are precisely the techniques that Rotuman teachers favor, despite the fact that they are discouraged from using them by the Colonial Administration. The reason is quite simple. As Rotumans they are well aware that these are the most effective techniques they can employ. Their wisdom became apparent to me recently while I was observing a middle-class elementary teacher attempting to maintain control over a group of Hawaiian children, who are like Rotuman children in many ways. She was using withdrawal of love and approval, admonishments, and various forms of threat, but was completely unsuccessful in gaining control of her class. The more she tried the more disinhibited the children became; ultimately they paid almost no attention to her at all. Instead of teaching, she was spending most of her time trying to control the class, and it was evident that she had become almost entirely punitive in her relations with the children. The catch was that her methods of punishment were so ineffective that she had to use a great deal more of it to obtain even a minimum degree of control. What is striking about Rotuman classrooms is that teachers rarely have to use punishment, in part because the mere threat of an effective measure is sufficient to maintain control. As a result, Rotuman teachers can spend most of their time teaching and rewarding student performances. I am not advocating that we must get tough with children who do not respond to our middle-class techniques of social control. Quite the contrary. The important point, as careful research has overwhelmingly demonstrated, is that rewards are far more effective stimuli to learning than punishment. What I am suggesting is that we must rationally appraise the effects of our actions when we are dealing with culturally different children.

American educators speak and write a great deal about the necessity of adjusting teaching techniques to "the individual child," but my observations lead me to believe that it has become an empty chiché, and is destined to remain so unless teacher-student ratios are drastically reduced from the typical norm. No teacher can intelligently diagnose thirty to forty children and then proceed to develop that many teaching strategies; few are willing to try. The alternative is not to treat everyone alike, though. Recognition of cultural and sub-cultural differences would permit us to develop a relatively limited set of teaching strategies, based upon differences in relational sensitivities, motivational structure, values, and the like. We could then begin to group students intelligently on the basis of the teaching strategies that work best with them. This is the *only* meaningful way to group students if the primary consideration is the transmission of knowledge. Our ideological emphasis on egalitarianism has led us astray in the field of education because it has made us blind to cultural differences. Even in Hawaii, where cultural differences are highly pronounced, it is nearly impossible to get teachers to admit that children of Hawaiian background are any different from those of Japanese ancestry, even though the academic performance of the latter is obviously and admittedly different. When asked about cultural differences, they almost invariably respond that "everyone is alike!"

My belief is that this egalitarian slogan masks one of the most pernicious Western ethnocentrisms—an inherent presumption that everything and everyone can be scaled along a single evaluative dimension of good and bad. Such linear thinking has dominated our religion, law, and much of social science as well as our educational system. It is pernicious because it precludes the notion that styles of life may be different without being better or worse. The message the teachers have been trying to convey with their assertion of equality is that they are not prejudiced, that they do not regard one group as superior to another. Unfortunately, they equate any recognition of differences with discriminatory judgments.

The pragmatic problem engendered by this mode of thought is that it results in such deficiency models as "cultural disadvantage." Such formulations are at best poor guides for action; the most they can tell us is why other groups do not behave like middle-class Americans. At worst they are the basis for bigoted judgments. A more noble goal is to understand differences in terms of each culture's own assumptions, values, and goals. Then perhaps we can place formal education in the service of making the world safe for diversity, rather than the homogenization of mankind.

Education based upon deficiency formulations is doomed to fail because it is based on incorrect assumptions. Children are not empty cups. Attempts to erase their background and replace it with ours merely compounds all of the problems associated with the transmission of knowledge. It will not be until educators recognize that American society is composed of many sub-cultural groups, and that the children produced by these groups are different—not better or worse, not culturally deprived, nor even unprepared for school—but *different*, that they will find themselves on the road to providing all American children with an equally valuable education.

Appendix A

Orthography and Glossary

ORTHOGRAPHY

The spelling of Rotuman words used in this study is based on the orthography introduced by Churchward.[1] The alphabet is as follows:

a	as in clam, but shorter, unless written ā
ạ	as in want
à	as in cat
ä	as in fan
e	as in bet
f	as in fish
g	as *ng* in sing
h	as in heart
i	as in sit
j	as *tch* in pitch
k	as in rake
l	as in laugh
m	as in mask
n	as in nine
o	as in obey
ö	pronounced as in German, somewhat like *er* in her
p	pronounced as in English, but blunted somewhat toward b
r	pronounced with a slight trill

[1] C. M. Churchward, *Rotuman Grammar and Dictionary* (Sydney: Australasian Medical Publishing Company, 1940), Part II.

s   between English s and *sh*

t   pronounced strictly dental, the tip of tongue being pressed
        against the back of the top teeth

u   as in put

ü   pronounced as in German. This sound may be approximated
        by endeavoring to pronounce *ee* as in see, with the lips
        rounded.

v   as in vat. When *v* falls at the end of a word, particularly
        when following an *a*, it is often imperfectly articulated and
        sounds like *o*.

'   glottal stop

GLOSSARY

'afa—basket (lit., basket woven from a palm leaf); [gift]

äfe—thousand

apei—finely woven white mate

as togi—togi = to succeed to (title, rank, office, etc.); [successor to
   the name]

'a'su—(lit., eating wedding feast); [also used to refer to: person chosen
   for place of honor at side of bridegroom and bride respectively]

'atua—ancestral ghost

'epa—mat; pandanus leaves prepared for mat-making

fa'es ho'aga—sub-chief of a district; [man of the *ho'aga*]

faiak se'ea—thank you

fakman'ia—to be conceited or proud

faksoro—to entreat, beseech; to apologize; to beg to be excused

fara—to beg, request, ask for

fekei moa—ten chickens cooked and then done up together in a
   coconut-leaf container; (*moa* = fowl)

figalelei—to be kindly disposed, merciful, or willing to oblige; to yield
   to entreaty; [please]

fūag ri—house-site or house-mound

fu'u—to remain or stay where one is

gagaja—person of high rank, chief, lord (*gagaj*)

gagaj'es itu'u—chief of a district

haina—wife (if no defining word follows), male speaking

hamfua—male's sister-in-law or female's brother-in-law; adj., to be
   ashamed, bashful, or shy, to feel uncomfortable in the presence of
   others, to suffer from stage-fright

hani—wife; woman, girl

hanisi—to feel pity, sorrow, sympathy, or solicitude; to take pity on,
   be kind to; to love

ho'aga—sometimes used in the sense of a district or village under the authority of a minor chief called a *gagaj 'es ho'aga*

hula—to wrestle

'i'ini—animal food (whether meat, fish, or eggs)

itu'u—district (with specific boundaries)

kainaga—clan, tribe; member of same clan; relationship; to be related, to belong to the same clan; race, nation; kind, sort, variety, species, class

kato'aga—public celebration, festive gathering, festival

kau noho'ag—(*kau* = group; *noho* = to dwell, reside); [household]

kava—a shrub from the roots of which a stimulating beverage is prepared; or the beverage itself

kiu—ten thousand

koua—earthen oven; cooked food, contents of native oven, meal of cooked food

le'e—offspring, son, daughter; child; person; [nephew, niece]; plural *lele'a*

le'efā—male child

le'ehani—female child

mäe—male's brother-in-law; female's sister-in-law

mafa—raw, uncooked

mamasa—feast given to a person after sea voyage or fishing, or after trip abroad

mane'a—to indulge in any form of recreation or relaxation; (to have illicit sexual intercourse)

ma'piag—grandparent or grandchild; (alternate pronunciation is *ma'kiga*); plural *ma'ma'piga, ma'ma'kiga*

ma'piag'aki—to be a grand-nephew, grand-niece, grand-uncle, or grand-aunt; (same as *ma'kiag'aki*)

marä'e—open space in the middle of a village, village green

ö'fā—father or uncle; plural *ö'ö'fā*

o'honi, ö'hön—mother or aunt; plural *ö'ö'haina*

o'i—general term used to describe distant relatives in the parents' generation, or even older non-relatives who are in positions of authority; plural *o'o'i*

'oj'aki—main feast given in honor of first-born child

'otou—possessive pronoun, my

puha—sweet tuberous root of the dracaena, used in sweetening native puddings

pure—to decide, rule, control, judge; (lit., one who decides)

sàghani—(male's) sister or female first cousin

sàgvävāne—(female's) brother or male first cousin

sapa—[custom of mockery]

sạsigi—often used in wide sense, including any or all of one's relatives of one's own generation and sex

sigoa—namesake

taupiri—to follow (lit. and fig.); to go to live without legal marriage

tē la 'ā—food, esp. starchy vegetables (yam, taro, etc.); (staples)

tē la 'ā mafa—the uncooked food (staples) that would go into a *koua* (yam, taro, etc.)

tika—dart-throwing; [dart is bamboo reed about 2 feet long with hardwood tip about 3 inches long]

togi—to succeed to (title, rank, office, etc.); [successor]

tokag'omoe—[annual presentation to show respect for chiefly status]

vạti—leafy vegetable

väväne—husband

—*Appendix B*———————————

Denotation of Rotuman
Kinship Terms

ma'piag—Any consanguineally related person in ego's grandparents'
generation; reciprocally, any consanguineally related person in ego's
grandchildren's generation.

This term is extended to consanguineally related persons beyond the second ascending generation and beyond the second descending generation. It is often used without distinction as to sex
of relative, but the suffixes *fā* (male) or *ḥani* (female) may be used
when sex distinctions are required.

An alternate pronuciation is *ma'kiga*. Plural forms are *ma'ma'piga*
and *ma'ma'kiga*.

ö'fā—Any consanguineally related male in ego's parents' generation.
Plural form is *ö'ö'fā*.

ö'hön—Any consanguineally related female in ego's parents' generation.
Plural form is *ö'ö'ḥaina*.

The more general term *o'i*, which does not distinguish sex of
relative, is rarely used to describe parents, but may be used to
describe distant relatives in the parents' generation, or even older
non-relatives who are in positions of authority. The plural form is
o'o'i.

le'e—Any consanguineally related person in ego's children's generation.
The term is often used without distinguishing sex of relative,
but may be used with the suffix *fā* to form *le'efā* (male child), or
ḥani to form *le'eḥani* (female child). *Le'e* is also used as a general
term to designate "child" without regard for relationship. The plural
form is *lele'a*.

sạsigi—Any consanguineally related person in ego's children's generation.

A distinction is sometimes made between ego's siblings of the
same sex who are younger (*sạsiga*) and those who are older, for
which the term *sạsigi* may be reserved. *Sạsigi* may also be used in
a more general sense to refer to all of ego's consanguineal relatives
in his own generation, regardless of sex.

sàgväväne—Female speaking, any consanguineally related male in ego's
generation.

sàghạni—Male speaking, any consanguineally related female in ego's
generation.

väväne—Female speaking, spouse.

hạina—Male speaking, spouse.

mäe—Male speaking, husbands of all persons referred to as *sàghạni*
and anyone known as *sàgväväne* to one's wife; also female speaking,
wives of all persons referred to as *sàgväväne*, and anyone known as
sàghạni to one's husband.

hạmfua—Male speaking, wives of all persons referred to as *sạsigi*, and
persons known as *sạsigi* to one's wife; also female speaking, husbands
of all persons referred to as *sạsigi*, and persons known as *sạsigi* to
one's husband.

Some other aspects of the terminological system are as follows:

1. There are no separate terms of address. Rotumans usually use persons' names when speaking to them, although small children sometimes address their elders by the terms of reference.
2. The Rotumans distinguish their actual parents, siblings, grandparents and children by adding the adjective *pu* (true) to a kinship
term. The suffix *-ak* may likewise be added to distinguish classifica-
tory kin, or to refer to adopted kin. The term *ö'fä'ak* may thus be
used in reference to such persons as mother's brother, father's
father's brother's son, or to a foster father.
3. Affinal relatives in ascending or descending generations are usually
referred to descriptively, i.e., by describing the relationship. Ego
thus refers to her husband's mother as *o'honi ne oto väväne* (the
mother of my husband), or to a father's brother's wife as *hạina ne
sạsigi ne oto ö'fä* (the wife of the brother of my father). Sometimes,
however, these people are referred to in the same fashion as adopted
relatives, in which case both husband's mother and father's brother's
wife are called *ö'hön'ak*.
4. The degree to which kinship terms are extended is indefinite and
depends upon recognition of individual ties.

—Appendix C—

Extract From *A Critical Examination of Education in Rotuma*

BY MAMAO P. MANAGREVE

"I paid visits to every one of the schools in Rotuma during the times of the experiment. I observed a few teachers giving lessons in reading, both in English and in Rotuman, arithmetic, geography and history. To my great surprise, none of them made much use of the blackboard and certainly nothing in the line of visual aids. One of the teachers was giving Class VII (New Zealand Form 1) the History of Sir Robert Clive and his struggle with the French in India. The whole lesson lasted thirty minutes. The teacher talked most of the time while the children listened or pretended to listen. I am not so sure that they did, but they sat facing the teacher for thirty minutes anyway. There was not a picture of Clive nor a map of India shown during the whole of the period. Another teacher with Class VIII pupils, made practically the same kind of teaching approach concerning the sugar industry in Fiji. No pictures or blackboard illustrations were used to depict various processes of making sugar.

"In a place like Rotuma where children have no access to such things, the use of visual aid techniques must be considered of vital importance. Teaching given to children in such a place without visual aids is in danger of being too formal and the performances of the children being educated in Rotuma in the tests seem to have proven that teaching in Rotuma is chiefly of a formal character.

"I made inquiries concerning what they have for the teaching of such subjects as history and geography for which the use of visual aid techniques is extremely valuable, and I discovered that they had

nothing besides textbooks and a few maps. Most of the teachers appear
to have had little training to put the school blackboard to better use
and in the absence of ready-made equipment for visual aid, their teaching tends, as it appears to be, formal.

"Some teachers have to live away from their schools because no
provision is made to provide accommodations for them near to where
they teach. Included in these are some women teachers, who have to
walk or cycle at least five miles on fairly stony roads to school every
morning.

"In Rotuma where the sun becomes very hot early or if the sun
is not shining then a tropical heavy downpour is likely to occur, these
teachers must find teaching a hard job at times. It should not be hard
to find accommodations for the teachers close to where they teach. As
a matter of fact one of the teachers has been provided with accommodations close by the school where he teaches. The same could be
done for other teachers too, having to travel long distances is not fair
for the teachers nor for the pupils they teach. The teachers may arrive
at school too tired and the children cannot be given the teaching they
require from those teachers.

"The objectives of the present education for the Rotuman people
are not all clear. It is said, the reason why the government took over
control of these schools and assumed the right to supervise the work in
schools, is to raise the standards of education. But after twenty years
under government supervision the standards of these schools are believed to be not much higher than when education was not compulsory under the churches. It is true that English is being taught today
whereas the schools under the churches, taught practically no English.
But the standard of English in these schools is so poor and the neglect
of the vernacular tends to produce children who leave school after eight
years compulsory education, good neither in English nor in Rotuman.
If the older generation cannot speak English because it was not taught
when they were in school, then they can at least speak, read and write
in Rotuman.

"It should be remembered, that only a very few of the children in
school today will go on to do secondary education. The majority will
leave at fourteen. If the schools cannot teach them something that will
be valuable to them for life out of school, their education is in danger
of being regarded as a waste of time. As a matter of fact, this attitude
is quite prevalent among the Rotuman people. The apparent lack of
cooperation between teachers and parents may be traced back to the
inability of the schools to do better.

"The position is frustrating to both teachers and their pupils. The
pupils do not get much encouragement from their parents and the

teachers find the different children hard to teach. To raise the standards of these schools, the Department of Education must give serious consideration to the present school organization in Rotuma. Unless something is done to improve the teaching in these schools the academic standards may continue to fall.

". . . [It] would be quite misleading for unscientific-minded people to make the rash judgment and conclusion that a particular person or group of persons is solely responsible for the unhappy findings of the present investigation. It should be kept well in mind that educational organization in Rotuma is complicated by the fact that it is under joint management of the Department of Education and the local school committees, and in the case of the Catholic schools, the department and the authorities of that church. While the results of the present research appear to indicate poor teaching in Rotuma, one should nevertheless remember that good teaching depends on certain factors, e.g., quality of the teachers, suitability of school buildings for learning, availability of good teaching facilities and so on. Therefore, it is not so simple a matter to pinpoint where the responsibility for the sad state of affairs lies."

[Managreve offers six recommendations for improving the standard of education in Rotuma:]

"(1) . . . [The] ability to read and understand what is being read is of vital importance to a child's school progress. Much of what is done in the school depends on reading efficiency, not 'barking at words,' but getting the meaning which is intended to be conveyed by what one reads. The efficiency in reading and understanding what is being read would appear by the reading test results to be in need of improvement.

"While it is true that children must be taught to read English, for English is essential on the higher rungs of the educational ladder, the probable danger that may result from teaching children reading in English at the beginning of their school careers should be kept well in sight. It is for this reason that it may be wise to begin reading with the language they understand. The use of primers in Hindustani and Fijian in Indian and Fijian schools may be a solution if primers in Rotuman could be procured. The major obstacle of course, to get things printed in Rotuman, is the adoption today of two different written forms of the language. To resolve this difficulty, the two churches should either agree to adopt one of the two or invite an expert specialized in this type of problem to see what can be done. The Department's assistance might be necessary in case of failure by the two churches to come to an agreement as to how the language should be written. If this problem is solved, then the Department may be asked to have, in the Fijian School

Journal, a few pages given to Rotuman for the benefit of the Rotuman children. It should be remembered that as things are now, the Department should not be asked to help and the possibility of obtaining reading materials in Rotuman is a remote one unless agreement is reached as above.

"(2) There is a need for teachers to hold meetings at least once each school term. This would allow them to discuss problems concerning their work and exchange ideas. In a place so isolated from better sources of information as regards teaching techniques such meetings would be valuable. These meetings should lead the teachers to prepare a report at the end of each year to be forwarded to the regional 'education officer' with suggestions for the improvements of their schools in Rotuma. The committee members may be included in these meetings if desired.

"The above suggestion may be found to be of great value to the 'education officer' in charge of this particular school area, especially when he cannot afford to come to visit these schools often enough nor to spend much time there during one visit.

"(3) In order to get the best returns from the money and labor expended on the erection of school buildings, it might be wise that plans for future school buildings could be approved by someone who knows the requirements of such buildings. Some of the buildings which are being used seem to be unsatisfactory because climatic and teaching requirements were not taken into consideration when they were built.

"The supervision of the work in building schools should remain as it is now, the responsibility of the school committee or committees, but the buildings should be erected according to plans as may be approved by an expert.

"(4) In view of the fact that teaching methods do change and rather often these days, it might be desirable not to let teachers remain in Rotuma too long at a time. If the standards of the schools in Rotuma should be kept at a desirable level, then a teacher when appointed to teach in Rotuma should be appointed for a set period, after which he should go to a school in Fiji where he can get in touch with new teaching techniques in order to bring up to date his teaching methods. It is generally believed that some teachers are inclined to be reluctant to undertake teaching in Rotuma and the reason is said to be that in Rotuma, facilities for the improvement of one's teaching techniques or general knowledge are not readily accessible so that is why some teachers prefer to be teaching in Fiji.

"There are a sufficient number of Rotuman teachers. Most of them are in Fiji schools. It might perhaps be a means of encouraging Rotuman teachers to come to Rotuma and to teach their people, if a teacher exchange scheme can be put into operation. This should if practicable achieve a double purpose, it would permit teachers to keep in touch with new developments and help keep the educational standard from falling behind that of Fiji. The only difficulty which seems likely to be a major one is the question of who is to pay the traveling expenses. This is perhaps the most difficult problem. But considering the number of Rotuman teachers being employed by the Department not only to staff schools in Rotuma but those in Fiji as well, it should be quite reasonable perhaps that the Department be expected to meet the expenses that may be involved in such a scheme.

"It should be remembered that there are schools called Government schools for Europeans, Indians and Fijians in Fiji, controlled and financed entirely by the government but none of that type of school in Rotuma for the Rotuman people. It was only a couple of years ago when the Rotuman people spent well over £1,000 to enable four Rotuman teachers to undertake further teacher training in New Zealand and of those four only one went back to Rotuma to teach. The other three are employed in Fiji to teach.

"(5) The schools are badly in need of proper educational facilities. To meet this need it should not be as difficult as it would seem. The relatively short distances separating these schools should enable them to share equipment that would be too expensive if each should have its own provided separately. Such equipment as physical training apparatus, school projector, a school library for the use of pupils and teachers can be bought on this basis. What is needed is for all parties concerned with the education of Rotumans to work out an equitable cost-sharing formula to meet the cost of such educational facilities. It may be difficult to find electric current for projectors. Catholic schools have such facilities and if it is not practicable for each school to have an electric plant, then perhaps arrangements could be made with those schools to assist the others.

"(6) There is a great need for cooperation among these schools. The teachers may perhaps be largely responsible for existing lack of cooperation. The endeavor to have school sports has failed not only once but many a time. It was not because the children did not like playing sports but the teachers themselves seemed to be more concerned for a win rather than to foster the social atmosphere. This is a contradiction of one of the fundamental principles in education which is that the schools should endeavor to instill in their pupils the spirit of cooperation.

"I suggest that if the schools cannot be made to play sports as normally done in other places, then they should combine and select team members from different schools instead of one school having its own team. This scheme should be tried for the time being to see if it can work, but even if it does work it should be regarded as a second best for the ultimate aim should be that children learn to play for their own respective schools and be able to take pleasure in victory and bear defeat in the right spirit.

"It is particularly essential that the schools cooperate in sports, for most of these schools have no proper playgrounds nor sports equipment. My suggestion for sharing of the use of teaching aids should also apply to the use of sports facilities. A good ground could be prepared for these schools at the Government Station at Ahou. There is one at this place where sports for all Rotuma are held, but it needs improvement. A cooperative effort by all the Rotumans should turn this place into a beautiful playground for everybody's need, the people of Rotuma and the schools alike."

Bibliography

Allen, William. "Rotuma." Report of Australian Association for Advancement of Science (sixth meeting). January 1895.

Churchward, C. Maxwell. "One Hundred Years of Christian Work in Rotuma." *Missionary Review,* Sydney. August 5, 1939.

————. *Rotuman Grammar and Dictionary.* Sydney: Australasian Medical Publishing Company, 1940.

————. *Tales of a Lonely Isle.* Sydney: Oceania Monographs, No. 4, 1940.

Coleman, James S. "Academic Achievement and the Structure of Competition." *Harvard Educational Review,* Vol. XXIX, No. 4 (Fall 1959), pp. 330–351.

Gallimore, Ronald and Alan Howard. *Dependency Training and Hawaiian Behavior: An Experimental Approach to Culture and Personality.* In press.

Hall, Edward T. *The Hidden Dimension.* Garden City: Doubleday & Company, Inc., 1966.

Historique de la Station St. Michel Upu Rotuma. Unpublished manuscript. Translated from the French by Irwin Howard.

Howard, Alan. "Adoption in Rotuma." In Vern Carroll (ed.), *Adoption in Eastern Oceania.* In press.

————. "Land Tenure and Social Change in Rotuma." *The Journal of the Polynesian Society.* Vol. LXIII (1964), pp. 26–52.

MacArthur. *Report on the Census of the Population, 1956.* Council Paper No. 1. of 1958, Government Press.

Ordinance No. 4 of 1958, Colony of Fiji. Suva: Government Press.

Outward Letters, Rotuma District Office. Annual Report of the Resident Commissioner for the year 1930. Central Archives, Suva.

————. Dispatch from Resident Commissioner H. E. Leefe to Colonial Secretary, January 14, 1899. Central Archives, Suva.

Sahlins, Marshall. *Moala*. Ann Arbor: University of Michigan Press, 1962.

Thompson, Laura. *Southern Lau, Fiji: An Ethnography*. Honolulu: Bernice P. Bishop Museum, Bulletin No. 162, 1940.

Wesleyan Missionary Notices, No. 37. October 1866.

Williams, Thomas and James Calvert. *Fiji and the Fijians; and Missionary Labours among the Cannibals*. 3rd edition. London: Hodder and Stoughton, 1870.